SYSTEMATIC INTERVENTION with DISTURBED CHILDREN

SYSTEMATIC INTERVENTION with DISTURBED CHILDREN

Edited by

Marvin J. Fine, Ph.D.

School of Education
University of Kansas
Lawrence, Kansas

SP MEDICAL & SCIENTIFIC BOOKS
a division of Spectrum Publications, Inc.
New York

SPECTRUM PUBLICATIONS, INC.
175-20 Wexford Terrace
Jamaica, NY 11432

Library of Congress Cataloging in Publication Data
Main entry under title:

Systematic intervention with disturbed children.

    Bibliography: p.
    Includes index.
    1. Child psychotherapy. I. Fine, Marvin J.   [DNLM:
1. Affective symptoms—In infancy and childhood.
2. Affective symptoms—Therapy. WS 350.6 S995]
RJ504.S89   1984   618.92'8914   83-21319
ISBN O-89335-199-7

Printed in the United States of America

Contributors

David Bogacki, Ph.D. Senior Clinical Psychologist, New Jersey Neuropsychiatric Institute, Princeton, New Jersey

Valerie J. Cook, Ph.D. Associate Professor of Psychology, George Peabody College of Vanderbilt University, Nashville, Tennessee

Ramon G. Corrales, Ph.D. Senior Supervisor, Family Institute of Kansas City, Inc., Kansas City, Missouri

Linda L. Edwards, Ed.D. Assistant Professor, Department of Special Education, University of Missouri-Kansas City, Kansas City, Missouri

Marvin J. Fine, Ph.D. Professor, Department of Educational Psychology and Research, School of Education, University of Kansas, Lawrence, Kansas

Barbara Gerson, Ph.D. Associate Professor, School Psychology Program, Department of Psychology, Yeshiva University, New York, New York

Robert G. Harrington, Ph.D. Assistant Professor, Department of Educational Psychology and Research, School of Education, University of Kansas, Lawrence, Kansas

Natalie Hill, Ph.D. Adjunct Associate Professor of Social Work, Smith College, Northampton, Massachusetts

Irwin A. Hyman, Ed.D. Professor, School Psychology Program, Temple University, Philadelphia, Pennsylvania

Margaret L. Marcus, Ph.D.   Senior Psychologist, Jewish Child Care Association, New York, New York

Frederic J. Medway, Ph.D.   Associate Professor, School Psychology Program, Department of Psychology, University of South Carolina, Columbia, South Carolina

Jeanne M. Plas, Ph.D.   Associate Professor of Psychology, George Peabody College of Vanderbilt University, Nashville, Tennessee

Laurence G. Ro-Trock, Ph.D.   Senior Supervisor, Family Institute of Kansas City, Inc., Kansas City, Missouri

Neil J. Salkind, Ph.D.   Professor, Department of Educational Psychology and Research, School of Education, University of Kansas, Lawrence, Kansas

Richard L. Simpson, Ed.D.   Associate Professor, Department of Special Education, Children's Rehabilitation Unit, Kansas University Medical Center, Kansas City, Kansas

Stephen T. Sirridge, Ph.D.   Associate Professor, Department of Education and Psychology, Avila College, Kansas City, Missouri

Preface

Disturbed children constitute a sizeable and varied percentage of the child population. Generally, two to three percent have severe, longstanding problems and 20 to 30 percent have current, more transient problems. While preventive efforts are needed, it also seems obvious that many children will continue to function in a disturbed and disturbing fashion and will continue to require various kinds of therapeutic interventions. These interventions will mainly occur in school and community settings.

This book attempts to present a picture of some fairly popular models of intervention and to consider important related issues. There are probably as many ways of coping with disturbed children as there are creative, caring persons attempting to do the coping. A growing literature exists on ways of conceptualizing and intervening with such children. It was believed by the editor that an organized body of information on these concepts and techniques would prove useful to student and practitioner.

A danger with such collections is that if they mainly portray novel or atypical techniques, while informative, the book quickly becomes passé and of limited value. This book's focus is on contemporary thought, but also on orientations that have stood the test of some time and the stability of the underlying theory.

In the first section of the book, the introductory chapter presents an historical overview of intervention concepts and methods. The chapters by Salkind and by Hyman and Bogacki, examine how social policy affects the direction of treatment and legal and ethical issues related to specific interventions.

The second section of the book examines several systematic orientations to intervention. For each approach, the rationale, objectives, and procedures are detailed with case examples. The approaches being discussed include behavioral, family therapy, psychoeducational, ecological, transactional analysis, and psychodynamic.

The third and final section includes important chapters on the efficacy of therapeutic intervention, assessment procedures, and home-school-clinic collaboration.

All of the authors have been actively involved in programs for disturbed children and bring their own rich background of experience along with their scholarship. The book, in total, should constitute a resource compendium of ideas and interventions, and of related professional issues and procedures. The book should stand as an advocate for humane and caring assistance for disturbed children.

Marvin J. Fine
February 1984.

Contents

SYSTEMATIC INTERVENTION with DISTURBED CHILDREN

PART I

Introduction

1

The Treatment of Disturbed Children: Introduction

MARVIN J. FINE AND RICHARD L. SIMPSON

Since the early 1900's there has been a rapid acceleration of interest and of theory and program development with emotionally disturbed children and youth. The proclamation of Ellen Key (1909) that this will be the century of the child has proved partly true.

Substantial advances in the treatment of disturbed children has indeed occurred. Yet there is no shortage of continued dehumanization of children. One need only to read statements by Blatt (1970, 1974) to be abrasively confronted with the grim and heartbreaking realities of institutional care. The national shame of child abuse (Kempe and Kempe, 1978; and Justice and Justice, 1976), the Supreme Court decision on corporal punishment in the schools (Piele, 1979), and the recent attempts to deregulate Public Law 94-142, reflect the nation's negative tendencies in relation to child care and the rights of children. But one ought not forget that the child abuse figures are revealed because of laws against it and requiring the reporting of suspected abuse. Also, Public Law 94-142 cannot be challenged with deregulation if it did not exist in the first place as a statement of national concern for the education of all handicapped children.

It is difficult at times to maintain a balanced view of the progress that has been made in light of the problems that still exist. Kauffman and Lewis (1974) have presented a rich chronicle of personal accounts by noted educators of disturbed children. What comes through is not only a personalized history of the field and the exciting diversity of efforts, but also the picture of personal dedication and the image of a network of training and influence that has permeated the field. Substantial progress has occurred even though there remains a crucial need to reach more children with effective preventive and therapeutic programs.

The forward by William Cruikshank in Kauffman and Lewis (1974) speaks of some important limitations in the field of service to disturbed children that are worth noting. He expressed concern with the absence of adequate longitudinal studies on specific interventions with specific populations. In light of the absence of such data, various programs are accepted on the strength of the reputation of their proponents. The chapter by Medway deals more extensively with issues of establishing the efficacy of therapeutic intervention. Another and more recent criticism was presented by Bower (1982). He decried the distortion of his earlier work on defining emotional disturbance (Bower, 1970) by Public Law 94-142. A major concern was with the artificial distinction between emotional disturbance and social maladjustment. Since his earlier data revealed that emotionally disturbed children experience social maladjustment, such a distinction would be in the service of bureaucrats and financial constraints rather than in the service of children. Clearly the field of treatment of disturbed children is not without controversy.

The term "emotionally disturbed" acutally did not enter the literature until the early 1900's (Reinert, 1972). While there have been numerous attempts to define the term over the years, a current and influential definition is the one proposed in Public Law 94-142, that Bower criticized as too limited.

> The term means a condition exhibiting one or more of the following characteristics over a long period of time and to a marked degree, which adversely affects educational performance: (a) an inability to learn which cannot be explained by intellectual, sensory or health factors; (b) an inability to build or maintain satisfactory interpersonal relationships with peers and teachers; (c) inappropriate types of behavior or feelings under normal circumstances; (d) a general pervasive mood of unhappiness or depression; or (e) a tendency to develop physical symptoms or fears associated with personal or school problems. The term includes children who are schizophrenic. The term does not include children who are socially maladjusted, unless it is determined that they are seriously emotional disturbed.
>
> (U.S. Federal Register, 42, August 23, 1977, pp. 42478-42479).

Anyone concerned with a detailed history of the treatment of disturbed children will find ample sources (Lewis, 1974; Kanner, 1962; Reinhart, 1972; Reynolds and Birch, 1982). This chapter does not focus on a general historical perspective but is organized around four themes that reveal significant movement in the field of treatment of the emotionally disturbed child. The four themes discussed are the demystification of behavior, the emergence of varied treatment modes, significant legislations, and growing emphasis on prevention.

DEMYSTIFICATION OF BEHAVIOR

Ehrenwald's book, *From Medicine Man to Freud* (1956) presents a fascinating account of attempts at understanding the human mind and mental healing from ancient cultures up to the Freudian era. Magic and religion have been man's historical ways of making sense out of his world (Frazer, 1922; Malinowski, 1954).

We can take a common definition of psychology, *the study of human behavior with the object of establishing understanding, control, and prediction*, and recognize that this indeed has been one of man's historical quests. Whereas a scientific approach to studying a phenomenon may lead to unanswered questions via "The data is inconclusive," or "We need to replicate the study before drawing a conclusion," magical or even religious viewpoints typically do not impose such limitations on the production of *truth*.

The progression of thought regarding deviant behavior seems to have moved from secret and mystical causes to more explicit and natural causes, and also from an illness model to a coping model. By the latter part of the nineteenth century, efforts to understand the disturbed child and to ferret out the functional reasons for the child's behavior began to occur. This was a great step from the more common views of inherent badness or "having the devil in you" which had opened the door to considerable physical abuse of children in the name of helping them.

Freud's influence at the turn of the century was far reaching (Jones, 1961). It led to the mental hygiene movement, prompted the development of mental health clinics, and presented persons as capable of being helped through essentially talking cures. These movements were carried forward by others but stimulated and directed very much by Freud's ideas. His intrapsychic theory presented disturbed behavior as the result of some disturbance in the individual's inner life, and as the person worked through his or her problems, so would the behavior improve. Environmental influences on behavior were not as seriously considered as were the intrapsychic mechanisms of the child and arrestments or aberrations of the child's psychological development. "Bad" behavior was viewed primarily as symptomatic of the inner disturbance.

The rise of behaviorism led to a more objective focus on the manifestations of emotional disturbance. While some internal activity was occurring, the key questions revolved around accurate descriptions of what the child was doing under what environmental conditions. Even persons not considering themselves behaviorists began dealing more explicitly and descriptively with the child's behavior.

The well popularized "eight ages of man" presented by Erikson (1950) did much to soften Freud's intrapsychic position and cast the person's behavior in a person-environment interaction light. At different developmental periods the child is faced with a developmental task and conflict; the inner world of the child interacts with the external reality as the child's ego development emerges. Achieving trust and a sense of personal autonomy, to name two of the developmental issues posed by Erikson, represent a more visible, less inferential view of early development, than the more classically presented view of psychosexual development.

Another important milestone in the demystifying of disturbed behavior was reached through the statements of Thomas Szasz (1960) on mental illness. He rejected the traditional view of mental illness as a disease entity and argued that we needed to think in terms of "problems in living." He was concerned that making right decisions and coping effectively were seen as the logical outgrowths of mental health when in fact it is effective coping that makes others regard us as having good mental health. From his point of view, teaching or helping people to cope and deal effectively with their problems of living was a more appropriate curative than traditional medical-psychiatric intervention.

Glasser's reality therapy (1965) with its strong emphasis on personal responsibility would seem to be a logical outgrowth of this line of thinking about "disordered behavior." His writings have significantly influenced the field of treatment and helped to shift the view of disturbed children as somehow being pawns of secret, uncontrollable inner forces, to persons who can and indeed should assume responsibility for themselves. One finds this same theme in the current writings of a pioneer in family therapy, Jay Haley (1980). In his recent book on the treatment of disturbed adolescents, he prefers to think of the person behaving irresponsibly rather than being sick or mentally ill. For Haley this way of framing the behavior is not only accurate, but identifies different and more productive roles for those concerned with the person's behavior.

The rise in popularity of family therapy and family system theory (Minuchin and Fishman, 1981; Madanes, 1981; Haley, 1980) has put individual disturbed behavior in another context. The deviant child is now seen as acting out some service to the family or individuals within the family. Examples would be a child whose problems brings his or her estranged parents back together, or a child in coalition with one parent who acts out that parent's anger toward another parent. While behavior viewed this way is less obvious in its meaning and more inferential than a behavioral stance, the child's behavior is nonetheless viewed in adaptive, interactive terms. That is, the causes are not mysterious or magical, but play themselves out in the interaction of the child with others and in the eventual consequences of the behavior.

The family systems frame of reference is in part an outgrowth of the broader socioecological position (Rhodes, 1970; Rhodes and Paul, 1978). This viewpoint looks at the match of child to environment. Rhodes was concerned with how children get labeled and categorized within systems. The meaning that an environment gives to the child's behavior will vary. Intervention would occur so as to modify those environmental structures that identify and maintain the child as a disturbed child. This could mean removing a child from a situation, such as a special class; it would mean through a consultative process having key people redefine the child's behavior such as from "hyperactive" to "curious and novelty seeking." For Rhodes, the locus of investigation would not be the child alone, but the environment within which the so-called disturbed behavior is identified and acts itself out.

A dynamic view of behavior, considering the child's inner psychological life, is still very much alive in the field of treating emotional disturbance. The shift historically has been from secret to more explicit and logical causes of behavior, and from an inner conflict to a coping model. The intrapsychic mechanisms underlying human motivation and behavior are seen now more in terms of how they support appropriate adaptive behavior and coping skills, rather than their somehow existing within the child and apart from the child's day to day interactions in the real world.

THE EMERGENCE OF VARIED TREATMENT MODES

As more attention was brought to bear on understanding and helping disturbed children, it was inevitable that varied treatment modes would emerge; some have just been mentioned. The diversity of approaches speaks on one hand to the creativity of mental health professionals, and also to the absence of a concensus on what works with what populations to what ends. Just considering the field of psychotherapy, it is of note that over 130 different approaches have been identified (Parloff, 1976).

There are several approaches to therapeutic intervention with children that have gained and maintained popularity. These will be briefly discussed and subsequently elaborated upon in later chapters.

The Psychodynamic Position

The postulates by Freud (1961) on the importance of the early years for the child have placed great emphasis on the child's early relationship with his or her parents. It is within the context of the home and prior to the age of approximately six years, that crucial psychosexual development occurs.

The initial object relationship with the mother is of particular importance in predicting how the child will relate with others in later life (Mahler, 1969). Erikson (1950), who did much to demystify Freud, spoke of the importance of the early trusting relationship between infant and parent. If the sense of basic trust does not occur, the child will continue to struggle with trust as an interpersonal issue. Also, as the child does not move satisfactorily through the process and stages of development, movement through subsequent stages will be affected.

The eventual separation of the child from the close bond of the parents and mother in particular must occur as the child moves from a symbiotic state to a state of great individuation and development (Mahler, 1968). Many of the problems that children experience can be seen as connected to unresolved symbiotic conflicts and inadequate ego development. One can observe the child utilizing different ego defenses and maintenance rather than resolution of his or her problems will occur. The behavior that parents, teachers, and others find problematic is viewed from a psychodynamic position as symptomatic of underlying or internal conflict rather than being the problem in and of itself.

This way of viewing a child's problem led to children being psychoanalyzed or at least treated with intensive psychotherapy, somehow exclusive of the difficulties they were having coping with daily life. An assumption was that as the inner turmoil or conflict was resolved, the child would have energy available to focus appropriately on day to day demands. A difficulty with this early psychodynamic view was the expanding and cumulative effects of disturbed behavior. As nondisturbed children were growing in cognitive learning and social skills, the disturbed child was falling further behind.

Certainly the contemporary picture of a psychodynamic approach considers the importance of the child acquiring appropriate social skills and succeeding in school learning as concommitants to a therapy program that stresses attainment of insight and resolution of internal conflicts.

Behavior Modification

Perhaps one of the more popular but historically controversial interventions is that of behavior modification (Fine and Walkenshaw, 1977). The controversy stems from the image of therapist or teacher mechanistically and in a dehumanizing way manipulating the behavior of the child. The basic premises of behavior modification, as it is mainly practiced today, are considerably different. Children are very often involved in goal setting and reinforcement selection, and a self-managed individual rather than an other-managed individual is the ultimate end goal of behavioral interventions.

The power of behavioral interventions is also a part of what seems scary to opponents of these approaches. Yet it is the power of reinforcement procedures that gives this approach its potency with a wide variety of behavior disorders. Perhaps no other therapeutic intervention has been approached in as scientific and data-based a way, with positive outcomes being reported across a wide spectrum of behaviors.

The basic assumption of behavior modification, that behavior is learned, is what ultimately sets the stage for the understanding and control of behavior. One need not be concerned with unseen inner causes, but can focus on the child's observable behavior and environmental elements that can impinge upon the child's behavior. The behavior modifier is not only then concerned with obtaining an accurate picture of the child's behavior by using systematic observation, but some quantitative understanding of the environment within which the behavior is nested is required. What specific events preceeded the emitting of the target behavior and what events or consequences followed the behavior?

The behavior is considered to be controlled by its relationship to those antecedent and consequent events; therefore some planned and systematic modification of the events will presumably lead to changes in the behavior. By being explained in terms of the target behavior and what is manipulated, and by collecting empirical data on the preceeding and consequent events and the target behavior, one can draw conclusions of an objective nature on what actually occurred. Impressions of improvement are essentially devalued as having validity because of the focus on objectivity, i.e., the direct measurement of behavior.

Behavior modification techniques have been utilized well not just with the elimination of undesirable behaviors but with the build-up of desirable behavior. There are also numerous reports of parents being trained to work with their children or at least to assume a partnership with the school in correcting problem behavior (Berkowitz and Graziano, 1972). The basic method also lends itself to the analysis of learning tasks as well as learning behaviors, so the child can be programmed into making appropriate discriminations and responding differentially in both learning and social settings. Behavioral interventions are useful in one-to-one counseling situations, especially in group settings, including group home environments (Fixen, Phillips, and Wolf, 1973; Patterson, 1971). There is also a current *discovering* of the child's inner life via cognitive behavior modification (Meichenbaum, 1977) leading to systematic attempts to shape a person's thinking concommitantly with, or as a precurser to behavior change.

Transactional Analysis

Initially developed by Eric Berne (1961) as a system of psychotherapy, Transactional Analysis (TA) achieved much attention and even professional notoriety for its pop psychology presentation. Some of Berne's books, *Games People Play* (1964), and *What Do You Say After You Say Hello* (1972), while containing very valuable substantive material, tended to further the view of TA as not quite legitimate in some professional quarters.

In fact, there is an extensive documenting of the therapeutic use of TA that argues its applicability with a wide variety of problems of children and youth (Amundson and Sawatzky, 1976; Maisenbacher and Erskine, 1976; Bendell and Fine, 1979). Unfortunately, much of the publication is of a theoretical or case study basis, rather than of a controlled, research nature. Nonetheless, TA constructs and techniques seem to have found their place in the broad picture of therapeutic treatment and deserves more study by persons seeking to expand their repetoire of skills.

The building blocks of personality from a TA perspective are the three major ego states—Parent, Adult, Child—and their sub-parts. An ego state is identified as a coherent pattern of thinking and feeling with related behaviors. Helping a person to identify his or her own ego states so as to enhance self-awareness, awareness of others, and various options in different situations, is referred to as *structural analysis*.

The term *transactional analysis*, in addition to representing the whole system, also represents the analysis of transactions among persons. By being aware of different types of transactions (complementary, crossed, and ulterior) and the principles of communication associated with each transaction, a person is better able to engineer and predict social outcomes.

Another important component of TA is *game analysis*. One way that a person structures time is through non-productive transactions that are predictable for that person, involve him or her with others, but lead to a continuation of an essentially self-defeating life pattern. An example would be game of "Kick Me," as played by a student in academic and social situations. This student somehow ends up getting put down or punished, denies his or her instrumentation in engineering the social interactions leading to those negative outcomes, and blames others for their unfairness or hostility.

The unifying construct that connects the various TA concepts is that of *life script*. The belief, much akin to a psychoanalytic view, is that in the early years of life, the child, through interaction with others, takes on some beliefs about self that become a kind of compass for future events. TA treatment will eventually involve the person in exploring his or her life script and in redeciding some important personal issues.

The basic objectives of TA therapy—spontanaiety, authenticity, and autonomy—represent life goals rather than short-term objectives. The descriptive and, at times, simplistic language of TA is very useful with children. The therapist is also in a position to function as a role model in terms of his or her own stroking patterns, strategies for coping with stress, and willingness to analyze his or her own behavior. TA therapy, perhaps as much as any other therapy, has the potential for being a fun and learning experience. It lends itself particularly well to a group format because of the quasi teacher-learner relationship of the therapist to a group, and the importance of interpersonal relationships and peer feedback.

As with any of the therapies being discussed, TA has schools of emphasis so that one practitioner may stress certain constructs or use certain techniques differently from another TA practitioner (Barnes, 1977). Perhaps one of the clearest distinctions would be between those using TA as a kind of behavior topography, dealing mainly with the analysis and learning of behavior, and those concerned with the structure of personality and developing therapeutic experiences calculated to achieve major intrapsychic change.

Family Therapy

Historically the stepchild of more traditional therapies, family therapy has escalated rapidly in its popularity within the psychotherapeutic community. Over the last decade in particular, the number of books, journals, professional organizations, and training programs have increased dramatically.

The predominant emphasis to contemporary family therapy is on a systems approach. The basic assumptions are that behavior needs to be understood contextually in terms of the purposes served by the behavior. Also, each of us grows up within some kind of family setting in which roles and relationships become established, and behavior patterns emerge that act out the power and control of relationships, supporting the rules of the family. There are hierarchies within families based on age and position; these influence behavior. Moreover, within any system there are homeostatic forces that serve to maintain the existing nature of the system and resist change.

Children are members of at least two main systems, home-family and school. These two systems overlap or interface and what happens in one system is likely to affect the child's behavior in the other. From a family systems viewpoint, one would be interested in how school and home organize perceptions and behaviors around the disturbed child.

One theme regarding intervention is that all the involved persons need to be present at counseling sessions. This would theoretically include the child who ostensibly has the problem, the parents, and the relevant school personnel. Such a meeting, conducted by a skilled mental health professional, would explore the meaning of the child's behavior in terms of the total set of relationships with which the child is involved. Some actual shifts in the structure of relationships could occur within these sessions as behavior gets reframed, assignments are given to individuals, and face to face communication occurs.

However, organizing such meetings can be difficult in terms of logistical problems. Since a systems viewpoint suggests that a change in one part of a system can influence other parts of the system, it is conceivable that by focusing on smaller units of change (i.e., the teacher, the child, or just the parents), other changes will be generated within the network of relationships. An example would be a *hyperactive* child who is relabeled by the teacher as a *high energy child with varied interests*. The teacher may then function differently in planning learning tasks and communicating with the parents. By initially changing his or her behavior, the teacher prompts behavior changes on the part of others, and the child's identity and behavior within the system is then modified.

From a systems viewpoint, the intrapsychic aspects of the disturbed child are considerably downplayed as one examines the roles and relationships assumed by the child and important others with whom (s)he interacts. Behavior is understood in terms of relationships and purposes served, and change implies change in the nature of the system.

Ecological Viewpoint

The ecological approach deals broadly with the emotionally disturbed child and his or her world. Cultural values, community beliefs, the impact of labels, and the message sent to an individual by virtue of a special program placement, all fall within the sphere of the ecological approach.

Of concern to the ecologically oriented helper is the match of the child to the environment. Why is it that a given child get labeled disturbed in one environment but not in another? Rhodes offers an answer in his definition of emotional disturbance.

> Disturbance is constituted from a reverberating circuit between the disturbing individual and various significant individuals within the environmental settings such as home, classroom, etc. The disturbance resides in the agitated exchange which takes place between individual and environment. Each contributes to the process. This exchange takes place both at the behavioral level and at the psycho-dynamic level. The so-called disturbed individual and his surrounding resonators are "in it together." It is their disturbing exchange which creates the problem.
>
> It follows from this view of disturbance that the environment must be given attention equal to that shown to the individual who has been singled out as "disturbed." (Rhodes, 1970, p. 44)

Ecological intervention might target on any aspect of the environment which could hypothetically influence the adaptation of the environment to the child and vice versa.

> Ecological intervention might then include the direct teaching of constructive social behavior to children; efforts to change the nature of social interactions in natural settings; helping children to gain competence in relevant areas of their daily lives; modifying environmental elements of a youngster's system; working to change the attitudes or behavior of the adults and children in an identified youngster's system; and, in general, any action designed to increase the goodness of fit between a child and his or her environments. (Apter, 1982, pp. 133-134).

Intervention from an ecological perspective does not really occur in terms of cure; it seeks to create a more propitious match between child and environment. This may require the involvement of community as well as family and school variables. Project ReEd (Hobbs, 1978; Hobbs, 1969) is a major example of this kind of school-family-community liason on behalf of the child.

Psychoeducational Intervention

As with other intervention models, the psychoeducational model has meant somewhat different things to different persons (Fagen, Long, and Stevens, 1975; Berkowitz and Rothman, 1960; and Fenichel, 1974). However, a common focus seems to be the recognition of the importance of productive learning as a therapeutic tool. Persons of a psychoeducational orientation may differ on the extent to which learning problems are seen as a direct manifestation of emotional disturbance. Agreement does occur on the need to assist the child in productive learning. The structure of the learning environment is what is seen as the heart of the psychoeducational orientation.

The text by Kauffman and Lewis (1974) on the personal perspectives of several noted educators of disturbed children is a representative view of the psychoeducational approach. Each of these educators with backgrounds ranging from clinical psychology to special education discovered the therapeutic importance of both learning and the structure of the learning environment for disturbed children and youth.

An example of a more psychodynamically oriented approach was offered by Berkowitz and Rothman (1960). Their text dealt extensively with the nature of child pathology and then extended itself into the psychoeducational treatment of disturbed children. But even with her background of extensive clinical training, Berkowitz (1974) wrote on the usefulness of behavior modification in the educational programming of disturbed children.

Whelan (1974) received some training and work experience with disturbed children in a highly psychoanalytic setting and moved to a more behavorial approach without losing his sensitivity to the individuality of children. The psychoeducational programs offered at the University of Kansas Medical Center under Whelan were attempts to offer the disturbed child the external structure and organization the child lacked, as well as an individualized educational program geared carefully to the child's educational needs. Behavior modification was the key tool for promoting more appropriate social and academic behavior.

Fenichel's observations seem to hold true for most persons involved in psychoeducational programming and underscores what has already been said regarding structure. His early days in educating deeply disturbed children were based on the belief that these children had weak, fragile egos and needed a gentle, permissive approach that would aid them in working through their conflicts.

Our children taught us otherwise. . . We learned that disorganized children need someone to organize their world for them. We began to recognize that disturbed children fear their own loss of control and need protection against their own impulses; that what they needed were teachers who knew how to limit as well as accept them. We learned the need for a highly organized program of education and training that could bring order, stability, and direction to minds that are disorganized, unstable and unpredicable. (Fenichel, 1974, p. 64)

LEGAL AND LEGISLATIVE CONSIDERATIONS

Legislative enactments and judicial decisions have had decisive impact on the development of programs and policies for emotionally disturbed children/youth. These various acts and judgments, supported and preceded by advocacy groups and legislative campaigns, have significantly expanded the availability and quality of direct service programs for emotionally and behaviorally handicapped persons and their families.

One enactment associated with expanded and improved services for emotionally disturbed individuals and their families has been the Community Mental Health Centers Act of 1963. As a result of this Act there are at present thousands of community health centers throughout this country. As a result of this expanded resource behaviorally disordered and emotionally disturbed children/youth and their families are able to utilize and secure services which will allow them to function in an optimal manner in as normalized a setting as possible. At the time of its enactment President John F. Kennedy called for a preventative emphasis in the field of mental health. Kennedy observed, "prevention is far more desirable for all concerned. It is far more economical and it is far more likely to be successful. Prevention will require both selected specific programs directed especially at known causes, and the strengthening of our fundamental community, social welfare, and vocational programs which can do much to eliminate or correct the harsh environmental conditions which are often associated with mental illness (1963)". While the overall efficacy of community mental health center programs has been questioned (Heller, Price, and Sher, 1980), there is general agreement that this Act has effectively served children and families with emotional problems (Hobbs, 1975).

In addition to the community mental health movement, there have been numerous other measures taken to enhance the services available to the emotionally handicapped and their families. Interestingly, particularly at the federal level, the emotionally disturbed have been indirect beneficiaries of several of these policies and enactments. For example, the original Social Security Act of 1935 was subsequently amended to provide services and support to families of disabled persons. Also, Medicare and the Supplementary Security Income Programs were eventually amended to allow for benefits and services to handicapped persons. In a similar manner, the 1963 National Defense Education Act, designed to enhance the training of scientists whose eventual work would be in the interest of national defense, supported in principle the notion of educational provisions and treatment alternatives for exceptional children and youth.

While the federal government played a relatively passive role in the development of policies and programs for emotionally disturbed and other handicapped children through the mid-1960s, it has subsequently been a dominant influence. This federal interest and influence culminated in the passage of the Education for All Handicapped Children Act of 1975, the most significant and comprehensive for all enactments which have impacted on emotionally disturbed and other exceptional children and adolescents. This regulation, which is supported by Section 504 of the Rehabilitation Act of 1975, was written as an amendment to the Education of the Handicapped Amendments of 1975 (Public Law 93-380). The latter, in turn, was developed in an effort to expand and clarify the Elementary and Secondary Education Act of 1966 (Public Law 39-10). Public Law 94-142 was designed to ensure a free and appropriate education for all handicapped children and youth. It has more significantly affected the educational provisions and treatment alternatives for handicapped young people, including the emotionally disturbed, than any other prior enactment.

Included in this historical Act are:

(a). Provision of a free and appropriate education for handicapped children
(b). Protection against discriminatory assessment
(c). Right to placement in the least restrictive setting
(d). Right to due process
(e). The provision of an individually developed treatment plan for each student
(f). Right to Parent involvement.

The Provision of a Free and Appropriate Education
for all Handicapped Children

The intent of this underlying principle of the mandate is to prevent the exclusion of any handicapped child/youth from appropriate services. While this broad ranging provision has not been fully implemented (*Levine v New Jersey*, 1980), it has resulted in most schools and programs acknowledging that children and youth cannot be denied suitable and needed educationally related services due to lack of resources or a child's condition. Beyond the promulgation of improved educational and related treatment provisions for behaviorally disordered children, this provision has also resulted in the development of programs for the severely emotionally disturbed (schizophrenic, autistic, etc.) and incarcerated youth (*Green v Johnson*, 1981). While the emotionally disturbed population remains the most underserved among handicapped and youth (Kauffman, 1977), its lot has significantly improved as a function of Public Law 94-142.

One significant result of the court's interpretation of the Act has been that schools are prohibited from expelling a handicapped child or adolescent if the behavior leading to the proposed expulsion was related to the handicap (*Stuart v Nappi*, 1978). This interpretation has been particularly beneficial for the emotionally disturbed, who have historically been denied suitable school services for behavior directly associated with their emotional disorders. While short-term suspension and expulsion for behavior not related to a child's handicap are allowed, the categorical expulsion of disturbed individuals because of their behavioral excesses and deficits has been eliminated.

Protection Against Discriminatory Assessment

This aspect of the act is designed to guard children and youth from inaccurate identification and the possible detrimental effects of segregated or overly restrictive placement alternatives. Hence, handicapped individuals of school age, including those with emotional and behavioral disorders, must be served in the least structured setting allowed by their handicap. While not mandating mainstreaming, this provision has been interpreted to mean that the desired setting for all children and youth is the regular classroom. Thus, this element of the Act has served as the primary impetus for the development of appropriate school based programs for the emotionally disturbed and for the elimination of state institutional and other residential programs as the sole option for placement and treatment.

Right to Due Process

This safeguard allows parents, the handicapped, their advocates, and school personnel to challenge decisions on which disagreement exists, and for which no compromise can be achieved. The basic elements of due process were initially presented in *Pennsylvania Association for Retarded Children v Commonwealth of Pennsylvania* (1972). In making deposition on this case the court noted that "no child who is mentally retarded can be assigned initially or reassigned to either a regular or special education status, or excluded from a public education without a prior recorded hearing before a special hearing officer." The same provisions were later assumed to apply to all exceptional populations, including the emotionally disturbed. The Pennsylvania decision also provided a series of due process procedures, many of which are conceptually a part of Public Law 94-142. These include parental access to records, independent evaluations, the right to surrogate parents, the right to parental notice prior to evaluations or educational program changes, and the right to a hearing. Each of these elements has significantly expanded the rights, procedural guidelines, and services available to emotionally disturbed children and their families.

Individualized Education Programs (I. E. P.)

The purpose of this procedure is to assure high quality services based on individualized needs. Accordingly, each exceptional child, including the emotionally disturbed, must be provided an individually designed instructional and treatment plan. Further, these IEPs (individual education plans) must be developed by professionals in conjunction with parents who are afforded the right to accept or reject the plan.

The interpretation of the degree to which seriously emotionally disturbed children and adolescents are to receive psychotherapy has led to significant concern and debate. Much of the disagreement has focused on whether or not psychotherapy is required for a child to benefit from special education, as per the related services operational definition of Public Law 94-142. The issue is extremely difficult to determine, even on a case by case basis. For example, in *North v District of Columbia Board of Education* (1979), the judge, in attempting to assign responsibility for services for an emotionally disturbed child, noted that, "The claim inextricability of medical and educational grounds for certain services does not signal court abdication from decisionmaking in difficult matters. Rather, unseverability for such needs is the very basis for holding that the services are an essential preprequisite for learning." Accordingly, it appears that psychotherapy has been accepted as a legitimate related service for emotionally disturbed children and youth.

However, even if psychotherapy is needed for a child to benefit from special education, does such treatment represent a psychological or medical service? The significance of this issue is great. If psychotherapy is shown to be a psychological or counseling service then it is required for a student to benefit from special education. However, if it is determined to be a medical service, it must be provided only for diagnostic or evaluative purposes. While this matter remains unsettled, a consistent set of court decisions suggest that psychotherapy is an acceptable related service as per the regulations of the enactment. These court decisions have largely allowed for psychological and counseling services for the emotionally disturbed in situations where such services have historically been withheld. As a result, many emotionally handicapped children and adolescents have been able to function effectively in less restrictive settings than might have been otherwise possible.

Parents as an Integral Component of the Planning Process

The very core of the Education for All Handicapped Children Act is founded on the concept that parents represent an integral part of the planning and implementation system for exceptional children. Hence, parents of emotionally disturbed children and adolescents are being persuaded to function as treatment and planning partners in order for the planned services delivery system to operate successfully.

Other Policies and Enactments

Finally, residentially placed emotionally disturbed individuals and their parents have benefited from a group of policies and enactments generally referred to as *partner rights*. Included are the development of procedural safeguards which have clarified such matters as right to treatment; treatment alternatives; self-harming conduct; release requirements; and the parents patriae doctrine.

PREVENTIVE INFLUENCES

While it would be inaccurate to suggest that current programs and treatment options for emotionally handicapped individuals are sufficient to meet the demand for such services, the availability of treatment and intervention alternatives has indeed increased substantially. Further, paralleling the promulgation of treatment options for emotionally handicapped children and youth has been an increased emphasis on preventive methods. These include: (1) parent involvement and training programs, (2) affective and other humanistic efforts, (3) greater awareness of differing values and behavior patterns, and (4) increased availability of school and community counseling services.

Parent Involvement and Training Programs

A salient preventive measure has been the increased willingness of many professionals to include parents as legitimate manpower resources and a means of extending treatment and intervention programs beyond the confines of schools and clinics. Thus, a number of professionals have expanded their roles to include parent training. As a function of such training, many parents have been able to apply therapeutic and intervention procedures across a number of natural environments with their own children. With increasing frequency professionals involved in treating and educating emotionally disturbed young people seem to be heeding Hobbs' (1978) admonishment that, "Parents have to be recognized as special educators, the true experts on their children, and professional people—teachers, pediatricians, psychologists and others—have to learn to be consultants to parents" (p. 486).

In particular, parents have successfully used behavioral procedures as a preventive measure (Berkowitz and Graziano, 1972). Perhaps because of its wide applicability and general utility this methodology has been particularly effective in dealing with problems that , if left untreated, might have resulted in serious behavioral disorders. Although as few as two percent of all children and youth may be considered seriously emotionally disturbed (McDowell, 1982), this does not suggest that the remaining population has no problems. Many parents of normal children would strongly agree that they are in need of effective and appropriate child management skills. Further, this technology has allowed professionals to train parents to treat the behavioral excesses and deficits of their children without requiring that those children first be labeled emotionally disturbed, behaviorally disordered, etc.

In addition to behavioral procedures, parents have been exposed to programs designed to facilitate communication and to enhance their relationship with their children and family members. Programs such as Gordon's (1970) *Parent Effectiveness Training* (PET) and Dinkmeyer and McKay's (1976) *Systematic Training for Effective Parenting* (STEP) have been used successfully by parents to facilitate communication with their children and to reduce family conflict. A contemporary and comprehensive overview of parenting programs is offered by Fine (1980).

Affective and Other Humanistic Efforts

Only within the past several years have affective education programs become the focus of careful study and implementation. Thus, these multifaceted and elusive procedures which are designed to facilitate understanding of human feelings, emotions and behavior, have been introduced to children and youth in a variety of settings, including schools, communities, and clinics. Because of their emphasis on self-understanding, ego development and enhancement of self-esteem, affective programs appear to reduce a child's vulnerability to emotional and behavioral problems (Medway and Smith, 1978; Topley and Drennen, 1980).

Presented under various names, such as human relations training (Berenson, 1971); humanistic education (Pine and Boy, 1977); values clarification (Simon, Howe and Kirschenbaum, 1972); and self-control (Fagen, Long and Stevens, 1975), affective processes and procedures have been introduced to children and adolescents in an effort to enhance their self-esteem and specific social and academic behaviors.

The empirical efficacy of affective education programs still remains unsettled (Hodgins, 1979). However, it remains feasible that programs and procedures which successfully facilitate communication and personal understanding and can make children and adolescents feel more comfortable about themselves may serve well their mental health needs. Without argument affective programs may have played an important preventative role in the area of emotional disturbance.

Greater Acceptance of Differing Values and Behavior

As observed by Weintraub and Abeson (1976), "From ancient to modern times the physically, mentally or emotionally disabled have been alternatively viewed by the majority as dangers to be destroyed, as nuisances to be driven out, or as burdens to be confined" (p. 71). Nonetheless, even though the present general attitude toward persons with behavioral peculiarities and emotional problems is less than enlightened, there is an increased willingness among many individuals to attempt to understand and tolerate ideosyncratic behavior, and specifically those exhibited by children and adolescents with emotional and behavioral problems. Further, there appears to be greater awareness of the rights of individuals to challenge mere conformity; similarly persons are more willing to demonstrate their own uniqueness without the immediate fear of being ostracized or referred to a mental health clinic. While tenuous in some respects, this trend appears to be associated with the increased willingness of many individuals to reconceptualize their perceptions of abnormality resulting, in some instances, in the rejection of the notion that conformity is always equivalent to mental health. Such attitude modification appears to have obvious preventative benefits, particularly for those children who might otherwise to exposed to severe rejection for relatively insignificant episodes of exceptional behavior. In the same manner, this attitude appears to be increasingly associated with successful deinstitutionalization, normalization and mainstreaming programs.

Similarly, efforts to help individuals better understand and accept their own values and the values of others have facilitated the development of empathy toward problem children and have served as a basis for the interpretation of many interpersonal conflicts. Because values are a primary means by which individuals (including children and adolescents) make decisions and structure their lives, there is obvious benefit to programs which aid persons in recognizing their own beliefs and those of others. In spite of the technological advances and social changes of the past decades which have tended to obfuscate many basic values and beliefs, the values clarification movement has served to facilitate greater self-understanding and acceptance of others. Such empathic understanding, acceptance, and sensitivity have been particularly beneficial to disturbed and disturbing children and youth, and have, in some instances, served a preventive role.

Increased Availability of School and Community Services

Although the problems presented by emotionally and behaviorally impaired children and adolescents have been present throughout the ages, orchestrated community and school programs for such are a reasonably new phenomenon. Historically, professionals as well as lay people have assumed that emotionally disturbed children were the responsibility of their parents, the medical community or, when available, the mental health system. In the 1960s the need for and role of school programs for emotionally disturbed children became increasingly accepted. Simultaneously, it was emphasized that educators and mental health specialists must work together for maximum impact on troubled children. In 1963, this movement was facilitated by President John Kennedy who drew attention to the needs of emotionally disturbed children. Further, Kennedy actively supported legislation aimed at combating mental illness through the development of community service programs.

Historically, these factors have played an active preventive role and have served to meet some of the most basic needs of emotionally disturbed individuals and their families. While these initial efforts have not begun to meet all the needs of emotionally disturbed children, they do demonstrate the preventive influence of coordinated school and community programs.

SUMMARY

The emotionally disturbed child has been misunderstood and accordingly rather dramatically mistreated. Primitive notions of "devils within" and isolated asylum confinement have given way in this century to more humane and objective views and treatment of the emotionally disturbed. There is enough evidence in terms of legislation, program development, emergence of varied treatment modes, and broadened community involvement in the care of treatment of the disturbed child to believe that substantial progress has occurred.

Problems remain in the areas of diagnosis, identification and treatment. There are efforts to repeal important provisions of legislation that had generated advances in the treatment of disturbed children. It is to be hoped that such efforts will be successfully resisted and effective and humane progress will continue in the therapeutic treatment of disturbed children.

REFERENCES

Amundsen, N. and Sawatzky, D. A summative evaluation of the Transactional Analysis with children educational program. *Transactional Analysis Journal*, 1976, *6*, 326-327.

Apter, S. *Troubled children: Troubled systems*. New York: Pergamon Press, 1982.

Barnes, G. (Ed.) *Transactional Analysis after Eric Berne: Teaching and practices of three TA schools*. New York:Harper's College Press, 1977.

Bendell, D., and Fine, M. Increasing personality responsibility in acting-out boys. *Transactional Analysis Journal*, 1979, *9*, 85-87.

Berenson, D. H. The effects of systematic human relations training upon the classroom performance of elementary school teachers. *Journal of Research and Development in Education*, 1971, *4*, 70–85.

Berkowitz, B., and Graziano, A. Training parents as behavior therapists: A review. *Behavior Research and Therapy*, 1972, *10*, 297-317.

Berkowitz, P. and Rothman, E. *The disturbed child*. New York, New York: New York University, 1960.

Berkowitz, P. Pearl H. Berkowitz. In J. Kauffman and C. Lewis (Eds.). *Teaching children with behavior disorders: Personal Perspectives*. Columbus, Ohio: Charles E. Merrill, 1974.

Berne, E. *Games people play*. New York, New York: Grove Press, 1964.

Berne, E. *Transactional Analysis in psychotherapy*. New York, New York, Grove Press, 1961.

Berne, E. *What do you say after you say hello*? New York, New York: Grove Press, 1972.

Blatt, B. Human treatment and public policy. In G. William and S. Gordon (Eds.), *Clinical child psychology*. New York, New York: Behavioral Publications, 1974.

Blatt, B. *Exodus from pandemonium: Human abuse and reformation of public policy*. Boston, Massachusetts: Allyn and Bacon, 1970.

Bower, E. Defining emotional disturbance: Public policy and research. *Psychology in the schools*, *1982, 19*, 55–60.

Cruikshank, W. Forward. In J. Kauffman and C. Lewis (Eds.), *Teaching children with behavior disorders: Personal perspectives*. Columbus, Ohio: Charles C. Merrill, 1974.

Dinkmeyer, D. and McKay, G. *STEP, Systematic training in effective parenting*. Circle Pines, Minnesota: Americal Guidance Service, 1976.

Ehrenwald, J. *From medicine man to Freud*. New York, New York: Dell, 1956.

Erickson, E. Eight stages of man. In E. Erickson (Ed.), *Childhood and society*. New York, New York: Norton, 1950.

Fagen, S., Long, N., and Stevens, P. *Teaching self-control in the elementary school: A curriculum for preventing learning and emotional problems*. Columbus, Ohio: Charles E. Merrill, 1975.

Fenichel, C. Carl Fenichel. In J. Kauffman and C. Lewis (Eds.), *Teaching children with behavior disorders: Personal perspectives*. Columbus, Ohio: Charles E. Merrill, 1974.

Fine, M. (Ed.) *The handbook on parent education*. New York, New York, Academic Press, 1980.

Fine, M. and Walkenshaw, M. *The teacher's role in classroom management* (2nd ed.). Dubuque, Iowa: 1977.

Fixen, D., Phillips, E., and Wolf, M. Achievement place: Experiments in self-government, with pre-delinquents. Journal of Applied Behavioral Analysis, 1973, *6*, 31–47.

Frazer, J. *The golden bough*. New York, New York: The MacMillan Co., 1922.

Freud, S. *The psychopathology of everyday life*. New York, New York: Signet, 1961 (Originally published 1901).

Glasser, W. *Reality therapy*. New York, New York: Harper and Row, 1965.

Gordon, T. *P. E. T. Parent effectiveness training*. New York, New York: Peter Wyden, 1970.

Green v. Johnson, 515 F. Supp. 965 (D. Mass., 1981).

Haley, J. *Leaving home*. New York, New York: McGraw-Hill, 1980.

Heller, K., Price, R., and Sher, K. Research and evaluation in primary preventions: Issues and guidelines. In R. Price, R. Ketterer, B. Bader, and J. Monahan (Eds.), *Prevention in mental health: Research, policy and practice*. Beverly Hills, California: SAGE Publications, 1980.

Hobbs, N. Helping disturbed children: Psychological and ecological strategies. In H. Dupont (Ed.), *Educating emotionally disturbed children: Readings*, New York, New York: Holt, Rinehart and Winston, 1969.

Hobbs, N. Perspectives on re-education. *Behavior Disorders*, 1978, *3*, 65-6.

Hobbs, N. Classification options: A conversation with Nicholas Hobbs on exceptional child education. *Exceptional Children*, 1978, *44*, 494–497.

Hobbs, N. *The futures of children*. San Francisco, California: Jossey-Bass, 1975.

Hodgins, E. W. Examining the effectiveness of affective education. *Psychology in the Schools*, 1979, *16*, 581–585.

Jones, E. *The life and work of Sigmund Freud*. (Edited and abridged by L. Trilling and S. Marcus) New York, New York: Basic Books, 1961.

Justice, B. and Justice, R. *The abusing family*. New York, New York: Human Sciences Press, 1976.

Kanner, L. Emotionally disturbed children: A historical review. *Child Development*, 1962, *33*, 97-102.

Kauffman, J. M. *Characteristics of children's behavior disorders*. Columbus, Ohio: Charles E. Merrill, 1980.

Kauffman, J. *Characteristics of children's behavior disorders*. Columbus, Ohio: Charles E. Merrill, 1980.

Kempe, R. and Kempe, C. *Child abuse*. Cambridge, Massachusetts: Harvard University Press, 1978.

Kennedy, J. A talk on serving the needs of the handicapped. Washington, D.C.:, Unpublished speech, 1963.

Key, E. *The century of the child*. New York, New York: Putnam, 1909.

Larry P. v. Riles, 495 F. Supp. 926 (N. D. Cal., 1979).

Levine V NJ, No. A-55 (Sup. Ct. N.J., July 30, 1980).

Lewis, C. Introduction: Landmarks. In J. Kauffman and C. Lewis (Eds.), *Teaching children with behavior disorders: Personal perspectives*. Columbus, Ohio: Charles E. Merrill, 1974.

McDowell, R. Prologue. In R. McDowell, G. Adamson, and F. Woods (Eds.), *Teaching emotionally disturbed children*. Boston, Massachusetts: Little, Brown Co., 1982.

Madanes, C. *Strategic family therapy*. San Francisco, California: Jossey-Bass, 1981.

Mahler, M. *On human sybiosis and the vicissitudes of individuation, Volume I: Infantile psychosis*. New York, New York: International Universities Press, 1968.

Maisenbacher, J. and Erskine, R. Time structuring for problem students. *Transactional Analysis Journal*, 1976, 6, 196–198.

Malinowski, B. *Magic, science and religion*. New York, New York: Doubleday, 1954.

Medway, F. and Smith, R. An examination of contemporary elementary school affective education programs. *Psychology in the Schools*, 1978, *15* (2), 260-269.

Meichenbaum, D. *Cognitive-behavior modification: An integrative approach.* New York, New York: Plenum, 1977.

Minuchin, S. and Fishman, H. *Family therapy techniques.* Cambridge, Massachusetts: Harvard University Press, 1981.

North v. District of Columbia Board of Education, 471 F. Supp. 136 (D. D. C., 1979).

Parloff, M. Shopping for the right therapy. *Saturday Review,* 1976, Feb. 21, 14–16.

PASE vs. Hannon, 506 F. Supp. 831 (N.D. Ill., 1980).

Patterson, G. *Families' applications of social learning to family life.* Champagne, Illinois: Research Press, 1971.

Pennsylvania Association for Retarded Children v. Commonwealth of Pennsylvania, 343 F. Supp. 279 (D. Penn., 1972).

Piele, P. Neither corporal punishment curel nor due process due: The United States Supreme Court's decision in Ingraham v. Wright. In I. Hyman and J. Wise (Eds.), *Corporal Punishment in American education: Readings in history, practice, and alternatives.* Philadelphia, Pennsylvania: Temple University Press, 1979.

Pine, G. and Boy, A. *Learner centered teaching: A humanistic view.* Denver, Colorado: Love, 1977.

Reinert, H. The emotionally disturbed. In B. Gearhart (Ed.), *Education of the exceptional child: History, present practices and trends.* Scranton, Pennsylvania: Intext Education Publishers, 1972.

Reynolds, M. and Birch, J. *Teaching exceptional children in all America's schools.* Reston, Virginia: The Council for Exceptional Children, 1982.

Rhodes, W. *The emotionally disturbed student and guidance.* New York, New York: Houghton Mifflin, 1970.

Rhodes, W. C., and Paul, J. L. *Emotionally disturbed and deviant children: New views and approaches.* Englewood Cliffs, New Jersey: Prentice-Hall, 1978.

Simon, S., Howe, L. and Kirschenbaum, H. *Values clarification: A handbook of practical strategies for teachers and students.* New York, New York: Hart, 1972.

Stuart v. Nappi, 443 F. Supp. 1235 (D. Conn., 1978).

Szasz, T. The myth of mental illness. *American Psychologist,* 1960, *15,* 113–118.

Topley, K. and Drenner, W. The influence of an affective curriculum on the cognitive performance of four and five year olds. *Child Care Quarterly,* 1980, *9* (4), 251–257.

Weintraub, E. and Abeson, A. New education policies for the handicapped: The quiet revolution. In F. Weintraub, A. Abeson, J. Ballard, and M. Lavor (Eds.), *Public policy and the education of exceptional children.* Reston, Virginia: Council for Exceptional Children, 1976.

Whelan, R. Richard J. Whelan. In J. Kauffman and C. Lewis (Eds.), *Teaching children with behavior disorders: Personal perspectives.* Columbus, Ohio: Charles E. Merrill, 1974.

2

The Role of Policy
in Dealing with Disturbed Children

NEIL J. SALKIND

POLICY AND POLICY ANALYSIS

The relationships between the public schools in this country and other institutions such as the family, the legal system, and political groups are becoming increasingly complex. With rapid technological and sociological changes taking place—such as the introduction of the computer as a learning aid, legal and ethical considerations in the education of children, and the changing nature of the family itself—everyone involved in the educational process is faced with important questions that, more often than not, have answers with far reaching implications.

It often appears, however, that much of the decision making that takes place as far as school issues are concerned is based more on opinion and personal experience rather than the systematic consideration of all the available information. Such a situation presents problems when we are considering the child who is "normal" or not disturbed, but is exacerbated when the special child brings non-academic problems to the classroom. These children, who are in the minority as far as numbers, are caught in the middle of debates at various levels as to what is the best course of action to follow as far as their future progress and well being are concerned. Indeed what has often been left out of the equation in dealing with disturbed children in the majority of school settings is the development, implementation and evaluation of policies that are directly attuned to the needs of these children.

199611

The purpose of this chapter is to discuss how the development of policy and the use of policy analysis as a tool can provide a more effective and equitable strategy in developing intervention techniques with disturbed children. This chapter is somewhat unique to this book since it does not focus on a particular theory or therapy, nor does it focus specifically on the topic of intervention. It does, however, cut across the substantive areas under consideration and presents general guidelines and criteria that should be used when decisions regarding the education of children are made. More specifically, it aids us in evaluating the use of interventions as techniques for assisting disturbed children.

THE IMPORTANCE OF POLICY

In the most general sense, a policy can be deferred as "a course of action significantly affecting large numbers of people" (MacRae and Wilde, 1979, p. 4). By spending a short amount of time in any public school, we can easily see how many such policies are in effect, both at an explicit level as well as those that more or less go unspoken and are established through tradition. For example, policies regarding graduation from high school generally require the completion of a certain number of credit hours and are clearly understood by almost all of those that it affects. On the other hand, the use of individualized Educational Programs or IEPs) for children in special education settings might be a less clearly understood policy.

Few of us would argue that whether policies are explicitly detailed and understood or not, they do exist and in many cases have an important influence on what actions are carried out and on, in general terms, what happens in school. Although we can acknowledge their existence we should be better equipped to understand them. A discussion of why policies are important and worth pursuing is the first step in this process.

First, the use of policy in the education of children and in the development of interventions with disturbed children helps to *avoid the arbitrary decisions* that are often more injurious than helpful to the special child. Before implementation of Public Law 94-142 for example, and the tacit assurance of education for all children, children with special needs might have been assigned to programs that are inappropriate given their disability and/or level of functioning. In the absence of policy guidelines, arbitrary decisions based on personally generated criteria more often than not serve as a basis for these decisions. We should not overlook the case where policy decisions affecting very large numbers of children can be as arbitrary as well.

Another important reason why policies are necessary is that they *provide guidelines* for parents, students, and teachers to help calrify and understand what is expected of and by them. In turn, this allows poeple to have an awareness of how they should behave, what alternatives may be available to them, and what sanctions and associated penalities might exist as well. For example, the student knows that out-of-seat behavior results in some type of punishment. As for the teacher, he or she knows that the preparation of an IEP and the maintenance of a program directed at meeting the plan's goals are a major professional responsibility. The less uncertainty there is in any situation, especially new ones, the less anxiety is generated and the easier it is to successfully reach designated objectives.

Closely related to this last reason why policies are vital to the success of any school or intervention program is that they *force the accountability of actions*. The development and evaluation of a policy incorporates several different criteria into what is called a decision matrix. As a part of this matrix, alternative policies are compared across several criteria. If a specific policy is clearly articulated, and the parties understand what is involved, accountability of actions becomes easier to insure, as well as a less threatening and less volatile issue.

One of the most important reasons for the use of policies as it relates to interventions with disturbed children is that it *encourages the systematic consideration of the effects of an intervention* (or a set of such strategies). It also encourages us to look down the road and consider the implications of the actions that we are about to take or are dictated by the policy under consideration. More often than not, hastily thought out policies that are not based on solid information are ineffective through lack of planning and foresight in the policy making process. Constructing an intervention program that is likely to be effective in the short run, but which has consequences that are undesirable at a later point in time, is not an effective way to plan or implement policy decisions.

The use of policy in a school setting as a tool for change, can also *motivate the general community* to become more involved in school decisions. Although we often associate the term policy and policy analysis with large corporations, executive positions and the government, policy is perhaps the most effective tool for the private citizen to use as he or she sees rules and regulations affecting institutions within the community.

Finally, and perhaps the most important reason why policy development should be encouraged and all parties in the educational system knowledgable about the process, is its use as an effective way to *advocate for certain causes*. For example, at one time the policy of immunizing children against infectious diseases was questioned based on a variety of concerns. One of the most significant was the presumed right of the government to impose what some people saw as restrictive conditions on the degree of parental control over their child's health. The implementation of a policy that results in the suspension of children from school who are not immunized has served to increase the percentage of immunized children, resulting in further support of that policy. Perhaps the most effective way a parent can advocate for children in general, and his or her child in particular, is through the use of policy related activities.

These previous six reasons help justify the role that policy might play in an education setting. They become even more important when we consider the very special place that children with emotional, psychological, or social problems might face.

When nonextreme populations are involved, it often seems that the less explicit policies are somehow created and perpetuate themselves since the majority tends to rule. Its an entirely different case, however, when the special child is concerned. Here the action on the part of the teacher, school board, parents' rights organizations, or even the state, may single out (and thereby stigmatize) a particular child or set of children, often introducing additional stress into an already too rigid, fixed, and overloaded system.

But given a specific policy or set of policies, how might we go about evaluating them? In order for us to understand a policy, we of course need to fully consider its implications. In order for us to most effectively use policy, we also have to be responsive to what these evaluative steps tell us, and to be able to respond in kind with alterations in the particular policy that we are considering. To find for example, that a behavioral program, given the nature of certain punishers, is unacceptable to parents, we should strive to reevaluate our approach and adjust it accordingly.

Given the arguments we have just made, policies are an important part of any effective school program. However, a policy without any kind of accountability system leaves us much to be desired as no policy at all. Basically, this is because the formation and refinement of policy can only take place most effectively in conjunction with the process of policy analysis.

HOW POLICY IS ANALYZED

Policies in public schools exist for many different reasons. Sometimes, the policies are based on a great deal of forethought, and sometimes they are almost knee-jerk reactions to problem situations.

In either case, for us to better understand their impact on children, it would be helpful to develop some kind of a policy analysis strategy for comparing different alternatives to one another using some set of predetermined criteria. For example, we might want to examine the relative strengths and weaknesses from a policy perspective of mainstreaming handicapped children into the classroom rather than keeping them segregated, or the relative merits of including parents in all phases of an evaluation and treatment of a disturbed child.

Definition of the Problem

The first step in the analysis of a policy deals with the specification or definition of the problem that is to be addressed. This is of critical importance, for without a clear idea of the problem that we believe needs attention, it is difficult, if not impossible, to derive a solution. We want to be as sure as possible that final recommendations attend to the problem, and that we have not strayed too far from our original purpose.

We must also address our attention however to the level at which the problem appears. We can define a problem at the general, intermediate, or specific level (MacRae and Wilde, 1979). At the more intermediate level, the problem of interest to us might be how to deal with disruptive children in the classroom. A different tier of the same problem might lead us to better understanding the kinds of problems presented by specific types of emotionally disturbed children, and possible treatment alternatives.

In general, the more specifically we define a problem, the more directly the policies that are put forth to ameliorate that problem can be examined. We can then use the information from the analysis to reconsider proposed solutions, and if necessary alter the policy or policies under consideration.

Selection of Criteria

After defining the problem, our next concern should be the selection of criteria we will use to evaluate the policy (or policies) under consideration. For example, if a school system has in effect a policy to deal with truancy, how can we evaluate the effectiveness of that policy? Should we examine the effect the policy has on number of days of school missed? on academic achievement? on attitude towards school? These are all questions that relate directly to the way in which the problem is defined.

Earlier in this chapter we noted how policy analysis uses *reason and evidence* to reach a choice among several alternative policies. Criteria represent those dimensions of reason and evidence across which several different policies can be compared. Criteria are valuative in the sense that they are often selected based on the implicit values underlying the particular policy that is being discussed. It is important for any student or practitioner of policy analysis to keep in mind that the clarification of such values should be an integral part of any analysis. In both cases, clarifying the criteria we select and the values underlying the selection of these criteria are crucial to a full understanding of the different policy alternatives under consideration.

Regardless of the problem however, there are two general classes of criteria. The first is often referred to as *universal criteria* and can be applied to almost any kind of policy problem. Such criteria as preference satisfaction, equity, efficiency, and stigma fall into this group. Likewise, there are criteria that are *specific* to the policy or policies under consideration. Only when we can define the specific nature of the problem, (as we will do later in the chapter) can we discuss the policy specific criteria.

Preference satisfaction is based on the economic notion of a free market as it applies to human behavior. That is, people will do those things that have the largest payoffs and avoid those things that do not. In other words, people will tend to gravitate towards those policy alternatives that they find most attractive for whatever reason that their own past experiences and present needs might dictate. From a policy point of view, we are talking mostly about the attractiveness of one policy alternative versus the attractiveness of another to the people who will be administering the policy as well as those who will be affected most by whatever policy is implemented. For example, while "time out" might not be very attractive to the child as an alternative for dealing with disruptive behavior, it may be exactly what both the teacher and the parent need and find most attractive if the goal is to reduce the frequency of some previously specified behavior.

Another criterion that is universally used in the analysis of policy is that of *equity*. In general, the criterion of equity addresses how people with similar or different needs are treated, and consists of both horizontal and vertical equity.

In the case of an emotionally disturbed child, the criterion of *horizontal equity* would not be violated if that child received services at the same level and degree of attention that another child with the same type of problem receives. On the other hand, if there are children who are in need of additional services, *vertical equity* (unequal treatment of unequals) would not be violated if the child with the greater need indeed receives additional attention. It is certainly very difficult to decide level of equality as it relates to specific problems that children might have, but the use of equity as an evaluate criterion will help insure successful implementation of the policy in spite of the individual differences that so often become a serious stumbling point in the policy process.

The criterion that we most often hear referred to in these times of fiscal constraint is *efficiency*, which includes both *benefit-costs analysis*, and *cost-effectiveness*. In both cases, the criterion of efficiency is premised on the fact that we want to maximize the return we see on any policy given a certain committment of resources. For example, we want the money allocated for our schools to be spent in the most cost-effective way. In common parlance, we want the "biggest bang for the bucks."

When we can assess both the input and the outcome of a certain policy in terms of dollars, we can discuss the benefit-costs of a particular policy. An excellent example of how benefits-cost applies can be seen in the examination of the outcomes associated with the Perry Preschool Project (Schweinhart and Weikart, 1980). The costs of this project that are associated with two years of preschool per child are $5,984. The benefits in terms of mother's release time (to do things such as work, go to school, etc.) increases in lifetime earnings which result, in part, from this released time; decreased costs of special education for these children who were in the preschool program amount to $14,810, clearly outdistancing the costs.

If one is to argue about the relative merits of a program or policy based on economic factors, this very well might be the most appropriate criterion to use. However, we find that the benefit-costs criterion may not always be the most appropriate one to use. If we are not interested primarily in the economic outcomes, or have the necessary information to complete such an analysis, we need to look elsewhere. For example, let's consider a policy such as the availability of counseling services to families through the public schools. To compute the costs of these services, we have to consider such things as counselor salaries, perhaps the cost of an administrator's time to help run the program, and the costs of space for the counseling and other related factors. The outcomes, however, are much more difficult to measure in terms of straight economic terms. Let's assume for example that such a program prevented the dissolution of some marriages, helped increase a child's school performance, and, in general, helped other families to cope better with school related problems that their children are having. All of these outcomes are very difficult to assess in an objective way, and are virtually impossible to assess economically. The efficiency here is what is important, and can be discussed in line with the costs (hence cost-efficiency), but is not as precise as the benefit-costs criterion we mentioned earlier. Hence, we may discuss other outcomes such as quality of family relationships.

In deciding which of these two criteria might be best to use in the analysis of a policy two things should be kept in mind. First, if the units of input and output are similar, benefit-costs analysis may be appropriate. In this case, we can express the input and the outcomes in terms of some economic measure such as dollars. If on the other hand, the input and output units are not similar, cost-effectiveness might be more appropriate. For example, input may be dollars, but quality of life might be the outcome that we are measuring. Second, the criteria that we choose to evaluate efficiency will depend, of course, on the question we are asking, and the way in which we have defined the policy problem.

Another universal criterion that we will discuss here is *stigma*, or the assignment of a negative label to an individual. This is often overlooked as a consequence of implementing a policy, but can have a powerful impact on the overall evaluation of the policy. For example, when a disruptive child is singled out and labeled negatively, not only is that child's self-esteem threatened, but his or her character in the perceptions of surrounding peers is altered for the worse more often than not.

In his classic book on stigma, Erving Goffman (1963) discusses stigma in terms of "spoiled identity" and the enormous impact that such psychological factors can have on one's emotional health and social adjustment. Policies that deal with human service problems almost invariably have to single out a group of people in the delivery of those services necessary to help ameliorate the problem. It is how this is accomplished that either results in an introduction of stigma and associated perverse effects, or minimizes the attachment of negative values to the services and hence to the people involved. In seeking a just and effective treatment method, we should strive to minimize the stigma associated with the treatment of hyperactivity.

Finally, there is the universal criterion of *unanticipated consequences*. These are those things that policy implementors, and those affected by policy cannot anticipate happening prior to the actual implementation of the policy. These consequences can take on a negative or positive valence. In the present case, an example of an unintended consequence in the use of drugs to control hyperactivity is the associated side effects such as suppression of growth or loss of appetite (Ross and Ross, 1976).

GENERATION OF ALTERNATIVE POLICIES

When we are faced with the specific problem that we know needs attention, we rarely have only one possible solution available. More often than not, there are many different strategies (or policies) that might be appropriate. Indeed we have spent the last section of this paper discussing what criteria we would use to evaluate any one policy. We are now at a point in our analysis, where we want to discuss how different policies can be compared to one another using the set of universal criteria that we have discussed, and the use of some policy specific criteria as well.

To accomplish this comparison we can combine the different criteria we specified along with all of the alternatives we would consider into what is commonly referred to as a decision matrix (Haskins, 1980). A decision matrix is simply a combination of all policies judged by all criteria into a tabular form that allows us to weigh or assign some value to each of the policies according to each criterion.

Decision matrices are not unlike the decision trees that characterize most systems analysis procedures, yet they are different in at least two significant ways. In the policy analysis model that we are discussing here, decisions are not made at a series of different points as they are in the tree system or the linear flow models frequently used. Second, because of this, decisions that are made are not hierarchical or dependent upon one another. One could consider the various criteria as different levels of a decision, and indeed this may be the case when one criterion is more important than another. Even in this case, however, the value that is assigned to one criterion as it might effect eventual adoption and effectiveness of the policy is not directly affected by the value assigned to other criteria.

A SAMPLE ANALYSIS: THE TREATMENT OF HYPERACTIVITY

In an earlier part of this chapter, we discussed the importance and value of using policy analysis as a tool in better understanding and using different intervention techniques with disturbed children. To continue with this discussion, it is useful to illustrate an application of this analytic technique to a specific problem—childhood hyperactivity or hyperkinesis.

Understanding the Problem

There is extensive and complex literature on the diagnosis and treatment of the hyperactive child. Falling under the general concern of behavior disturbances in young children, we can narrow our focus to the more specific area of what we will define as a "persistent pattern of excessive activity in situations requiring motor inhibition" (Safer and Allen, 1976, p. 7).

On of the major problems in reaching and defining the problem statement is the clarity with which the subject of the policy issue itself can be defined. As readers of this book surely recognize, the difficulty in defining hyperactivity has certainly been great. To a large extent, the lack of clearly defined basic terms when incorporated into policy work can lead to nothing other than lack of clarity in the articulation of goals.

Nye (1974) made a concerted attempt to identify four types of hyperkinesis, and to associate different signs or factors of psychiatric significance with each one. The four types are; genetic (or constitutional), behavioral (or conditioned), minimal brain dysfunctional (or chemical), and reactive (or chaotic). This is an attempt to segregate these different types of hyperactivity into categories thereby making diagnosis more accurate and treatment more effective.

But what about hyperactivity might we consider of sufficient interest or need, if such be the case, that we might formulate a policy? Given the often controversial nature of the topic, it seems we have many choices, including, the various ways in which hyperactivity is measured, the related diagnostic procedures that are used, or the different treatment paradigms that have developed over the past fifty years to deal with the problem. All of these are viable topic areas to which we can address our policy concerns. They are also viable since they appeal to different audiences.

For the purposes of this chapter, our policy question examines the various models and techniques available for dealing with the hyperactive child. We ask the question that, given the variety of therapies that are available, which is the most effective in decreasing childhood hyperactivity in young children? We are defining effectiveness though the use of several criteria, some of which we have discussed earlier (universal criteria), and some of which are policy specific.

Keep in mind, however, that rarely does a policy question become formulated without input from a variety of different sources that all have influence on the final question. For example, if we recall the history of the use of psychopharmocological agents as a treatment method, we might remember the extensive discussion that followed news reports of five to ten percent of school children in Omaha receiving drugs (Maynard, 1970). The policy question in this case might become the use of this one therapeutic approach or even perhaps the side effects of such drugs on children's health.

Another very important component of clearly formulating the policy question that we want answered is the historical issues behind the question. In our case here, the way in which hyperactivity was defined and handled by various professional communities sheds light on the development of current methodologies, and their advantages and disadvantages as well. A little history then, might serve to further illuminate the nature of the problem.

More than 100 years ago Hoffman (1845) described children who today would be classified as hyperactive. For perhaps the next 70 years, these types of children were segregated and placed in groups that more or less kept them away from the mainstream of everyday life. They are certainly excluded from those children who more easily fit into the design of a society that stressed normality in its educational and religious institutions.

With the increased popularity of the child guidance clinics in the 1930s, these types of "neurotic" behaviors took on sufficient significance to be recognized as a treatable problem, and were defined within a medical model that postulated some type of organic dysfunction to be responsible for the overactivity. This period of time also saw the introduction and systematic examination of the effect of amphetamines on this behavior by Bradley (1937).

With the importance of education as a mediating influence becoming more dominant, the 1940s and 1950s were characterized by a dependence upon the schools to help in the diagnosis and treatment of the disturbed child. The 1960s witnessed an enormous increase in the use of drugs to control behavior, an issue that was surfacing across our society in general, coupled with some serious questioning of their effectiveness, and the morality of using such controlling means especially with young children (Hentoff, 1972). Finally, it seems as if the last ten years has seen more and more emphasis on behavioral methods of treating hyperactivity in an effort to move away from drug or psychotherapeutic approaches.

In effect, over the last 50 years, several different approaches have been taken in dealing with childhood hyperactivity. For our purposes here, we will examine three of the most popular, namely, psychopharmocological or drug therapy, diet, and behavioral techniques. The status quo or "as is" policy alternative can also be examined to help establish a baseline for comparison.

At this point, an extensive policy analysis would detail a review of the literature that is available within each of these four approaches. Since space restrictions do not permit such a lengthy exposition, the reader is referred to other sources for an overview of this information such as Ross and Ross (1976), Safer and Allen (1976), and Loney (in press).

Selection of Criteria

In our example here, we are concerned with the general effectiveness of each of these four intervention or treatment models as they relate to hyperactivity in children.

To complete this evaluation, we need to specify a set of criteria across each of these alternatives that will be compared. Given the purpose of the analysis, *cost-effectiveness* and *stigma* will be used as universal criteria. We will also consider the *unanticipated consequences* associated with each of the policy alternatives. As far as policy specific criteria are concerned, the one of greatest importance is the *effectiveness* of the various treatment systems as it reduces actual level of hyperactivity. Keep in mind that different intervention models may assume difficult definitions of hyperactivity, an issue that besets many policy analyses.

Each of these criteria have been incorporated into the decision matrix that is presented in Figure one. Before we begin discussing each of the individual cells of the figure, it is important to note the substantive nature of the cell entries. Each policy is rated on each of the criteria as low, moderate or high. A rating of high (note it is not a ranking, although this might be another strategy that an analyst might assume) across the criteria would mean, highly cost efficient, a high degree of stigma is associated with that particular treatment, there are many or serious unanticipated consequences, and the alternative is effective in reducing hyperactivity.

It is very important to point out that the content of the cells, in terms of qualitative or quantitative ratings, can be as precise or global as the policy analyst sees fit. One example is the audience, who will be using the policy analysis itself to make a decision.

Evaluation of Policy Alternatives

There are two ways each of the alternative policies can be evaluated via the criteria we specified in the last section of this paper. The first is by discussing each of the criteria sequentially within a particular policy, while the second is by discussing each of the criteria across all policies. While the second option would serve the purpose of discussing criteria more so than policies, our analysis (often called the synthesis of information stage) examines each policy in turn a la each separate unknown.

Pharmocological Management of Hyperactivity

There is little doubt that the use of pharmocological agents (especially central nervous system stimulants) are at least, in the short run, effective as treatment for many cases involving hyperactivity (Steinberg, et al., 1971). Yet, in spite of the effectiveness of the drugs, many questions remain regarding the mechanism through which they affect attention and/or activity level, the duration of treatment, the need for monitoring, and the somewhat troublesome side effects.

As far as the cost-effectiveness of medications such as Ritalin or Dexedrine, the cost of the medication, given the enormous volume of amphetamine usage in the United States, is quite low. This low cost, coupled with the documented evidence that this therapy routine is somewhat effective (Safer and Allen, 1973), the cost-effectiveness ratio is very high. That is, given the cost, the effectiveness of the treatment is quite high.

The stigma however associated with such a treatment modality is high and should be a major consideration in the use of this intervention strategy. It is not common for young children to be on a routine schedule of taking medication, especially when the reason for such is the behavioral differences that exist between the child and his or her peers. What an adult might see as a simple task of taking medication can turn out to be a source of severe and traumatizing embarrassment for the child. Ross and Ross (1976) discuss the feelings of an eight year old about his required pill taking. The boy not only was chided by his peers, but one wrote the following poem that taunted the child to the degree he wanted to "go to another school and start over" (p. 102).

David Hill
Did you take your pill
That makes you work
And keeps you still
Take your pill, Hill
(Ross and Ross, 1976, p. 102)

Other less obtrusive strategies for taking medication, where sensitive school personnel might be available, could help ameliorate this problem. However, school guidelines on who holds drugs and distributes them (usually someone in the front office) often prevent possibly more lax, but more responsive practices. Because of these kinds of outcomes, the use of drugs as a management routine is highly stigmatizing.

The unanticipated consequences associated with pharmocological treatment raise some troublesome issues as well. Most of these are physical in nature and often present in unattractive and intolerable set of outcomes that rule out such a therapy for many families. Among such side effects are insomnia and headaches (Connors, Taylor, Meo, Kurtz, and Fournier, (1972), suppression of growth (Safer and Allen, 1973), changes in heart function and the potential for later drug abuse (Safer, Allen, and Barr, 1972), and a "panda effect" first reported by Solomons (1971) characterizing the child with a sunken dark look around the eyes. All of these effects tend to be short lived once the medication is removed, yet there is little evidence on the long range effects of such medication on young children. Clearly, there is legitimate concern over the use of these drugs for an extended period of time when some of these consequences or side effects can be extreme.

Finally, and perhaps equal in importance to any of the criteria we have so far discussed is the reduction in hyperactivity. As we mentioned earlier, there is no question that the short term efficiency of the program is high, and that the more hyperactive the child is, in general, the better the response to the medication (Steinberg, Troshinsky, and Steinberg, 1971). However, there are no real estimates as to the long term benefits of such treatment. To estimate such, we have to move outside of the actual drug treatment and view one long term benefit resulting from increased attention and increased learning time (and perhaps learning as well!). Safer and Allen (1973) estimate that dramatic effects are achieved in 35-50% of the children, moderate effects in 30-40%, and no effect in 15-20%. In addition, Wender (1971) has discussed how the use of some drugs actually have a negative effect. All in all, it seems that the treatment is moderately effective, even given the lack of information as to any long term benefits.

Management of Hyperactivity by Diet

When Benjamin Feingold, a food allergist from San Francisco, made his presentation on food additives and hyperactive children to the American Medical Association (June, 1974) it started a controversy involving physicians, the food industry, and parents that is still continuing at an intense level.

His hypothesis is that hyperactivity, and a wide range of associated learning disorders, are the result of ingesting foods that are artificially colored and artificially flavored. He proposed a salicylate free diet which excluded "not only foods containing natural salicylates, but also all sources of artificial flavors and colors, with and without the salicylate radical" (Feingold, 1974).

Probably the most costly component of this treatment method is that almost all foods that the child eats need to be prepared at home from scratch. This is because commercially prepared foods almost always contain some amount of artificial ingredients. Reading the labels of commercial foods is not sufficient since not all ingredients are always stated, nor are the amounts of each. While preparation at home, using allowable ingredients, is somewhat costly in terms of time and effort, one recommendation of the treatment regime includes preparing the same foods for the entire family, an even more costly undertaking. There are few estimates of what maintenance on such a diet might cost, but relative to the diet's effectiveness as a treatment (which has been shown to be inconsistent), the cost-effectiveness of the program seems low to moderate at best.

While there is relatively little stigma attached to the consumption of such prepared foods, the circumstances surrounding eating lunch at school can sometimes present a problem. To begin with, all foods prepared by school personnel would be prohibited, therefore excluding buying in the school cafeteria. Buying from vending machines or a snack on the way home from school is prohibited as well. Eating out for the individual child (attending birthday parties, etc.) and for the whole family also becomes very difficult. It is important to keep in mind that the diet is not easy to follow, and such commonly acceptable foods as almonds, cherries, oranges, catsup, margarine, all manufactured candy, aspirin, and even toothpaste are not allowed.

One of the major advantages of this diet however, is that for the individual child there are few unanticipated consequences that might arise. If anything, the reduction of a diet high in fat and sugar might lead to greater health and well being.

Finally, we have to examine how effective the treatment is in the reduction of the child's hyperactivity. Remember, that this diet was accepted and is still advocated by a large number of parents and parent groups around the country who have found it to be very effective. In a recent book that reviews the effectiveness of controlling food additives as a means of dealing the hyperactive children, Connors (1980) presents an extensive review of available literature and concludes that although the treatment may be effective in some cases, overall it tends to be inconsistent. While Feingold found that upwards of 50% of his clinical sample improved (Feingold, 1974), Connors reports on 12 studies that report inconsistent results. Although the anecdotal information on a case by case basis (which generally is the way that parents are referred) has a significant validity, the "hard" scientific evidence is as yet questionable. In final judgment as to the efficacy of the diet however, we should not exclude the possibility that altering to the diet in a nonexperimental setting is so difficult for the child that a true test of the hypothesis would be impossible.

Behavioral Treatment of Hyperactivity

Of the three different interventions that we are considering, a behavioral approach is probably the least invasive for the child, and the most cost-efficient as well. To begin with, there are no "real" costs associated with the intervention, although we might consider the expense of training parents and others in the techniques of behavior modification and modeling as a cost. Even in this case, training can more often than not be accomplished through self study and a relatively small degree of formal instruction. Costs for training materials and the time that the instructor would spend should be taken into account. Keep in mind, however, that it is the pediatrician or family doctor who maintains surveillance over any drug regime; and with the increasing awareness of the part of the medical community as to the availability of behavioral approaches as an alternative, the health practitioner's skills and time can be focused on assisting parents and teachers in implementing such programs.

The fact that costs are minimized within this policy alternative is definitely a plus in its favor. The stigma associated with this intervention technique tends however to be moderate, and depending upon the contingencies on the child's behavior, could even be high. For example, if the child's behavior is not very extreme (or disruptive in the classroom), the effective time out procedures (using self-control techniques) would tend to minimize the degree of stigma. If on the other hand the child's behavior is extreme and very difficult to control, then more imposing controls need to be used, and the possibility that the child is stigmatized as a trouble maker or fidgety kind, increases. Some behavioral therapists would argue however, that if the behavior is allowed to get to the point where extreme contingencies are necessary, then the management program is not effective to begin with.

There are minimal unanticipated consequences as far as the application of a behavioral model to the treatment of hyperactivity. This is primarily because it is a relatively unobtrusive intervention. There are, however, side effects noted in the literature, especially as they impact on the family of the child. Most noteworthy here is that these effects can be positive in nature.

Patterson, McNeal, Hawkins, and Phelps (1967) identified what they call a *chain reaction* or an *avalanche effect* which refers to their finding that the use of behavior modification which results in a change in the child's behavior, also results in changes in the behavior of those people in the child's environment. They provide an example of how teaching a mother to effectively use time out as a way to control her hyperactive child resulted in an avalanche or positive benefits including, reduced anxiety on her part, reduction in the child's hyperactive behavior, a more pleasant household environment, increased social activity for the mother, increased use of positive social reinforcers, and a reduction in adversive types of controlling practices such as scolding and yelling. Patterson et al. notes how the simple teaching of time out could not "directly produce all these dramatic changes. The procedure merely initiated the first step in a chain reaction" (Patterson, McNeal, Hawkins, and Phelps, 1967. p. 193). It would, of course, be very difficult to ascertain whether the mother's use of time out for her child was not mediated by the host of other indirectly related factors associated with the treatment such as increased contact with other adults teaching her the method, and other potentially interactive factors.

The key question that remains, however, concerns the effectiveness of this intervention technique for reducing hyperactive behavior. Wahler, Winkel, Peterson, and Morrison (1965) and Becker, Madsen, Arnold, and Thomas (1967) recognize the effectiveness of behavioral intervention strategies but question their generalizability to other settings. This inability to be generalized to new settings is an often heard criticism of the behavioral model in general. It becomes especially relevant here, when we consider that specific types of behaviors that would need control tend to be different in different settings, such as at home and at school. Although time out and other related techniques might be very effective, their efficiency in terms of how well the specific program transfers from one setting to another is low. This is not as much a criticism of the strategy as much as a statement of fact, and is especially true during the initial stages of any such program. The reader should keep in mind however, that the ability to be generalized is often not a problem since highly similar types of behaviors can and do occur across different settings.

SUMMARY AND CONCLUSIONS

There are many different ways to use policy analysis as a tool in making a decision as to which of many alternative strategies is the best one to select in dealing with a certain human services problem. In this chapter we followed a model that requires the identification of a problem, the selection of criteria, the application of those criteria to a set of alternatives, and the final use of a decision matrix to better understanding the use of the criteria. As an example we chose the problem of hyperactivity in young children, and used absolute judgments rather than relative ones as far as the overall attractiveness of one policy versus another.

Our complicated decision matrix is illustrated in Figure one, where each of the policies is rated along each of the criteria as high, moderate, or low. Based on our analysis, it appears that the most attractive of the three policies that we have discussed is the behavioral approach. It seems to be cost-effective, minimizes stigma, and is moderately successful in reducing the incidence of hyperactive behavior. Most interesting, however, is that the associated unanticipated consequences of this strategy have a positive valence and a generally favorable impact as far as evaluating the program is concerned.

Cost-effectiveness	H	L	L
Stigma	H	L–M	M
Criteria			
Unanticipated Consequences	H	L	H
Reduction in Hyperactivity	M–H	L	M–H

Figure 1. Decision matrix on policy alternatives.

Whether the present swing towards courting policy in the field of education remains or not is impossible to predict. Educators, especially those who deal with the disturbed child, should look upon policy analysis as a tool that can effectively assist them in advocating whatever treatment or intervention paradigm they believe can best fit the needs of the child, the family, the school, and ultimately the entire community.

REFERENCES

Aman, M. G. and Werry, J. S. Methylphenidote in children: Effects upon cardiorespiratory. *International Journal of Mental Health*, 1975, *4*, 119-131.

Beck, L., Landord, W. S., MacKay, M., and Sum, G. Childhood chemotherapy and later drug abuse and growth curve: A follow-up study of 30 adolescents. *American Journal of Psychiatry*, 1975, *132*, 436-438.

Becker, W. C., Madsen, C. H., Arnold, C. R. and Thomas, D. R. The contingent use of teacher reinforcement and praise in reducing classroom behavior problems. *Journal of Special Education*, 1967, *1*, 287-307.

Bradley, C. The behavior of children receiving benzedrine. *American Journal of Psychiatry*, 1937, *94*, 577-585.

Connors, C. K. *Food additives and hyperactive children*. New York, New York: Plenum Press, 1980.

Connors, C., Taylor, E., Meo, G., Kurtz, M. and Fournier, M. Magnesium penoline and dextroamphetamine: A controlled study in children with minimal brand dysfunction. *Psychopharmocologia*, 1972, *26*, 321-336.

Eysenck, N. T. and Rachman, S. T. The application of learning theory to child psychiatry. In T. C. Howells (Ed.) *Modern perspectives in child psychiatry*. New York, New York: Brunner/Mazel, 1971.

Feingold, B. Hyperkinesis and learning difficultes (H–LD) linked to the ingestion of artificial colors and flavors. Paper presented at the American Medical Association annual meeting, June 1974.

Gittelman-Klein, R. Review of clinical psychopharmacological treatment of hyperkinesis. In Klein, D. F. and Guttelman-Klein, R. (Eds.) *Progress in psychiatric drug treatment*. New York, New York: Brunner/Mazel, 1975.

Gittleman-Klein, R., Klein, D. F., Abikoff, H., Katz, S., Gloisten, A. C., and Kates, W. Relative efficacy of methylphenidote and behavior modification in hyperkinetic children: An interim report. *Journal of Abnormal Child Psychology*, 1976, *4*, 361-379.

Goffman, E. *Stigma*. Englewood Cliffs, New Jersey: Prentice-Hall, 1963.

Haskins, R. Introduction–A model for analyzing social policies. In Ron Haskins and James J. Gallagher (Eds.) *Care and education of young children in America.* Norwood, New Jersey: ABLEX Publishing Company, 1980.

Hentoff, N. Drug pushing in the schools: The professionals. *The Village Voice,* May 25, 1972, p. 20–22.

Hoffman, H. *Der Struwwelpeter: Older lustige geschichten und drollige bilder.* Leipzig: Insel-Verlag, 1845.

Loney, J. Hyperkinesis comes of age: What do we know and where should we go? *American Journal of Orithopsychiatry* (in press).

MacRae, D. and Wilde, J. *Policy analysis for public decisions.* North Scituate, Massachusetts: SSachuselk: Duxbury Pren, 1979.

Maynard, R. Omaha pupils given "behavior" drugs. *Washington Post,* June 29, 1970.

Nachamin, S. J. and Comly, H. M. The hyperkinetic or lethargic child with cerebral dysfunction. *Michigan Medicine,* 1964, *63,* 790–792.

Nye, P. G. Four types of hyperkinesis. *Canadian Psychiatric Association,* 1974, *19,* 543–550.

Patterson, G. R., McNeal, S., Hawkins, N. and Phelps, R. Programming the social environment. *Journal of Child Psychology and Psychiatry,* 1967, *8,* 181–195.

Ross, D. M. and Ross, S. A. *Hyperactivity: Research, and Theory and Action.* New York, New York: Wiley, 1976.

Safer, D. and Allen, R. Single daily dose methylphenidote in hyperactive children. *Diseases of the Nervous System,* 1973, *34,* 325–328.

Safer, D. J. and Allen, R. P. Factors influencing the suppresent effects of the stimulant drugs on the growth of hyperactive children. *Pediatrics,* 1973, *51,* 660–667.

Safer, D. J. and Allen, R. P. *Hyperactive children: Diagnosis and Management.* Baltimore, Maryland: University Park Press, 1976.

Safer, D., Allen, R., and Barr, E. Depression of growth in hyperactive children on stimulant drugs. *New England Journal of Medicine,* 1972, *287,* 217–220.

Schweinhart, L. H. and Weikart, D. P. *Young children grow up: The effects of the Perry preschool program on youths through age 15.* Ypsilanti, Michigan: High Scope Foundation, 1980.

Solomons, G. The role of methylphendote and dextroamphetamine in children. *Drug Letter* (University of Iowa Hospitals and Clinics), 1971, *10,* 7-9.

Solomons, G. Drug therapy: Invitation and follow-up. *Journal of New York Academy of Medicine,* 1973, *205,* 335–344.

Sprague, R. L. and Sleator, E. K. Effects of psychopharmacologic agents on learning disorders. *Pediatric Clinics of North America,* 1973, *20,* 719–735.

Sprague, E. L. and Sleator, E. K. What is the proper dose of stimulant drugs in children? *International Journal of Mental Health,* 1975, *4,* 75–104.

Steinberg, G. G. Troshinsky, C., and Steinberg, H. R. Dextroamphetamine-response behavior disorders in school children. *American Journal of Psychiatry,* 1971, *128,* 174–179.

Wahler, R. G., Winkel, G. H., Peterson, R. F. and Morrison, D. C. Mothers as behavior therapists for their own children. *Behavioral Research and Therapy,* 1965, *3,* 113–124.

Wender, P. H. *Minimal brain dysfunction in children.* New York, New York: Wiley-Interscience, 1971.

3

Legal and Ethical Issues in the Discipline of Emotionally Disturbed Children

IRWIN A. HYMAN AND DAVID BOGACKI

The purpose of this chapter is to present an overview of select legal and ethical issues of discipline procedures with emotionally disturbed children. The emphasis is on the public school and other institutional settings in which children receive educational services under Public Law 94-142. It is acknowledged that problems of confidentiality of information, parents' acceptance of the school's classification and definition of least restrictive environment, and parents' right to know all information regarding their children are issues involving ethical and legal questions. However, these problems have been dealt with extensively in the literature related to child advocacy and therefore will not be discussed here (Hyman and Schreiber, 1975; Mearig, 1978). Of greater concern to the writers are the day to day problems faced by educators and clinicians when dealing with those emotionally disturbed children who present maladaptive behavior which causes difficulties for themselves and others.

It will be noticed that the title of this chapter did not use the usual clinical euphemisms such as "behavioral management", "limit setting", or "therapeutic strategy" to describe the process more commonly called discipline. While professional nosology may offer the practitioner a more precise theoretical frame within which to operate, the interaction between the teacher and child may be reduced to a simple fact. One way or another, the teacher attempts to change the child's behavior so that it is either less disturbed or disturbing and therefore acceptable to the teacher.

The difference between "disturbed" and "disturbing" behavior is of more than passing interest to clinical and educational personnel dealing with children classified as emotionally disturbed. While the subtleties of psychiatric nomenclature, as expounded in the American Psychiatric Association's *Diagnostic and Statistical Manual of Mental Disorders–III*, may be approached from a variety of theoretical, diagnostic and treatment frameworks, the teacher and school administrator usually reduce the clinical information available into a very simple paradigm regarding the child's ability to learn in a classroom. Since the ultimate goal of schooling is the education of children to at least a minimal level of literacy and socialization, most educators view the classroom as a place in which children learn to adjust to an ordered and orderly society in which there are acceptable and proscribed behaviors. That is, a great deal of effort is usually expended to develop a disciplined person who will be able to function in the community. And there is no question that the philosophy of the public is reflected in the behaviors of educators who will not accept deviant behavior which is seriously disturbing or disruptive to others. For once a school child's actions begin to challenge the authority of the school, whether the classroom teacher or an administrator, there generally occurs a chain of events which are oriented towards the reestablishment of the homeostasis perceived by most educators to be necessary for a proper learning climate. Reduced to simplistic terms, both educators and the public consider the maintenance of discipline as a major enterprise of schools. This is reflected in the repeated results of the Gallup Polls on Education (1978) which consistently reveal that the public considers discipline the number one problem in schools. It is no wonder then, that any experienced school psychologist knows that a majority of referrals for diagnosis and classification begin with some sort of disruptive behavior that is disturbing to the teacher. Most often, the teacher's attempts to discipline the child have been futile and the teacher is either asking for better methods of intervention or for the removal of the child from the classroom. The school administrator is often the next person in line to attempt to discipline the child. When all attempts fail, the school staff are always frustrated, often angry, and frequently desirous of removing the child from the school. If the child is diagnosed and classified under Public Law 94-142, the behavior that is designated as either disturbed or disturbing, or both, falls within the realm of a set of legally prescribed procedures for amelioration. While clinicians are concerned with the treatment intricacies of their recommendations, teachers are concerned with their effectiveness in helping to bring order to the child and the class. In other words, how helpful the recommendations are to assure good discipline. Both clinicians and teachers want to change deviant or unacceptable behavior. When these attempts enlist voluntary cooperation of the child and parents through positive therapeutic strategies, ranging from psychotherapy to teacher-child contracts, there is generally little major legal or ethical problem. These aforementioned may, at times, involve situations relating to confidentiality, use of records, and appropriateness of treatment and educational plans; but the chief ethical and legal problems regarding intervention occur when punishment becomes involved. Unfortunately, the concept of punishment is inextricably intertwined with discipline in the minds of most Americans (Hyman, Bilus, Dennehy, Feldman, Flanagan, Lovoratano, Maital, and McDowell, 1979). The synonymous use of discipline and punishment have unfortunate consequences for many children in American education, but even more so for those who, as a group, may be identified by behaviors that are considered unacceptable (Hyman and Wise, 1979). It is therefore important to recognize that the material discussed in the rest of this chapter must be understood within the context of a society which strongly supports the use of punishment as a pedagogical technique and is still steeped in the historical and religious belief that sparing the rod spoils the child (Hyman, Flanagan, and Smith, 1982).

In conclusion, we have suggested that much of the misbehavior that occurs among students may be classified by educators as either disturbed or disturbing and is viewed by many as being in need of discipline. However, once a child is classified as emotionally disturbed, the procedures available to the educators to remediate previously unacceptable behavior come within the purview of Public Law 94-142; and although semantic differences between educators and clinicians may exist, both groups must move toward helping children to change their behavior. In relation to this problem, we have selected three topics of interest which focus on the schools' and institutions' attempts to deal with disturbing behavior. The rest of this chapter presents legal and ethical issues related to the following: (1) suspension and expulsion, (2) physical restraint, and (3) corporal punishment and aversive techniques. Where possible, and within the scope of page limitations, we have presented related historical, scientific and policy implications.

SUSPENSION AND EXPULSION

The passage of Public Law 94-142 presented problems for educators who have tended to rely on suspensions as a way of dealing with disruptive behavior. While in theory, special educators allow for a variety of deviant behaviors and are trained to deal with them appropriately, the reality is that the more disruptive the actions of a child, especially when they challenge the authority of the teacher, the more likely there will be pressure for removal. While time out procedures and methods of restraint are used, most teachers and child care workers do not have adequate institutional support systems to deal quickly and efficiently with constant disruption. Very often, the removal of a child from the class becomes an emotional issue for all concerned.

The use of suspension or expulsion of any student is controlled by Supreme Court rulings in a number of important cases. In the case *in re Gault* (1967), the Court ruled that students are entitled to the same procedural rights of due process as adults. Students are entitled to (1) a notice of the charges, (2) the right to counsel, (3) the right to confrontation and cross examination of witnesses, (4) the right to avoid self incrimination, (5) the right to a transcript of the proceedings, and (6) the right to appellate review.

In *Goss v Lopez* (1975) the Court struck down an Ohio law which allowed school officials to suspend students for more than 10 days without proper due process safeguards. An important issue in the Goss case was that it established the precedent that federal courts, rather than school administration and state legislatures, have authority to determine appropriate rules of school discipline. Despite these and other rulings, the courts are not eager to become involved in school discipline, and if administrators offer minimal rights to students, they will generally not have problems (Bolmere, 1976). But if they are unreasonable in depriving children of their rights in disciplinary cases, the Supreme Court held in *Wood v Strickland* (1975) that even school board members may be held liable. While all school children are guaranteed minimal protection in the form of procedural safeguards, this does not guarantee that they will receive fair and equitable treatment on a daily basis. Recognizing that safeguards for nonhandicapped children are often not available considering problems inherent in dealing with discipline, Congress made special provisions regarding handicapped students (Lichtenstein, 1980). In Public Law 94-142, Congress reflected the belief that handicapped children are subject to discrimination, that they are often easily distinguished from others, that they are often perceived as discipline problems, and that they are often excluded by ignoring mandatory attendance laws. A number of legislative and judicial rulings have followed the passage of Public Law 94-142 and these indicate that handicapped students may not be deprived of their education for more than two days in the public schools, unless appropriate private placement is provided (Lichtenstein, 1980). Actual expulsion can become extremely difficult since parents may use their due process rights to force the school to provide appropriate treatment to deal with the child's disruptive behavior. This right was affirmed in the case of *Stuart v Nappi* (1978). In this case the Court clearly delineated the school board's responsibility to follow all legal and educational procedures to provide the least restrictive environment for handicapped children and would not allow for expulsion until that was accomplished. These rulings are tempered by the limitation that if a child presents a clear danger to others, himself or herself, removal may be used. However, this must be documented, and the child must be helped within the framework of the educational plan prescribed by the child study personnel.

Considering the above, it is obvious that it is to the advantage of school personnel to provide a range of possibilities and procedures within the school to deal with disturbing behavior of emotionally disturbed students. The psychologist or other clinician has a clear ethical responsibility to protect the child's rights by informing parents of the law and insisting that the school adhere to it. However, the psychologist also has a responsibility to the school to provide staff with an appropriate repertoire of procedures to handle disciplinary problems.

The following section deals with ethical and legal issues of a practical nature. What to consider when a student begins or is actually into a behavioral episode which is so disruptive that it requires physical restraint.

PHYSICAL RESTRAINT

Until the recent mandate of Public Law 94-142, issues concerning the procedural safeguards involved in restraining individuals who manifest aggressive behavior have primarily been a concern of mental health professionals working in institutional settings. With the influx of students with special needs and problems into the public schools, this issue has become important to public school educators as well.

It is imperative that educators understand the critical difference between the proper application of restraint procedures and corporal punishment. A primary distinction is the purpose for which the restraint procedure is used. Physical restraint is conceived as serving both control and therapeutic objectives. It is readily apparent that therapeutic restraint procedures are intended to preserve both the physical and psychological welfare of the child while serving as a means of protection for the child's teacher, other children, and school property. Educationally, corporal punishment has been generally defined as the infliction of pain by a teacher or other educational official upon the body of a student as a penalty for doing something which has been disapproved of by the punisher (Wineman and James, 1967). A special instance of corporal punishment involves the controlled use of aversive techniques. These are discussed later, but it is important to recognize the difference between punishment and restraint. The distinction is quite clear. Physical restraint procedures attempt to preserve the rights of both client and clinician, with an overiding emphasis placed on the maintenance of a positive relationship between them with all precautions taken to avoid the *infliction of pain*. Implicit in this definition is the responsibility of the teacher to act in a rational way in order to safeguard against the indiscriminate use of restraint for the purpose of punishing the student. Clearly, the advocacy of training school personnel to properly administer restraint procedures under well-defined circumstances is conceptually the antithesis of corporal punishment. More important, however, is the notion that injury sustained from the improper utilization of restraint techniques may in some cases constitute child abuse (Wexler, 1975).

Restraint as a means of controlling student behavior has been empirically demonstrated. For example, O'Brien, Azrin, and Bugle (1972) decreased crawling and increased walking in profoundly retarded children by holding them around the waist for five seconds when they crawled, prompting walking. Hendricksen and Doughty (1967) modified eating behavior by briefly holding the child's arm to prevent inappropriate eating and then shaping appropriate eating skills. Abusive language and violent behavior was extinguished in a 29 year old man in a state mental hospital with the use of physical restraint as a timeout procedure for aggressive behavior (Edwards, 1974). Other studies (Foxx, 1976; Thomas, Becker, and Armstrong, 1968; Barkley, 1976) suggest the successful modification of undesirable behavior by employing physical restraining procedures. It is apparent that both academic achievement and behavioral management can be positively affected by the utilization of therapeutic restraint.

Legal Considerations

An entire paper could be devoted to the implications of ethical and legal issues involved in the use or misuse of physical restraint. What is presented, however, is a guiding rationale for the use of such procedures in a way that they are commensurate with the spirit and the letter of the law which protects children and institutionalized persons from abusive treatment.

There is legislation which advocates rigid controls on the use of behavior modification techniques of which physical restraint is a part (American Bar Association, 1977; Friedman, 1975; Wexler, 1975). While all school personnel should be cognizant of such matters, it is the primary responsibility of the administration of the employing agency to ensure their proper consideration (Griffith, 1979).

All legal considerations indicate that interventions such as physical restraint must be governed by a reasonable set of guidelines. Properly developed, these will ensure procedural safeguards and guarantee rights to both staff and client. In addition, guidelines governing potentially harmful programs will also render staff immune from liability absent of malicious or neglectful behavior (Griffith, 1979).

The mandate of Public Law 94-142 regarding the right of an educational placement in the "least restrictive environment" is well known by educators. What may not be as clear is the implication that this environment must be a legaly safe environment as well. That is, clients are entitled to an environment which takes reasonable precautions to protect the client from dangerous circumstances or risk. Griffith (1979) outlines a rationale for proper guidelines that help monitor programs that place clients at risk. Issues involving administrative policy statements, provisions for program development, peer review, client consent, and staff training are a few of the components necessary for the maintenance of a legally safe environment. The psychologist's role in helping to shape administrative policy in this regard is that of consultant. If a proposed program presents unusual risk of controversy, the psychologist's expert opinion may be warranted. Additionally, the school psychologist can present needed data that will demonstrate the appropriateness or potential harm of a procedure. The psychologist may also be responsible for maintaining accurate records and data concerning a procedure in order to monitor its effectiveness.

Another important legal concern regards federal and state laws which relate to child abuse. Under state regulated child abuse laws, children are protected from maltreatment by their parent, guardian, or any person responsible for a child's care. Included in most definitions are employees of a public or private residential home, institution, day treatment program, school or agency. An example of child abuse related to physical restraint is specifically stated in the New Jersey Child Abuse Laws: physical abuse occurs when a staff member may sit on a child or *inappropirately* restrain or *inappropriately* apply restraints (such as camisole or leg and arm restraints) to a child which may result in bruises, welts, or other injuries. This also includes subsequent emotional abuse. The spirit and intent of child abuse laws are quire clear. Restraint must be applied in an *appropriate* manner, and in a way that guarantees reasonable safeguards for the physical and emotional protection of the child. Toward this end, procedural guidelines for maintaining a legally safe environment are of considerable importance. A review of cases involving child abuse in New Jersey and Pennsylvania revealed that courts weigh heavily the intent of the defendant's actions toward the child, as well as the situational context under which reported abuse took place. It is quite likely that the consideration of situational consequences by the court may include whether the defendant was provided with reasonable training efforts to safeguard against child abuse. Without such efforts, an agency or school will be hard pressed to defend the use of interventions that put clients at risk (Griffith, 1979).

Ethical Issues

Beyond technical and legal problems in the application of physical restraint, there remains the issue of the ethics of its use. May we legitimately impose discomfort on other people to alter their behavior? More specifically, may we impose such procedures on children who are too young or intellectually impaired to give their informed consent? Harris and Hershfield (1978) present an excellent review of these issues as they relate to methods of punishment, but their arguments apply equally well to restraint. The answers to the above questions have been seriously debated (Senate Subcommittee on Constitutional Rights, 1974). A review of the literature reveals that the behavior modifier cannot impose punitive or harmful procedures without consulting the child, legal guardian, or in some cases, the court (Harris and Hershfield, 1978). Of course, the case of an assault on a teacher by an aggressive student is somewhat different in that the teacher has the legal right of self defense provided that sound judgment is used in the manner in which the defense is employed.

There is also a body of literature which suggests that under appropriate conditions one may institute unpleasant procedures if they are perceived to be for the client's benefit (Buddenhagen, 1971; Warren, 1971). Whether or not guidelines should exist for the regulation of behavior modification procedures such as physical restraint remains an issue of controversy which is discussed in a following section of this chapter (Ayllon, 1975).

Another ethical consideration related to physical restraint is embodied in the preamble of the American Psychological Association's *Ethical Standards of Psychologists* (1979): "psychologists respect the dignity and worth of the individual and honor the preservation and protection of fundamental human rights" (p. 1). In this regard, the sanction of inappropriate methods of restraining children by untrained staff who are not supervised or observed by the psychologist constitutes a breach of ethics. Under such circumstances, the psychologist is required to assume the role of child advocate and take part in rectifying the situation to its full resolution. The role of the school psychologist as a child advocate is fully elaborated elsewhere (Hyman and Schreiber, 1975). The point here is that a fundamental role of school psychologists is to protect the welfare of children, and actively involve themselves in ways which provide input for the development of a sound administrative policy regarding a legally safe environment for children. They also have a responsibility to conduct inservice training for school personnel in the proper implementation of restraint procedures.

It is imperative that professionals responsible for treatment services have a working knowledge of federal and state laws which regulate their programs and practices. Responsibilities for incorporating this knowledge into school policy is the primary concern of administrators. The input of the school toward this end is mandated by sound professional judgment and ethical considerations.

CORPORAL PUNISHMENT AND AVERSIVE TECHNIQUES

The concept of "in loco parentis" has offered historical justification for educators' rights to inflict pain upon children to the same extent that the law allows parents that prerogative. This practice, derived from English law, might well be considered an anachronism, since it was established at a time when parents had complete control over the tutors they employed to educate their children. The early adherents of "in loco parentis" surely did not envision the modern bureaucratic education system that has a history of eliminating parents from pedagogical decision making.

The Anglo-Saxon tradition of inflicting pain on school children has led to an interesting paradox when considering this practice within the modern context of civilized nations. While it is true that English-speaking schools continue as luminaries in offering examples of child punishment worthy of any gallery of horrors, these schools exist in nations which form a major portion of the countries which offer constitutional protection of civil liberties for adults. The English-speaking countries have steadfastly refused to abolish the infliction of physical pain upon school children, despite its elimination in much of the civilized world. In the United States, only four states have legally abolished the use of corporal punishment in schools. In the Supreme Court's ruling in *Ingraham v Wright* (1977) the Court, in a 5-4 majority, denied consitutional protection for school children from the use of corporal punishment. This, of course, would apply to emotionally disturbed children in schools, but in residential institutions most states prohibit the use of corporal punishment.

Corporal punishment, defined within a legal frame, is the infliction of pain, loss or confinement of the human body as a penalty for some offence (Barnhart, 1963). Black's Law Dictionary (1968) defines corporal punishment as "physical punishment as distinguished from pecuniary punishment or a fine; any kind of punishment of or inflicted on the body, such as whipping or the pillary."

Corporal punishment in the schools is not implied when (1) the teacher uses force to protect himself or herself, the pupil or others from physical injury, (2) to obtain possession of a weapon or other dangerous objects or, (3) to protect property from damage. While educational use of corporal punishment is most often confined to the use of a wooden paddle, it must be noted that any excessive use of time out procedures would also be considered within this definition. *Reasonable* becomes *excessive* when the time out procedure causes pain or physical discomfort.

There is an extensive body of literature, involving both theory and research, indicating that corporal punishment should not be used with school children (Hyman and Wise, 1979). A review of Bongiavanni (1979) indicates that the use of corporal punishment by school personnel provides the child with a real-life model of aggressive behavior which has been demonstrated to be imitated by young children (Bandura, 1962; Bandura, Ross, and Ross, 1961; 1963). Not only do children imitate such aggressive behavior, but they also tend to employ these aggressive behaviors when faced with frustration in their own lives. In a study in which children observed a model being punished, a learned fear reaction was demonstrated to have occurred, although they were not recipients of any punishment (Berger, 1962). The implication for school personnel is that the use of corporal punishment may provide a living model of aggression which may be imitated by the classroom children. Such a model may provide a problem solving method which can be utilized by the child in various settings. In addition, by visibly punishing a child in the presence of others, the other children may become fearful and anxious. Such conditions are not conducive to socialization or learning.

The available research on punishment, when applied to schools, suggests that it is ineffective in producing durable behavior change; it is potentially harmful to students and staff; and it is highly impractical in the light of the controls necessary for maximal effectiveness. Maximum effectiveness of any punishment procedure can only be achieved by close adherence to the basic principles and factors which have been shown to influence the reduction or elimination of unwanted behaviors. In light of the role of school personnel to educate children and provide for their proper socialization, corporal punishment appears to be impractical, time consuming, and contrary to the goals of education. The potential for social disruption constitutes a primary disadvantage of punishment. Because of negative side effects, the possible reduction of undesirable behavior should clearly be secondary in importance.

Those who defend the use of corporal punishment as a practical method tend to view the practicality issue from the perspective of the classroom teacher or disciplinarian only. As a method, it can be applied to anyone, there is no need for any type of specialized training. It can be applied to all settings, and no special equipment except a paddle is necessary. The fact that most school personnel are physically stronger than their students makes corporal punishment especially attractive.

Despite the vast amount of research indicating the superiority of reward in changing behavior, there have been a small number of behavioral scientists who see a place for the use of aversive methods with severely disturbed children. The techniques and procedures described must be carefully separated from the issue of corporal punishment in the schools as a practice which is supported by 60 to 80% of the American Public (Hyman and Wise, 1979). It must be remembered that it is only within the last four decades that Thorndike, Skinner, Bandura and others systematically studied the effects of reward and punishment on learning and personality development. In reality, contrasted to over 2,000 years of belief, we have about forty years of research effort representing attempts to examine in both animal and human subjects, the merits of two opposing views, and to consider and generate new questions concerning the complexity of the role of pain in learning.

While the writers are overwhelmingly against the use of corporal punishment with emotionally disturbed children, it is clear that there are legal precedents. The majority of court cases involving its use indicate that it should: (1) be exercised within the limits of state statutes, (2) be for the purpose of correction and not be administered with malice and in anger, (3) not be cruel or excessive, and (4) be appropriate to the age and sex of the student (Bolmere, 1976). However, even within these legal safeguards, there is enough abuse (discussed later in this chapter) to cause concern. These should cause professionals to consider the ethical implications of supporting the use of painful procedures with students. Even though the writers strongly believe that punishment serves no legitimate educational purpose in teaching new behaviors, research suggests it may be useful for suppressing undesirable behavior. While we recognize that researchers such as Solomon (1964), MacMillan, Forness, and Trumbull, (1973), Parke (1970) and others point to some of the limitations of the punishment research, and we recognize that the full story, from an experimental point of view, may not be in, there is another body of literature to be examined.

In a systematic review of programs used for training teachers to handle discipline problems in the schools Hyman (1979) and Hyman and Lally (1980) found that almost all programs used positive motivational techniques for changing behavior. While the body of research has many more methodological problems than the laboratory research, it still offers evidence that punitive methods are not successful in the schools when compared to positive techniques.

Mayer, Sulzer and Cody (1968), Rutherford and Neel (1978), and Maurer (1974) offer a whole list of negative consequences of the use of painful/aversive techniques of control in educational settings.

While there is overwhelming evidence against the use of aversive techniques in normal or even special educational settings, what about their use with severely disturbed children? More specifically, is it justifiable to use approaches such as contingent electric shock (CES) to prevent severe, even life threatening, self-destructive behavior of autistic or severely retarded, blind or hearing impaired children? Our reading of the research suggests that these techniques, as with punishment in general, can be useful for short term elimination of destructive behavior (Wood and Lakin, 1978). However, they are of little use if "a new set of adaptive competing behaviors are not taught" (Neel, 1978, p. 79). Also, in many of the studies it is not always clear that all other possible techniques have been tried before the use of aversive procedures. There are many other contingencies regarding the use of CES and other aversive procedures and it is clear that only in carefully controlled settings can their usefulness be documented. An important consideration in the use of aversive techniques deals with the reinforcing effect on the person using them (Scholl, 1980). Once the technique is successful, a teacher, technician, or other caretaker may very easily become more and more prone to the use of punishment, leading to its eventual ineffectiveness.

Social Concerns and Policy Implications

Any discussion of the development and implementation of new technologies cannot realistically be confined to considerations of methodology and efficacy. This is an especially important consideration in contemplating the use of aversive techniques to control human behavior. The social considerations are apparent, even when one considers the attempt at scientific clarity attached to the term "aversive". Aversive is really a vague euphemism for a more accurate adjective which would be the term "painful". In addition to considering the social implications of the semantic and the historical contexts of the use of pain on children, it is important to ponder the problem of objectivity within the framework of science.

It is probably safe to say that most scientists and much of the informed public no longer ascribe to the belief that researchers function in an atmosphere of detached objectivity, unfettered by problems of emotional involvement that plague the work of mere mortals.

Further, the consumer movement and investigative reporting have promoted media coverage of debates which have exposed the public to opposing testimony by distinguished scientists on a variety of important issues from the efficacy of vitamin "C" to the safety of genetic engineering. It would be naive to assume that scientific differences of opinion would be ignored by the many interest groups which await the smallest hint of scientific evidence which might support their social and religious values. In the political arena, advocates will use any bit of scientific evidence to influence social policy. Those educators favoring the use of pain to change behavior await every scientific, carefully worked statement regarding the use of aversive techniques so that they may use them to justify hitting children, and most often the evidence is cited out of context.

An interesting study by Clarke, Liberman-Lascoe, and Hyman (1980) researched press clippings from 1976 to 1979 to see what type of painful punishment procedures were described in the press. It is wondered how objective a behavioral scientist who is a proponent of aversive techniques would feel if any of the following documented methods were used on his or her own children. These are all documented cases by Clarke, Liberman-Lascoe, and Hyman (1980).

Students in American schools have been subjected to the use of the paddle, strap, hand, arrow, stick, rope, belt and/or fist. They have been subjected to the cutting off of hair; put in storerooms, boxes, cloak rooms, closets and/or school vaults; and thrown against walls, desks and/or concrete pillars. Other aversive techniques that are documented include being subject to forced running of the "gauntlet" or "belt line"; forced punishment push-ups—military style; sticking a pin in a child's body; taping mouth, hands and/or body; making children stand on their toes for long periods of time; punching; dragging by the arm and/or hair; withholding meals; forcing children to stand in pajamas in 20 degree weather; choking; forcing children to lay on a wet shower floor in clothing; eating cigarettes and being tied to a chair with a rope.

It is realized that the preceding smacks of sensationalism, but it also smacks of reality. It is an issue that anyone must consider when reporting data on the use of aversive techniques. It is important to know that in far too many cases of uncontrolled and cruel uses of aversive procedures, the public supports the school rather than the victim. We certainly have a responsibility in all these cases to speak out in order to clarify the differences between beating children and using carefully controlled aversive procedures to eliminate self-mutilating behavior. This is an ethical imperative to which we will now turn.

Ethical Issues

Obviously, anyone reading the above would consider it highly charged writing against the use of corporal punishment in any form. Yet one must also consider that there is scientific and humane merit in efforts which attempt to prevent severely disturbed children from self destructive activities. How can we allow for research and not open the door to provide justification for excessive abuse, sadism and irrational experimentation, all under color of law. We see the situation as in need of a set of preliminary statements and guidelines which are offered as follows:

1. The evidence to support the use of physically painful aversive techniques in the schools is extremely meager at best. The overwhelming evidence from both theory and research indicate that it is unethical for any psychologist to use, support, or encourage the use of painful techniques in the public school setting except in very special situations described below. The use of corporal punishment, especially as it is normally practiced should never be accepted by clinically trained personnel or knowledgeable educators.

2. The only support for the use of physically painful aversive techniques exists in the elimination of self-destructive behavior displayed by severely disturbed children and youth. While the data is far from conclusive regarding permanence, its ability to be generalized and other factors, a growing body of literature supports the use of carefully controlled aversive techniques with extremely disturbed individuals. This population has previously been almost entirely institutionalized but as severely disturbed children begin to enter schools under Public Law 94-142, they form a special case. While the literature on the use of aversive techniques is far from complete, there is enough evidence that these procedures *may* be useful to prevent children from causing much more pain and physical damage than they would receive under carefully controlled aversive procedures. Therefore, research should continue in these cases. The following safeguards are based in part on the recommendations of Adah Maurer (personal communication to author, 1980) and suggestions of Wood and Lakin (1978).

3. The American Psychological Association and other relevant groups should develop guidelines to spell out appropriate credentials for those "authorized" to use aversive techniques (A-T).

4. The use of aversive techniques (A-T) should be conducted only under the direct supervision of senior level professionals with sufficient credentials.

5. A-T should not be used when a history of abuse to the child exists.

6. When the threat of A-T is effective to deter self-destructive behavior, actual A-T should not be administered.

7. A-T should not be used when the targeted behavior change is primarily meant for institutional convenience.

8. A-T should not be administered outside of a research setting, with the exception that any field based use meets all the conditions for controlled experimentation.

9. Procedures such as contingent electric shocks (CES) should be discontinued after sufficient trials demonstrate them to be ineffective. Guidelines for this cessation should be developed by an appropriate group of experts.

10. Painful stimuli should never be administered if they are more painful than the targeted behavior to be eliminated.

11. The use of A-T should only be allowed when all other appropriate techniques have been unsuccessful. A group of experts should develop a check list from the literature and from practice regarding what techniques might be used for specific self-destructive behaviors. This should also include guidelines for developing appropriate individual historical and contextual information concerning the child.

12. A-T should only be used in conjunction with attempts to provide new acts of adaptive competing behaviors.

13. A-T should only be used with approval and ongoing review by an appropriate board made up of professionals, parents and a client advocate. The model should be similar in legal and supervisory aspects to the granting of court approval for such practices as wire tapping and search warrants. In fact, a legal advocate for the child should be involved at all times.

14. Because time out is often abused, this procedure should be considered as a punishment procedure and similar guidelines should be developed as those suggested above.

The above are not, and cannot, offer a guarantee that no abuses will occur in the use of aversive techniques. The suggestions are proposed only as an interim measure to allow for the opportunity to develop what may be effective techniques. Given a sufficient time period, perhaps five years, if sufficient supporting evidence is not available, complete legal and ethical sanctions should be imposed.

SUMMARY AND CONCLUSIONS

This chapter has presented selected issues dealing with the discipline of emotionally disturbed students. We have pointed out that the behavior of children which is disturbing to others is most often the focus of interaction between students, parents, educators and clinicians. We have discussed major legal and ethical implications of the most common practices in education associated with the disciplining of extreme misbehavior. Most important is that Public Law 94-142 offers additional safeguards from abuse for emotionally disturbed children in regard to suspension, expulsion and the use of physical punishment because of due process and parents' rights to know. We recognize that there are other issues worthy of discussion under this general topic such as the use and abuse of time out procedures, verbal and psychological abuse, and the problems of parents' versus childrens' rights in determining treatment procedures. However, it is hoped that this chapter helped to stir the reader's interest and sensitize him or her to the many problems attendent upon protecting emotionally disturbed children from the most common abuses associated with school discipline.

REFERENCES

American Bar Association, Commission on the Mentally Disabled. Mental health standards and human rights. *Mental Disability Law Reporter*, 1977, *2*, 219-303.

American Psychological Association, *Ethical Standards of Psychologists*. Washington, D.C.: Author, 1979.

Ayllon, T. Behavior modification in institutional settings. *Arizona Law Review*, 1975, *17*, 3-19.

Bandura, A. Social learning through imitation. In M. R. Jones (Ed.) *Nebraska Symposium on Motivation*. Lincoln, Nebraska: University of Nebraska Press, 1962.

Bandura, A., Ross, D., and Ross, S. A. Transmission of aggression through imitation of aggressive models. *Journal of Abnormal Social Psychology*, 1961, *63*, 575-582.

Bandura, A., Ross, D. and Ross, S. A. Imitation of film-mediated aggressive models. *Journal of Abnormal Social Psychology*, 1963.

Barkely, R. Reduction of stereotypic body contortions using physical restraint and DRO. *Journal of Behavior Therapy and Experimental Psychiatry*, 1976, *8*, 167-170.

Barnhart, C. L. *American college dictionary*. New York: Random House, 1963.

Berger, S. M. Conditioning through vicarious instigation, *Psychological Review*, 1962, *69*, 450-466.

Black, Henry C. *Black's Law Dictionary*. Minnesota: West Publishing Co., 1968, (4th edition).

Bolmere, E. *Legality of student disciplinary practices*. Charlottesville, Virginia: The Michie Company, 1976.

Bongiavanni, A. An analysis of research on punishment and its relation to the use of corporal punishment in schools. In I. Hyman and J. Wise (Eds.) *Corporal Punishment in American Education*, Philadelphia: Pennsylvania Temple University Press, 1979.

Buddenhagen, R. Until electric shocks are legal. *Mental Retardation*, 1971, *9*, 48–50.

Clarke, J., Liberman-Lascoe, R. and Hyman, I. An analysis of corporal punishment cases as reported in nationwide newspapers: Types, incidents, and outcomes. Paper presented at the annual convention of the National Association of School Psychologists, Washington, D.C., April 10, 1980.

Edwards, K. Physical restraint as time-out in therapy. *Psychological Record*, 1974, *24* (3), 393–297.

Foxx, R. The use of overcorrection to eliminate the public disrobing (stripping) of retarded women. *Behavior Research and Therapy*, 1976, *14*, 53–67.

Friedman, P. Legal regulation of applied behavior analysis in mental institutions and prisons. *Arizona Law Review*, 1975, *17*, 39–102.

Gallup, G. H. The tenth annual Gallup poll of the public's attitudes toward the public schools. *Phi Delta Kappan*, September 1978, *60* (1), 33–46.

Goss v. Lopez, 419 U. S. 565, 95 S. Ct. 729 (1975).

Griffith, R. An administrative perspective on guidelines for behavior modification: The creation of a legally safe environment. *Behavior Therapist*, 1979, *3* (1), 5–7.

Harris, S. and Herschfield, R. Behavioral suppression of seriously disruptive behavior in psychotic and retarded patients: A review of punishment and its alternatives. *Psychological Bulletin*, 1978, *85*, 1352–1375.

Hendricksen, K. and Doughty, R. Decelerating undesirable mealtime behavior in a group of retarded boys. *American Journal of Mental Deficiency*, 1967, *72*, 40–44.

Hyman, I. (Ed.) An analysis of studies on effectiveness of training and staffing to help schools manage student conflict and alienation (NIE-P-78-0036) Washington, D. C.: National Institute of Education, 1979.

Hyman, I., and Lally, D. Effectiveness of staff development programs to improve school discipline. Presented at the annual convention of the American Psychological Convention, Montreal, Canada, Septemper 2, 1980.

Hyman I. and Schrieber, K. Selected concepts and practices of child advocacy in school psychology. *Psychology in the Schools*, 1975, *2* (1), 50–58.

Hyman, I. and Wise, J. *Corporal Punishment in American Education: Readings in History, Practice, and Alternatives*. Philadelphia, Pennsylvania: Temple University Press, 1979.

Hyman, I., McDowell, E., Raines, B. Corporal punishment and alternatives in the schools: An overview of theoretical and practical issues. *Inequality in Education*, 1978, *23*, 5–20.

Hyman, I., Bilus, F., Dennehy, N., Feldman, G., Flanagan, D., Lavoratano, J., Maital, S., and McDowell, E. Discipline in American education: An overview and analysis. *Journal of Education*, Spring 1979, *161* (2), 51–70.

Hyman, I., Flanagan, D., and Smith, K. Discipline in the schools. In C. Reynolds and T. Gutkin (Eds.) *Handbook of school psychology*. New York, New York: Wiley, 1982.

Ingraham v. Wright, 430 U. S. 651 (1977).

In re Gault, 387 U. S. 1 (1967).

Lichtenstein, E. Suspensions, expulsion, and the special education student. *Phi Delta Kappan*. March 1980, *61* (7), 459–461.

MacMillan, D., Forness, F., and Trumbull, B. The role of punishment in the classroom. *Exceptional Children*, 1973, *40*, 85-96.

Maurer, H. Corporal Punishment. *American Psychologist*, 1975, *29*, 614–626.

Mayer, G. Sulzer, B., and Cody, J. The use of punishment in modifying student behavior. *Journal of Special Education*, 1968, *2*(3), 323-328.

Mearig, J. (ed.) *Working for children: Ethical issues beyond professional guidelines*. San Francisco, California: Jossey-Bass Inc., 1978.

Neel, R. Research findings regarding the use of punishment procedures with severely disturbed behavior disordered children. In F. Wood and K. Lakin, (Eds.) *Punishment and aversive stimulation in special education*. Minneapolis, Minnesota: Advance Training Institute, University of Minnesota, 1978.

O'Brien, F., Azrin, N., and Bugle, C. Training profoundly retarded children to stop crawling. *Journal of Applied Behavior Analysis*, 1972, *5*, 131-137.

Parke, R. D. The role of punishment in the socialization process. In R. A. Hoppe, G. A. Milton, and E. C. Summel (Eds.), *Early experience and the process of socialization*. New York, New York: Academic Press, 1970.

Rutherford, R. and Neel, R. The role of punishment with behaviorally disordered children. In R. B. Rutherford and A. Preto (Eds.), *Severe behavior disorders of children and youth*. Lafayette, Pennsylvania: Council for Children with Behavior Disorders, 1978.

Scholl, A. The effectiveness of aversive techniques in education. Unpublished paper, Temple University, Department of School Psychology, 1980.

Senate Subcommittee on Constitutional Rights. Individual rights and the federal role in behavior modification. Washington, D.C.: U.S. Government Printing Office, 1974.

Solomon, R. L. Punishment, *American Psychologist*, 1964, *19*, 239-253.

Stuart v. Nappi, 443 F. Supp. 1235 (1978).

Thomas, D., Becker, W., and Armstrong, M. Production and elimination of disruptive classroom behavior by systematically varying teacher's behavior. *Journal of Applied Behavior Analysis*, 1968, *1*, 35-35.

Warren, S. Behavior modification-boon, bane, or both? *Mental Retardation*, 1971, *9*, 2.

Wexler, D. Reflections on the legal regulation of behavior modification in institutional settings. *Arizona Law Review*, 1975, *17*, 132-143.

Wineman, D. and James, A. *Policy statement: Corporal punishment in the public schools*. Detroit, Michigan: Metropolitan Detroit branch of the American Civil Liberties Union of Michigan, 1967.

Wood, F., and Lakin, K. *Punishment and aversive stimulation in special education*. Minneapolis, Minnesota: Advance Training Institute, University of Minnesota, 1978.

Wood v. Strickland, 420 U.S. 308, 95 S. Ct. 992 (1975).

PART II

Models of Therapeutic Intervention

4

The Psychoeducational Approach

THEORETICAL ASSUMPTIONS

The term psychoeducation as it applies to the treatment of emotionally disturbed children usually refers to an approach which attempts to balance educational and clinical influences "with educational decisions made after considering the underlying motivation of children" (Fagen, Long, and Stevens, 1975, p. 51). An early categorization paradigm by Morse, Cutler, and Fink (1964), based upon observation of operational programs for distrubed children shows the placement of the psychoeducational approach along a continuum in the following manner:

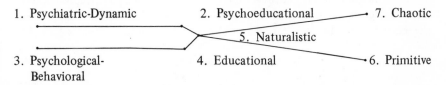

1. Psychiatric-Dynamic   2. Psychoeducational   7. Chaotic

5. Naturalistic

3. Psychological-   4. Educational   6. Primitive
    Behavioral

The relatively close position of psychoeducational to psychiatric-dynamic intervention in this diagram is symbolic of the thought that the two approaches share theoretical origins and that psychoeducation is an outgrowth and/or refinement of the psychodynamic orientation. Several authors use these two terms synonymously, believing that psychoeducation is the process of integrating psy-

Copyright © 1984 by Spectrum Publications, Inc. Systematic Intervention with Disturbed Children, Edited by M. Fine.

chodynamic theory into educational practice (Swanson and Reinert, 1979). In other words, the theoretical underpinnings of psychoeducation rest on the analytical thought of Freud and others and psychoeducation becomes a delivery system, i.e., a way of converting these allied theories into practice in the classroom. It is true that both these approaches are intrapsychic in nature and focus to varying degrees on affective aspects of children's behavior. However, to view psychoeducation as merely a practical application of psychoanalytic theory and one which is relevant only to classroom intervention seems unnecessarily limiting. There appear to be rather clearly formulated theoretical assumptions which though derivative, serve to distinguish psychoeducation from psychoanalytic theory and classroom intervention. In addition, the practices based on psychoeducational thought have applicability to many treatment settings for emotionally disturbed children, the mental health center, the camp, the residential "cottage" as well as the classroom.

As noted by Rezmierski, Knoblock, and Bloom (1982):

> Although the psychoeducator uses the tools of education and works in the educational setting, these aspects of the approach are not used solely to promote the education or achievement of children. In the psychoeducational model, the educational component is used to achieve other therapeutic results for the child (p. 50).

However, these authors further note that the model is not adequately described by the term *psychoanalytic treatment* or the program of education traditionally associated with this term, since psychoanalytic treatment has emphasized almost entirely therapeutic aspects of the program with education regarded as secondary or as an arena where conflicts were identified from which therapists pursued treatment goals. "...A fundamental precept of the psychoeducational model is the balance and dynamic interplay between education and therapy" (p. 51).

Differences in Theoretical Assumptions

While the psychoeducational approach has much in common with psychoanalytic theory in that both are concerned with the inner life of the child, with the impact of past events on present behaviors and with conscious and unconscious motivations, there are important differences of emphases. Eighteen principles basic to the psychoeducational approach and which serve to distinguish this model from others have been outlined by Long, Morse, and Newman (1976). Among these are: there is a dynamic interaction between affect and cognition, between the educational process and each child's unique needs; there are patterns in observable behavior which reflect a child's needs; there are efforts made to identify the pattern reflecting the needs that the behaviors represent and to assist the child in meeting his or her needs more constructively; needs are changeable in nature; and prescriptive interventions have the potential for restoring psychological growth.

THE CONFLICT CYCLE

One useful way of conceptualizing the dynamics behind the inappropriate, maladaptive behaviors of emotionally disturbed children from the psychoeducational position has been formulated by Long (1974). It evolved from his work at Hillcrest Children's Center during the 1960's, a time in which the medical (psychodynamic) model was coming under severe criticism for its focus on individual therapy, its cost, and the psychological damage inflicted upon a child by labeling him as having a psychiatric illness. The Conflict Cycle model describes how the interaction between a child and adult follows a circular process in which the attitudes, feelings and behaviors of the adult are influenced and in turn influence the attitudes, feelings and behaviors of the child. A cyclical "power struggle" results during which the aims of helping and understanding on the part of the adult disappear and "winning" becomes the desired outcome for both child and adult (Figure 1).

The cycle is based on the assumption that troubled and troublesome behavior is circular in nature and to some extent perpetuated by the environment. It is based on the following concepts, which though written with the classroom teacher in mind, have applicability to others who treat disturbed children.

1. A child in conflict views the classroom through the eyes of his or her life history.

2. A child in conflict has learned to be vulnerable to specific school tasks (i.e., competition, separation, etc.).

3. Acceptance of positive and negative feelings within and between children is normal, healthy and necessary to a fulfilling life.

4. Each child has been socialized to process feelings by direct expression, defense mechanisms or coping techniques.

5. Under severe stress, a child in conflict will regress from coping techniques, to defensive techniques and to primitive expressions of feelings.

6. The problem behavior of a child in conflict represents his or her present solution to stress, although it may cause difficulty with adults, peers, learning, rules, and self.

7. A child in conflict creates feelings and behaviors in others (peers and adults) which almost always perpetuate his or her problem.

8. The child's awareness and skills in perpetuating negative environmental reaction to his or her behavior justifies his or her conviction that it is not safe to change his or her view of the world or of himself or herself. In other words, she

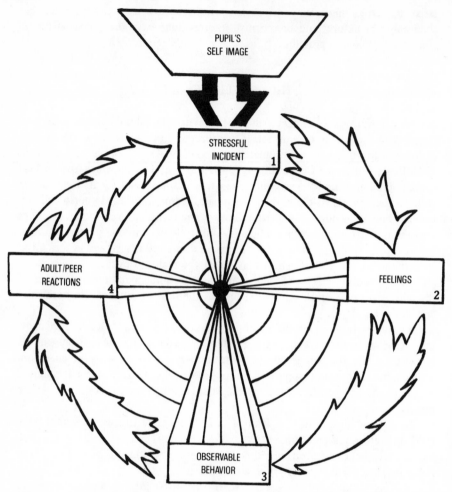

Figure 1   The pupil's conflict cycle. From Long, 1974. Copyright © 1974 by Charles E. Merrill Co. Reprinted by permission.

has been successful in maintaining his or her self-fulfilling prophecy of self and his or her world (Long, p. 182).

Defining the terminology of the Conflict Cycle may also aid in understanding the psychoeducational position. A child's self-concept or self-image plays a central role. It consists of all self-perceptions, values, and beliefs about the kind of person she feels she is. "What a child believes about himself is more important in determining his behavior that is any list of objective facts about him" (Long, 1979, p. 8).

Stress is an emotional reaction to external conditions which may be real, anticipated, or imagined and which cause physical and/or psychological discomfort. Four types of conditions may be causes of stress: (a) physical, e.g., lack of sleep or activity, (b) psychological, e.g., boredom, acts of rejection, (c) reality, e.g., breaking something, an accident, and (d) developmental, e.g., meeting someone new, separating from friends. Stress can be cumulative which would result in a higher level of intensity. Children with vulnerable self-concepts tolerate stress very poorly and will react to it in immature ways.

In the psychoeducational approach, a child's feelings are extremely important. Many children have learned that certain feelings are bad or unacceptable and that they shouldn't have them. By denying feelings, children will get rid of them in distorted ways: by projecting them onto others or disguising them as something else. Psychoeducational practitioners believe that feelings are natural to the individual and that "it is important for every pupil to learn to 'own' his feelings" (Long, 1974, p. 8). However, it is important to distinguish between feelings and behavior. For example, it is healthy to feel guilty when one has behaved in a way that one knows is unacceptable, but it is not useful to act out so that others will punish one. The existence of feelings and the importance of accepting them are incontestable. The critical issue is how they are expressed in behavior.

The observable behavior of children in conflict may be viewed as a result of the way they are coping with feelings of stress. Acting out behaviors such as hitting, running away or lying, or passive, withdrawn activities such as not paying attention or not responding, will cause children to be at odds with peers and adults in the classroom and other settings. A child may witness his or her parent's violent fights night after night and project hostility for his or her parents on his or her teacher. The result may be a relationship and/or learning problem. In this way, "the problems children cause in school may not always be the cause of their problems" (Long, 1979, p. 9). The child is coping with stress by creating trouble in the classroom.

Disturbed children are viewed as having learned to associate adult intervention with adult rejection. For some this is a distortion but for others it may be a reality. A child in stress is capable of creating his or her own feelings and behaviors in others. A withdrawn child will be successful in having an adult ignore him or her; a hostile, acting out child will generate feelings of anger and thus sometimes reprisal from peers or adults. A self-fulfilling prophecy results, encouraging the child in his or her defence against change. When an adult reacts in a punitive way, the child's feelings of rejection will increase which intensifies stress. The conflict cycle is now operating in full force with the potential of escalating; it has reached the level of the power struggle.

By understanding the Conflict Cycle, the adult can gain insight into causes of an existing problem and formulate methods of solving it. The following vignette is an illustration of the conflict cycle in operation, evolving through nine cycles before its completion. It is interesting to note that it began not with rejection or frustration but with an incident which had positive potential. In each cycle, the child's feelings, stress and behavior and the teacher's reaction are identified.

Setting

The scene is a math class in a public school junior high; Mr. Zee is the teacher.

Background Stresses on Tom

(1) Tom is a cute, blonde 13-year-old who has a growing interest in girls. (2) He is a bright boy but learning disabled, under the psychological stresses of a failure cycle and school disapproval. (3) His father is presently on military assignment away from home. Tom's fondness for his father is causing him much stress.

Tom's Self Image

Tom sees himself as inadequate, incapable of succeeding in school work, a failure. As his classroom tutor, I am attempting to alter this perception. However, success is new to him, and he copes with it poorly.

His Perception of His World

He sees his teachers as being against him, and he perceives himself as a failure in their eyes. The attention he seeks comes from his peer group, girls in particular, because he is the class cut-up.

Background Stresses on the Teacher

Mr. Zee feels hostile to Tom because he disrupts the class with his cutting-up; he also feels frustrated by Tom's unusually high math performance. He felt that this test score of Tom's was just a lucky fluke.

The Incident

It is Monday, and Mr. Zee is handing out the graded exam papers; Tom's grade is an A.

CYCLE I

Tom's Stress: Apprehension as he awaits his paper.
Feelings: Feelings of relief, disbelief, then exuberance at the A grade.
Behavior: Cutting-up in class is his normal mode of behavior for getting attention. Following a typical pattern, he lets out with the vocal disturbance, "Wha Who!" He cheers and takes a few bows.
Teacher's Reaction: "Tom, be quiet!"

CYCLE II

> *Feedback and New Stress:* Mr Zee's disapproval causes Tom some new stress.
> *Feelings:* Tom is angry. He feels entitled to approval, to praise, to attention from his teacher and peers.
> *Behavior:* Tom turns to a classmate nearby and says, "Look, Sal, I got them all right, out of sight, eh."
> *Teacher's Reaction:* "Tom, you were told to be quiet! How many times do I have to tell you."

CYCLE III

> *Feedback and New Stress:* This reprimand evokes more psychological stress in Tom.
> *Feelings:* He feels more anger because he feels he is being treated unfairly.
> *Behavior:* He turns to pal Billy and says out loud, "Hey, man, got them all right."
> *Teacher's Reaction:* "Tom, either you will be quiet, or you will have to go to the office. I knew you couldn't change. Your kind never do."

CYCLE IV

> *Feedback and New Stress:* The teacher's anger is escalating, causing Tom additional stress.
> *Feelings:* Tom's anger is likewise escalating.
> *Behavior:* Under his breath he says to Billy, "His kind never changes either."
> *Teacher's Reaction:* The teacher says, "I heard that—To the office, Tom."

CYCLE V

> *Feedback and New Stress:* The teacher escorts Tom to the principal and states that he is sarcastic and uncooperative. Mr. Zee leaves.
> Feelings: Tom experiences a feeling of fear.
> Behavior: Tom is quiet but very nervous.
> *Principal's Reaction:* The principal says, "You are a disgrace. What have you to say for yourself?"

CYCLE VI

> Feedback and New Stress: New stress from principal.
> Feelings: Scared half out of his wits.
> *Behavior*: "But, sir," Tom answered, "I don't know what I did wrong. I just got an A."

Principal's Reaction: "Don't give me that—your teacher wouldn't send you here for getting an A."

CYCLE VII

Feedback and New Stress: The reaction reinforces Tom's psychological stress.
Feelings: Confusion.
Behavior: "But he did, sir..."
Principal's Reaction: "I'll have no more of your sarcasm."

CYCLE VIII

Feedback and New Stress: (To find himself—"now I've done it.")
Feelings: He's scared half out of his wits and wishing very much he'd never got that A.
Behavior: Tom stares and says nothing.
Principal's Reaction: "I'm afraid you'll have to come up with a better reason, or I'll have to expel you."

CYCLE IX

Feedback and New Stress: This comment from the principal floors Tom.
Feelings: Fear and confusion as to what else to say leads him to repeat it.
Behavior: "But, sir, that is the reason."
Principal's Reaction: "Okay, you're expelled for one day until I can talk to your parents." (Easley, 1979, pp. 13-17.)

PSYCHOEDUCATION INTERVENTION

While psychoeducational intervention emanates from a theoretical position closely allied to psychodynamic theory, the process of helping emotionally disturbed children from this viewpoint has its own set of internally consistent, though somewhat widely ranging procedures. Much attention has been directed toward translating and interpreting theoretical tenets into practices which can be used by classroom teachers, both special and regular; however, many of these practices can be adapted by slightly shifting their emphases into relevant approaches for any adult attempting to help children in conflict. On the other hand, some procedures with a psychoeducational orientation have been specifically developed for use by adult professionals from other areas of the disturbed child's milieu, such as child care workers (Trieschman, Whittaker, and Brendtro, 1969).

A major principle guiding all psychoeducational intervention is the "circular and interacting relationship between thoughts and feelings such that cognitive experience and emotional experience affect each other simultaneously" (Long, 1976, p. 238). This statement reflects again the importance accorded in this approach to achieving a balance between educational and clinical influences. Other principles may be viewed as evolving from this central one:

(1) The adult/teacher's role is concerned with decoding, labeling and accepting children's feelings and in providing support. Teaching is the art of communication; the teacher must decipher the feelings that lie beneath surface behavior rather than focus entirely upon a behavioral event or symptom. Once feelings are decoded, they can be given a name or labeled for a child, e.g., "You look upset. Can I do anything to help?" Accepting feelings is also done verbally by the adult as in, "It's okay to feel nervous before a test." Psychoeducational practitioners believe that children learn through a process of unconscious identification with significant adults in their lives. Therefore, the relationship between child and adult is of primary importance since all learning takes place within this context. (Knoblock and Reinig, 1971).

(2) Crises are excellent times to teach and to learn. Such situations can be used to find new and more productive ways of coping with stress. Many failures in human relationships come from a reluctance to deal with or an attempt to ignore pain and unpleasantness. Experiences of pain and frustration are necessary for personal development (Fagen, Long, and Stevens, 1975).

(3) Learning must be invested with feelings to give it interest, meaning and purpose. Additionally, and equally important from an educational perspective, since each child learns differently, a careful assessment of strengths, weaknesses and interests must be carried out. The environment should be structured so that a child can succeed academically and socially at his or her present level. Successful mastery of these skills helps a child cope with a stressful environment.

(4) "Surface" behaviors (symptoms) need to be managed in a way that is supportive to the child. These are behaviors which need to be dealt with immediately without regard to underlying cause; however, procedures for surface management, such as physical restraint, must be carried out in a way that is caring and protective of the child.

(5) The criterion against which personal growth is evaluated is the extent to which positive behavior is derived from self control rather than external control (Fagen, Long, and Stevens, 1975). Self-control is more than simple absence of external control, however; it is a capacity to direct and regulate one's own behavior. A self-control curriculum has been designed by psychoeducators which will be discussed later in this chapter. A primary objective of the curriculum is reduction of anxiety over loss of control by increasing children's skill and confidence in regulating inner impulses and increasing skills for coping flexibly and realistically with their life situations.

(6) Collaboration and cooperation among the significant adults in a child's environment is essential. Everything that happens "to, for, with and against the pupil during the 24 hours of each day is important and has therapeutic value. This includes wake-up routine, art, music therapy, school assignments, food, play, etc." (Long, 1974). This point of view makes open communication between adults dealing with troubled children critical since the total milieu has treatment possibilities.

(7) A final principle to be inferred from psychoeducational intervention strategies is that these are preventive as well as remedial in nature. For example, the self-control curriculum was designed to be implemented in the regular classroom with "normal" children as well as in the special class or other settings where disturbed children receive treatment. A long-term goal is to promote the healthy functioning of all children by integrating psychoeducation procedures into the public schools, mental health centers and other systems which serve children and their parents.

The preceding discussion has presented a brief overview of some of the principles guiding psychoeducational intervention. A more detailed elaboration of how these may be implemented in various settings now seems necessary for a more thorough understanding. Since there is such a wide variety of specific designs which fall under the umbrella of this approach, an exhaustive description is an almost impossible task. Therefore, the strategy here is to illustrate each principle with one procedure for intervention. It should be obvious, however, that most specific procedures will exemplify several or at least more than one principle chosen for illustration since there is an interrelationship among principles and since a well-designed intervention should incorporate many aspects of the psychoeducational approach.

HELPING CHILDREN COPE WITH FEELINGS

There has been, traditionally, somewhat of a dichotomy of focus between groups of professionals interested in the educational process. Teachers have been interested in promoting cognitive skills and in the acquisition of knowledge, whereas psychologists and mental health workers have emphasized the motivational and affective aspects of learning (Dembinski, Schultz and Walton, 1982). While, as stated several times in the discussion of this approach, psychoeducation seeks to integrate affect and cognition, there remains the question of emphasis. Academic instruction from the psychoeducational point of view requires affective modification, that is, curricular changes based on an understanding and application of the emotional variables affecting learning by the adult/teacher. Therefore, an affective component is integrated into content instruction. Direct instruction in affective areas (Dembinski, et al., 1982) is the second curricular strategy emanating from psychoeducational principles. While cognitive variables must be kept in mind in this latter strategy, it would appear that the affective variables influencing learning behavior have received a primary focus in psycho-education intervention.

Helping children cope with feelings (Long, Alpher, Butt, and Cully, 1976) as one of the primary responsibilities of the adult/teacher is an example both of this emphasis and of direct instruction in affective areas. Children often mask their feelings; the teacher can help them find "more acceptable ways of commu-nicating them without exploding, running away or denying that they have feel-ings" (Long, et al., 1976). This is done, not by focusing on a surface explanation of behavior, but by the process already briefly described of decoding, labeling and accepting feelings. A fourth step is redirecting behavior after feelings have been explored. Decoding means becoming aware of the child's verbal and non-verbal communications as they provide clues to his or her inner life. Listening to what a child says with his or her "body language" is as important as listening to the verbal message and one may contradict the other.

After the teacher has successfully interpreted the feeling message being sent by a child, has helped him or her put it into words (labeling) and expressed the idea that such feelings are normal, natural or typical (accepting) it is necessary to complete the process by a final, critical step: helping the child find appropriate ways of expressing the feeling in behavior (redirecting behavior). This is done through the techniques of ventilation, skill development and through encourag-ing verbal insight. Ventilation allows the child to "drain off" overwhelming feel-ings of anger, frustration and fear through being allowed to express them verb-ally. In skill development, the child is helped to release emotional blockage by the teacher helping him or her to find appropriate activities for indirect expres-sion of his or her feelings. An example of this would be bibliotherapy, e.g., read-ing a book about a famous person and his or her childhood problems, or an art activity such as drawing. Verbal insight is encouraged through a "life space inter-viewing" procedure which is discussed later in this chapter.

The following case example is offered as an illustration of the sensitive use of all of these procedures by a teacher of a public school special class for emo-tionally disturbed children.

Craig is a nine-year-old fourth grader in my class who was abruptly brought in to my room during my planning period by the principal with the words, "Here, I think you'd better handle this." Craig had been at recess on the playground with the rest of his class and the other fourth graders His head hung down and his body was tense from an obvious battle to keep from crying. When I asked him what happened, he just shook his head and wouldn't look at me. I told him I knew he was feeling awful, and that was okay, but we had to talk about it before I could help him. Still no response except for putting his head down on the table.

After we sat like this for a few minutes, I asked him if he could write down what happened. When he shook his head yes, I gave him paper and a pencil. He wrote that he got caught going to the bathroom outside. I said softly that that must have really embarrassed him, was that right? He took the pencil again and wrote in big letters: DUMB. I repeated, "dumb," and Craig began to talk.

He said that the teachers in this school make him feel dumb when he does something wrong because they usually tell him he should know better. He wished they would just spank him and forget it. I said I understood that he was angry at the teachers for catching him in these situations and it was okay to feel upset and embarrassed under the circumstances but it was not okay to urinate on the playground. We sat for a while longer until Craig asked if he could use the rest of the time to finish the math paper he'd started before recess (Schumacher, 1980).

LIFE SPACE INTERVIEWING

The life space interview (LSI) is a therapeutic, psychoeducational procedure developed by Fritz Redl (1971). It is a way of dealing constructively with the crises which arise in the "life space" of the emotionally disturbed child, that is, with the small or large events in the child's daily life which bring him or her into conflict with others. Conflict need not always interfere with learning. In fact, conflict is viewed in the psychoeducational approach as having unique potential for helping the child explore and understand the relationship between feelings and behavior. The susscessful practice of life space interviewing, a method of communicating effectively with children, requires a capacity on the part of the adult to be empathic, to relate to the feelings of the child. It is not as easy to carry out as reading may make it seem; LSI requires training and skill to be used effectively.

There are two major categories of life space interviews: the first is termed "emotional first aid on the spot," and the second, "clinical exploitation of life events." A determination of which type is to be utilized is based not on the nature of the precipitating event or conflict, or as Redl terms it, "the issue," but upon a decision as to how the issue is to be used. Emotional first aid is the interview strategy to be considered if the therapeutic aim is to support and help the child get temporarily through the crisis and back, intact, to the situation (s)he was in before it was precipitated. The example cited previously concerning the communication between Craig and his teacher might be viewed as an illustration of emotional first aid on the spot. On the other hand, clinical exploitation of life events might have been used in the same situation had the teacher had the time and felt that this particular incident lent itself to developing an awareness in

Craig of issues which he needed to come to grips with, e.g., his confusion of anger at the teachers with his feelings of embarrassment and insecurity. Craig's teacher might have used the playground crisis as a special opportunity to embark upon an interpretation, tying this event to other similar ones so that a behavioral pattern could be brought to light for Craig.

In summary, LSI is a counseling procedure using one incident from a child's immediate, direct life experience which is conducted by an adult who is important in the child's life space. Its purpose is to structure an event or crisis incident so that the child can begin to solve the problems facing him or her. If conducted by a competent person, the life space interview procedure has many advantages: It encourages and teaches the child to deal verbally with his or her feelings and to use language as a way of mediation; it approaches problems one at a time; it is conducted "on the spot" without having to wait until the therapeutic hour when the impact of the issue may have lessened; it helps the child become aware of his or her own behavior and its feeling components, and finally, it helps the child find alternatives to self-defeating behaviors.

LEARNING INVESTED WITH FEELINGS

Achievement in academic content areas is also viewed as important from the psychoeducation perspective of helping disturbed children. Successful mastery of new cognitive skills depends upon infusing the instructional process with knowledge about the individual learner, about his or her interests and abilities, self-concept and how material is processed. In other words, affective and process variables must be considered when making decisions about what to teach, how to teach it and how to evaluate what has been learned. Guiding principles in designing the learning situation is that it: "(1) Be appealing to the learner, (2) insure some degree of success for the learner and, (3) introduce a new piece of knowledge that the learner, on the basis of his earlier successful experience, would be interested in trying to master" (Dembinski, et al., 1982).

An example of how these principles are applied can be seen in the following case example adapted from Edwards and Simpson (1983).

Victor is an emotionally disturbed eleven year old boy. A careful evaluation yielded the following assessment information: Victor has a poor self-concept, is extremely withdrawn and will not interact much verbally with the teacher or other class members. His achievement is approximately two years below grade level in most subjects; he is large for his age and, in fact, much larger and somewhat older than other students in his class. Additionally he has a strength in listening comprehension; he can comprehend material read to him at about sixth grade level.

In attempting to design an individualized instructional reading program for

Victor, the teacher decided to try to increase his silent reading factual comprehension while at the same time trying to increase his verbal responses and self-concept, keeping his age and size differences in mind.

Content was selected that Victor was clearly interested in, in this case pro basketball players. Since he had been successful in listening comprehension, the teacher decided to use this strength to approach his factual comprehension deficit. She made a series of short audio tapes about pro basketball players, asking factual questions at the end of each selection, to which Victor responded also on tape, a kind of response that was less threatening to him initially than writing or telling it to the teacher.

After Victor had experienced success at these lessons, the teacher gradually began to ask a few questions herself. When this procedure could be tolerated without anxiety, the teacher began to give him short written passages at his independent reading level about which he also responded verbally to her. Finally, difficulty level was slightly increased and Victor began to read and respond to material at his instructional level.

At the same time, Victor was made an official teacher's aide for certain periods of the day. His responsibilities included grading some math papers using keys and helping one of the younger students with addition facts. This procedure also increased his verbal interactions with the teacher and at least one student, and by acknowledging his relatively mature status in this classroom, made him feel a little better about himself.

MANAGING SURFACE BEHAVIORS

According to Long and Newman (1976), there are four major alternatives to handling incidents of nonconstructive behavior: permitting, tolerating, interfering and preventive planning. There are times when full scale interference may not be the intervention of choice (assuming, of course, that the behavior is not dangerous), such as times when problems are reflective of a developmental stage, or of mistakes made as a child is in the process of learning new social or academic skills. Sometimes interference also may not be worth the group confusion that would arise, or the commotion created might disguise its real purpose. To help children maintain appropriate behavior over some rough spots, Long and Newman (1976) have formulated twelve "influence techniques" for preserving classroom order. Many of these are procedures teachers have used intuitively for as long as there have been children in classrooms; however, they have "often been used without conscious awareness of their effects on students" (Rich, Beck and Coleman, 1982). Long and Newman emphasize that these are merely stopgap methods and do not substitute for a well designed program or the teacher's knowledge of individual and group psychology. While some of the procedures may appear to be borrowed from other theoretical orientations, their primary intent, emphasizing the psychoeducational perspective, is to positively affect behavior without increasing the level of emotional discomfort in the disturbed child.

Planned Ignoring. Sometimes children's behavior is designed to get teacher attention. If it does not get the desired reaction, it may soon exhaust itself. At other times, the behavior may be a signal that a child needs help with an assignment or problem. The teacher may choose to ignore the behavior but attend to its motivation by assisting the child.

Signal Interference. These are nonverbal techniques such as eye contact, gestures, frowns or body posture that convey a feeling of disapproval and control to the child. Use of signals is a routine management technique, one most often used by teachers, many times ineffectively. It should be noted that its usefulness is limited to the very initial stages of misbehavior. One adaptation of this procedure is to develop a special individualized signal between the adult and a particular child, one which remains secret between them and is therefore a uniquely personal form of communication.

Proximity Control. For some children, particularly those of elementary age, the physical closeness of the teacher standing by them is effective in helping them control their impulses and anxiety. "The teacher operates as a source of protection, strength and identification" (Long and Newman, 1976, p. 446). Walking among the students, sometimes putting a hand gently on a child's shoulder, are also important sources of proximity control. These procedures have the advantage of not embarrassing the child in the group.

Interest Boosting. Showing a genuine knowledge of and concern for a particular child's personal interest or in an assignment (s)he is struggling with may help him or her "mobilize his or her forces" and view the teacher as someone (s)he wants to please. This procedure is helpful for a child showing signs of restlessness and inattention. The teacher might say, "that's an important assignment you are doing" or "that's a difficult problem but I know you can do it" (Rich, Beck, and Coleman, 1982).

Tension Decontamination Through Humor. This technique is another old one: clearing the air or releasing anxiety in a tense situation by enjoying a humorous remark. It can be used to convey that everything is all right and ensure a return to business as usual. It is important of course, that the remark not be sarcastic or made at the expense of an individual.

Hurdle Help. This procedure is similar to interest boosting in that it is used when a child may be having trouble getting started on a particular assignment, does not understand the directions or has become bogged down. Instead of asking for help and risking teacher disapproval, the child "is likely to establish contact with his neighbors, find some interesting trinket in his pocket, or draw on his desk. In other words he is likely to translate his frustrations into motor behavior" (Long and Newman, 1976, p. 448). A solution is to try to provide a few minutes of individual help before the problem gets to this stage.

Restructuring the Classroom Program. Altering instructional methods, assignment length, mode of response or deviating from a preplanned schedule may be effective interventions when a teacher feels that the tension level is increasing in an individual child or an entire classroom because of boredom, irritability or excitement.

Support from Routine. While restructuring routine can be effective in certain instances, may emotionally disturbed children function best in structured, predictable environments. A secure schedule and being able to predict what will happen next, whether, "this is teacher reaction to behavior," or, "math comes immediately after free time," serves to decrease anxiety and therefore prevent disruptive behavior. Providing a daily schedule or reviewing the day's activities early in the morning are also helpful procedures for those children who need a great deal of structure.

Direct Appeal to Values. Teachers can appeal to values a child has internalized without becoming angry and exacerbating a situation in several ways: by appealing to the student-teacher relationship ("Do you think I've been unfair to you?"), by appealing to the reality of cause and effect ("If you keep doing this, these things will probably happen") or by appealing to the child's awareness of peer group reaction ("What do you think the rest of the class would think about that?").

Removing Seductive Objects. Certain objects have a magnetic appeal to children and elicit particular kinds of behavior. A flashlight says, "turn me on," a base ball says, "throw me," a magnifying glass says, "reflect the sunlight." "These objects feed into the child's impulse system, making it harder for children to control their behavior" (Long and Newman, 1976, p. 450). Teachers cannot expect to compete with such objects or expect much learning to occur in their presence.

Antiseptic Bouncing. When a child is at the point of losing control, a positive, helping procedure is to ask him or her to leave the room for a few minutes to run an errand or get a drink of water. The intent of antiseptic bouncing is not punishment but to protect and help the child recover from feelings of anger, disappointment, uncontrollable laughter, etc.

Physcial Restraint. When a child occasionally loses control completely and threatens to hurt himself or herself or others, (s)he needs to be restrained. The preferred hold is for the adult to cross the child's arms in front of him or her and around his or her sides while the adult stands behind, holding the child's wrists. Once again, the intent of physical restraint is not punitive, but to give the child a sense of outside protection and help so that (s)he can regain his or her feelings of control.

These techniques of surface management of behaviors have been formulated for the classroom teacher but many have obvious relevance for other adult professionals who deal with disturbed children in group situations. They are organized in a somewhat hierarchial fashion, with the first procedures to be used with milder varieties of disturbing behavior and the later ones with increasingly severe episodes of loss of emotional control. The emphasis in surface management is on temporary intervention, and upon allowing the child to redirect his or her behavior and gain control without threat or punitive action. Recurring incidents demand a more thorough intervention approach.

TEACHING CHILDREN SELF CONTROL

The degree to which children's positive behavior is self-directed rather than managed by external controls is viewed as a measure of emotional, psychological growth. Many of the procedures outlined previously have been either directly or indirectly aimed toward helping children develop self-control. In addition, an entire curriculum has been developed by Fagen, Long, and Stevens (1975) which is entitled *Teaching Children Self-Control*. The emphasis of this material is preventive, but the model as described by the authors may also be used with children who are experiencing emotional difficulties.

The model used to teach self-control consists of eight clusters of interrelated skills which were derived through observation and analysis of disruptive behaviors in both special and regular classrooms. Four of the skill clusters rely heavily upon cognitive, intellectual development: Selection, storage, sequencing and ordering, and anticipating consequences. Affective, emotional development is emphasized in the other four: appreciating feelings, managing frustration, inhibition and delay, and relaxation. A brief description of each of these eight clusters is presented by Fagen and Long (1979).

> *Selection* - Ability to perceive incoming information accurately
> *Storage* - Ability to retain information received
> *Sequence and ordering* - Ability to organize actions on the basis of a planned order
> *Anticipating consequences* - Ability to relate actions to expected outcomes
> *Appreciate feelings* - Ability to identify and constructively use affective experience
> *Managing frustration* - Ability to cope with external obstacles that produce stress
> *Inhibition and delay* - Ability to postpone or restrain action tendencies
> *Relaxation* - Ability to reduce internal tension

Each component is divided into several units for teaching purposes; goals

Table 1 Overview of Self-Control Curriculum Areas and Units

Area	Unit	Number of learning tasks
Selection	Focusing and Concentrating	9
	Mastering figure-ground discrimination	4
	Mastering distractions and interference	3
	Processing complex patterns	3
Storage	Visual memory	11
	Auditory memory	12
Sequencing and Ordering	Time orientation	8
	Auditory and visual sequencing	7
	Sequential planning	8
Anticipating Consequences	Developing alternatives	11
	Evaluating consequences	7
Appreciating Feelings	Identifying and accepting feelings	7
	Developing positive feelings	8
	Managing feelings	10
	Reinterpreting feeling events	4
Managing Frustration	Accepting feelings of frustration	2
	Building coping resources	9
	Tolerating frustration	22
Inhibition and Delay	Controlling actions	13
	Developing part-goals	5
Relaxation	Body relaxation	5
	Thought relaxation	5
	Movement relaxation	3

and tasks are specified for each unit. To help the teacher evaluate students' self control skills as well as to aid in selection of appropriate instructional units within the curriculum, a self-control inventory has been developed (Fagen and Long, 1979). Component units and number of learning tasks involved are presented in Table 1.

THE MILIEU AS A THERAPEUTIC TOOL

Also emphasized in the psychoeducational model is the idea that all of the components of the environment (milieu) surrounding troubled children can be constructed and utilized as a therapeutic tool. Trieschman, Whittaker and Bendtro (1969) have formulated an approach drawing from Aichorn's (1955) and Redl and Wineman's (1957) original concept of milieu therapy which is directed to the "adults who people a milieu: child care workers, houseparents, counselors, nurses, social workers, group workers, psychologists and psychiatrists. It is meant for all adults who deal with children or plan for children's living conditions... Our major concern is the 23 hours outside the psychotherapy session—because that is when and where most of the milieu is" (p. 1).

The primary aims of this approach are to provide adults with an understanding of what is happening in the milieu and to give practical alternatives to structuring it. Specific attention is given to issues and problematic behaviors occuring, for example, at mealtimes, bedtime and wake up times and during program activities. Temper tantrum stages and management are also dealt with. After describing the dangers and anxieties evoked for disturbed children in these situations, practical, proven strategies for their therapeutic management are outlined.

PREVENTIVE STRATEGIES

Many of the strategies evolving from the psychoeducational approach may be viewed as focusing upon the prevention of mental health problems among children. Helping children cope with feelings and the ways in which this is accomplished has as much relevance for "normal" children as it does for those who may be considered disturbed. Teachers and parents, if acquainted with these procedures, can be effective in promoting emotional and social maturity for all children.

The self-control curriculum is subtitled "preventing emotional and learning problems in the elementary schools" (Fagen, Long, and Stevens, 1975). Its primary aim is to be a "school program of primary prevention in mental health" (p. 262). The authors note that in the past a great deal of professional time and skill has been expended on mental health "repair," in clinics, in psychotherapy or in special classrooms. Though these services are important, they cannot hope to reach all children who may be in need of them. An essential component of the psychoeducational approach, therefore, is to provide teachers and other adults with methods and curriculum which can strengthen children's coping skills and prevent the development of learning and behavior problems.

EVALUATING THE PSYCHOEDUCATIONAL APPROACH

There are many problems attached to assessing the effects of any systematic intervention with emotionally disturbed children. What variables are to be measured along with how measurement will be conducted are among the more important considerations. The emphasis of the psychoeducational approach upon emotional and cognitive interaction compounds the problems already inherent in evaluation in this field of endeavor.

Affective growth is difficult to measure. While some interventions rely upon direct observation of behavior and while psychoeducators acknowledge the importance of this technique, "the sociopsychological and intrapersonal orientation of the psychoeducational model requires more extensive evaluation procedures" (Rich, Beck, and Coleman, 1982, p. 158). Problems with relying upon measurement of specific behavioral changes in children are based on some of the psychoeducational principles already discussed which relate to evaluation. For example, assessment of change must go beyond the surface level of behavior and look at possible causes. The classroom environment itself may be the source of behavior and affect problems when it is not meeting the legitimate needs of the student. Specific behaviors are only one aspect of the whole student; therefore, evaluation of effects must somehow include the art of human relationship as a variable.

Self-reports are seen as an important evaluative technique since psychoeducators view the individual's self-perception as a central influencing factor upon behavior. Thus, success in the approach could be partially measured by positive interpersonal changes as perceived by the child. Many measures of self-concept, self-esteem and locus of control exist; however, the validity of these instruments is difficult to establish.

Evaluating the success of psychoeducational interventions is difficult at best. Critics have stated that the testimony of advocates of the approach is its only real support (Kauffman, 1977). A further drawback sometimes cited is that there is little scientific evidence to support the effectiveness of acceptance and expression of feelings in reducing aggression. In fact, accepting and expressing feelings, such as anger, without training in how to manage or change may serve to increase aggression as well as internal conflict. This criticism seems to overlook the fact that accepting and expressing feelings are only the first two steps in increasing children's ability to cope with stress through other means than acting out behaviors.

A further criticism is that insight into one's behavior, as promoted by life space interviewing, for example, does not necessarily produce behavioral change. Hobbs, (1974) once a proponent of therapeutic strategies designed to promote insight, has stated that, "...insight is not a cause of change but a possible result of change " (p. 149).

The self-control curriculum has been reviewed by several special educators (Haring, 1979; Morse, 1979). Both the definition of self-control as outlined by its authors (Fagen, Long, and Stevens, 1975) and the assumption that the eight component parts of the curriculum correspond to self control have been questioned by these reviewers. The difficulty of measurement in the affective domain was an additional problem posed. Despite these criticisms, both Haring and Morse applaud the curriculum as representing a systematic effort toward teaching self-control.

Fagen and Long (1979) report the results of one study assessing the impact of the self-control curriculum on two aspects of student behavior, general school adjustment and academic achievement. General school adjustment as measured by both teacher ratings and student self-reports was significantly higher among the group exposed to the curriculum than it was among the central group. No significant differences were found between the two groups in math and reading achievement, however. The authors note that unless long term programmatic effects can be investigated, research activity will continue to be piecemeal and uncoordinated.

SUMMARY

The psychoeducational approach is an intervention for emotionally disturbed children which attempts to balance educational and clinical, cognitive and affective influences. Many of its procedures are designed to enhance children's abilities to understand their feelings and achieve self-directed behavior in the classroom as well as in other settings. The child's relationship with the helping adult is a critical variable in attaining these desired aims. Continuing research activities are needed to further evaluate the effectiveness of psychoeducational procedures in the lives of troubled children.

REFERENCES

Aichorn, A. *Wayward Youth.* New York, New York: Meridian Books, 1955.

Dembinski, R. J., Schultz, E. W., and Walton, W. T. Curriculum intervention with the emotionally disturbed student: A psychoeducational perspective. In R. L. McDowell, G. W. Adamson and F. H. Woods (Eds.), *Teaching emotionally disturbed children.* Boston, Massachusetts: Little, Brown and Co., 1982.

Easley, M. No more A's Thank You. *The Pointer,* 1979, Fall, 13–17.

Edwards, L. L. and Simpson, J. Emotionally disturbed children. In E. Meyen, (Ed.). *Exceptional children.* Denver, Colorado: Love Publishing Co., 1983.

Fagen, S. A. and Long, N.J. A psychoeducational curriculum approach to teaching self-control. *Behavior Disorders,* 1979, *4,* 68–82.

Fagen, S. A., Long, N. J., and Stevens, D. J. *Teaching children self-control: Preventing emotional and learning problems in the elementary school.* Columbus, Ohio: Charles E. Merill Co., 1975.

Haring, N. G. Reply to Fagen-Long self-control curriculum. *Behavior Disorders,* 1979, *4,* 92–94.

Hobbs, N. In J. M. Kauffman and C. D. Lewis (Eds.), *Teaching children with behavior disorders: Personal perspectives.* Columbus, Ohio: Charles E. Merill Co., 1974.

Kauffman, J. M. *Characteristics of children's behavior disorders.* Columbus, Ohio: Charles E. Merill Co., 1977.

Knoblock, P. and Reinig, J. *Special project report: preparing psychoeducators for inner-city teaching.* Syracuse, New York: Syracuse University, Division of Special Education and Rehabilitation, 1971.

Long, N. J. An Approach to Initiating Social Change in Elementary Public School by the Development of a Demonstration School for Pupils with Learning and Behavioral Problems in a Community Mental Health Center. Unpublished Manuscript, 1974.

Long, N. J. In J. M. Kauffman and C. D. Lewis (Eds.), *Teaching children with behavior disorders: Personal perspectives.* Columbus, Ohio: Charles E. Merrill Co., 1974.

Long, N. J. The conflict cycle. *The Pointer,* 1979, Fall, 6–11.

Long, N. J. and Newman, R. G. Management of surface behaviors. In N. J. Long, W. C. Morse, and R. G. Newman (Eds.), *Conflict in the classroom* (3rd edition). Belmont, California: Wadsworth, 1976.

Long, N. J., Morse, W. C., and Newman, R. G. (Eds.), *Conflict in the classroom: The education of children with problems* (3rd edition). Belmont, California: Wadsworth, 1976.

Long, N. J., Alpher, R., Butt, F., and Cully, M. Helping children cope with feelings. In N. Long, W. Morse, and R. Newman (Eds.), *Conflict in the classroom* (3rd edition). Belmont, California: Wadsworth, 1976.

Morse, W. C. Self-control: The Fagen-Long curriculum. *Behavior Disorders,* 1979, *4,* 83–91.

Morse, W., Cutler, R., and Fink, A. *Public school classes for the emotionally handicapped: A research analysis.* CEC, NEA, Washington, D.C., 1964, p. 121-124.

Morse, W. C.; Cutler, R. L.; and Fink, A. H. Public school classes for the emotionally handicapped: A research analysis. In N. Long, W. Morse, and R. Newman (Eds.), *Conflict in the classroom* (2nd edition). Belmont, California: Wadsworth, 1972.

Redl, F. The concept of the life space interview. In N. Long, W. Morse, and R. Newman (Eds.), *Conflict in the classroom* (2nd edition). Belmont, California: Wadsworth, 1972.

Redl, F., and Wineman, D. *The aggressive child.* Glencoe, Illinois: Free Press, 1957.

Rezmierski, V. E., Knoblock, P., and Bloom, R. B. The psychoeducational model: Theory and historical perspective. In R. L. McDowell, G. W. Adamson and F. H. Wood (Eds.), *Teaching emotionally disturbed children.* Boston, Massachusetts: Little, Brown and Co., 1982.

Rich, H. L., Beck, M. A., and Coleman, T. W. Behavior management: The psychoeducational model. In R. L. McDowell, G. W. Adamson, and F. H. Woods (Eds.), *Teaching emotionally disturbed children.* Boston: Massachusetts: Little, Brown and Co., 1982.

Schumacher, E. Crisis Interview. Unpublished manuscript, University of Missouri-Kansas City, 1980.

Swanson, H. L. and Reinert, H. R. *Teaching strategies for children in conflict: Curriculum, methods and materials.* St. Louis, Missouri: C. V. Mosby Co., 1979.

Trieschman, A. E., Whittaker, J. K., and Brendtro, L. K. *The other 23 hours.* Chicago, Illinois: Aldine Publishing Co., 1969.

Wineman, D. The life-space interview. *Social Work,* 1979, *4,* 3–17.

5

Behavior Modification
with Emotionally Disturbed Children

RICHARD L. SIMPSON

Emotionally disturbed or behaviorally disordered children are distinguished by patterns of behavioral excess and deficit (Bower, 1960; Graubard, 1973; Kauffman, 1977). Zabel (1981) noted, for instance, that emotionally disturbed pupils "engage in too many inappropriate, disruptive, disagreeable behaviors and too few appropriate, cooperative, agreeable behaviors" (p. 192). Along similar lines, Ross (1974), observed that a psychological disorder is thought to exist when children emit certain behaviors "with a frequency or intensity that authoritative adults in the child's environment judge, under the circumstances, to be either too high or too low" (p. 14). Hence, apart from a small percentage of psychotic, autistic, and other types of severely emotionally disturbed children who present qualitatively unique characteristics, the vast majority of school age emotionally handicapped children are distinguished by socially and culturally determined excesses and deficits of otherwise normal patterns of behavior. Such children may be of concern to parents, teachers or others in their environment because of an inability or unwillingness to remain in their assigned seats at school, to talk out without permission, to quarrel immoderately with their peers; etc. In addition to such manifestations of behavioral excess, emotionally handicapped youngsters may display a variety of response deficits such as not developing and maintaining friendships, not completing homework assignments, or not participating in classroom discussions.

The common element of all these characteristics is that each represents a quantitative rather than a qualitative or conceptual difference from what is typically regarded as normal behavior. That is, emotionally disturbed children are much more likely to be characterized by socially determined excesses or deficits of some essentially normal behavior pattern than by highly aberrant responses. What parent or professional, for example, could argue that even the most well adjusted child will not occasionally encounter difficulty staying in his or her seat at school or interacting appropriately with peers or classmates? Accordingly, the most distinctive difference between the behavior or emotionally disturbed children and their nonexceptional peers is based on the frequency of such behaviors.

One highly successful strategy for intervening with emotionally disturbed children in terms of managing a variety of behavioral excesses and deficits is behavior modification. This procedure, which stems from the work of John Watson (1913), involves the application of learning theory principles for the purpose of manipulating the duration, frequency, rate, or intensity of behavioral excesses and deficits. This approach has been successfully employed in a variety of settings and with equally diverse groups of subjects (Heaton, Safer, Allen, Spinnato, and Prumo, 1976; Whelan and Haring, 1966). Successful intervention programs have been conducted in hospital and clinical settings (McGrath, Marshall, and Prior, 1979) as well as in public schools (Broden, Hall, Dunlap, and Clark, 1970; O'Leary and Drabman, 1971). Behavioral techniques have been successfully employed to decrease aggressive patterns of behavior (Kauffman and Hallahan, 1973; O'Leary and O'Leary, 1976), problems associated with social withdrawal (Buell, Stoddard, Harris, and Baer, 1968; Hall and Broden, 1967), academic difficulties (Copeland, Brown, and Hall, 1974; Hallahan and Kauffman, 1975), hyperactivity (Doubros and Daniels, 1966; Reith, 1976), and to facilitate speech and language development in severely emotionally handicapped children (Kerr, Meyerson, and Michael, 1965; Risley and Wolf, 1967; Wheeler and Sulzer, 1970). Further, such behavioral procedures have been found to be effective with a variety of age groups (Peed and Pinsker, 1978; Williams, 1959) and levels of severity (Foxx and Azrin, 1973; Nolen, Kunzelmann, and Haring, 1967; Simpson and Sasso, 1978). All in all, the model has proven to be among the most versatile and functional of the intervention strategies available to professionals involved with treatment and education of behaviorally disordered children and youth.

MODEL ASSUMPTIONS

A behavioral approach to conceptualizing and managing the behavior of children with emotional and behavioral disorders can be effectively utilized only when one recognizes and comprehends the principles and assumptions underlying such a model, e.g., virtually all human behavior is learned; understanding and manipulating observable stimuli and behavior are of primary concern; diagnostic labels are not prerequisite to treatment; the utility of intervention procedures is empirically determined; and operant behavior is determined by related antecedent and consequent events.

Most Patterns of Human Behavior Are Learned

According to this basic tenet of behavior modification, the maladaptive responses manifested by emotionally and behaviorally handicapped children are learned and, in fact, are acquired and maintained in much the same fashion as are more adaptive behaviors. Hence, according to this assumption, nearly all operant responses, whether it is an adaptive behavior such as attending to task in a classroom setting or a socially maladaptive behavior such as chronically fighting with other children, are learned and controlled by the same principles. The implications of this assumption are very clear: First, it allows for planned change to take place whereby maladaptive responses can be "unlearned" and replaced by more socially appropriate behavior. Second, this optimistic position negates the argument that emotionally disturbed children engage in certain inappropriate behaviors because of uncontrollable or unobservable events or that behavioral progress must await a psychiatric or psychological treatment of a child's ego.

Importance of Understanding and Manipulating Observable Stimuli and Behavior Rather than Unobservable and Undefined Phenomena

Behavior modification involves the systematic application of learning theory principles to change the occurrence of specific behavior patterns. In order to effectively apply the necessary procedures and to determine the effects of the intervention, an overt target behavior must be selected for change. If, for instance, a teacher or psychologist were to focus on facilitating the "self-actualization" of a child with a conduct disorder, (s)he would most likely encounter difficulty not only in securing agreement among independent participants on the nature and meaning of the problem, but also in evaluating the effectiveness of a given intervention program. However, by focusing on an observable behavior, such as complying with the directions of a psychiatric aide, the general concept of self-actualization may be translated into a form that is amenable to intervention via a behavioral approach.

The behavioral models' emphasis on observable responses and stimuli, in turn, leads to the selection of applied procedures and directly relevant methodology. That is, the assumption is made that a target behavior is not a byproduct of a broader, unobservable problem (e.g., limited ego intergration, unresolved Oedipal complex) which will be corrected only after the more generally underlying issue is resolved. Rather, the overt behavioral excess or deficit is the basic consideration. Consequently, the behavioral engineer disregards considerations associated with nondirected treatment programs (e.g., attempts at strengthening a child's ego for the purpose of improving compliance) in favor of direct intervention applicable to a given issue. While a child's ego might, in fact, become more integrated as a result of a behavioral program, the primary intent of any intervention is only to modify an observable and measurable behavioral excess or deficit.

The emphasis on observable stimuli and responses is also compatible with and facilitative of the basic principle of the behavioral model that operant responses are a function of observable environmental events which precede and follow a response. In other words, this principle further promotes the accentuation of those items which can be observed, monitored and potentially modified, and which are more closely aligned with children's situational present than their historical past. Accordingly, this emphasis of the behavioral model offers further assurances that individuals providing treatment will not lose sight of the primary issues confronting them.

Finally, the overtness and practicality of the behavioral approach facilitates appropriate application of these principles by paraprofessionals, parents and other individuals who interact with emotionally disturbed children. Thus, the applicability of the model is extended beyond a single therapeutic or educational setting. Psychotherapeutic and more traditional intervention approaches, on the other hand, not only rely on relatively esoteric and technical procedures but often emphasize unconscious and unobservable phenomena. Consequently, such methods can only be applied by clinicians and other highly trained mental health experts.

Diagnostic Labels Are Not a Prerequisite to Treatment

One of the basic strengths of the behavioral approach is that the principles may be applied to the problems of a given child without requiring that the child first be diagnosed or labeled as emotionally disturbed or behaviorally disordered. Rather, the focus of the procedures is on the identification and examination of those observable and measurable behavioral excesses and deficits which are interfering with optimal adjustment, and the application of methods of assisting a child in acquiring more adaptive responses. Because behavior modification focuses attention on observable behavioral excesses and deficits, as opposed to labeling the child demonstrating the pattern, educational personnel may use the principles without much concern about the social relevance of "disturbed" behavior and without paying a great deal of attention to differential diagnosis and labeling issues. The fact that educators, clinicians and other personnel responsible for the education and treatment of emotionally handicapped children are primarily interested in promoting appropriate behavior, as opposed to selecting an acceptable label for a pupil, makes the strategy all the more functional. In summary, this approach combines the advantage of restricting the use of potentially pernicious labels with significant implications for preventative treatment of emotionally handicapped youngsters, such as the use of behavioral techniques with children prior to, and as a deterent to, labeling.

The Utility of Intervention Procedures is Empirically Determined

Based on this assumption, users of the model disregard the notion that the effectiveness of a procedure with one child automatically guarantees its applicability and success with others. Accordingly, no behavioral intervention strategy is assumed to be universally applicable. Although judged to be potentially effective based on previous experience, a procedure is nonetheless evaluated each time it is applied to a child.

Hall, Hawkins, and Axelrod (1975) commented on the advantages of careful measurement and empirical validation as part of the application of behavior modification procedures. In particular they noted:

A. Measurement forces the teacher to define target behaviors more precisely.

B. It [measurement] results in a precise assessment of performance that is a more relevant form of diagnosis than most psychological testing.

C. It focuses the teacher's efforts on the specific behavior and thus, is more likely to achieve the desired changes.

D. The frequent—usually daily—measurement and charting of data on a graphic record encourages the teacher to persist with the technique until its effect is adequately tested, rather than to give up when immediate and obvious results cannot be seen.

E. With frequent measurement, the teacher is stimulated to make small improvements in his technique and to note the effects; the final form of the technique achieved may be much more effective than the original.

F. Measurement increases the likelyhood that a teacher will apply a planned technique consistently and exclusively; often teachers who do not measure behavior will contaminate a promising technique by introducing other procedures along with it or vacillating between it and one or more other techniques that counteract its effect. (pp. 195-196).

Operant Behavior Is Controlled by Related
Antecedent and Consequent Events

According to this tenet of the behavioral model the learning of nearly all operant responses is a function of stimulus events occurring before and after a particular operant behavior. That is, the operant behavior of behaviorally disordered children is associated with stimuli which promotes its occurence (Patterson, 1974) or follow a response (Skinner, 1953). Such environmental events can take the form of stimulus cues, reinforcers, punishers or extinction procedures. The significance of this assumption for the behavioral model is that if the environmental stimuli associated with a particular response can be identified and manipulated, a child's behavioral excesses and deficits can be replaced with more adaptive behavior.

THE APPLICATION OF THE BEHAVIORAL MODEL WITH
EMOTIONALLY DISTURBED CHILDREN AND YOUTH

This section provides an overview of the methods and procedures involved in employing behaviorally oriented procedures with emotionally disturbed pupils. While a cursory outline of the procedures required to develop and implement a behavior management program is presented, it must be recognized that the success of any application is a function of the skill with which the various components of the technology are applied as well as the level of rapport, communication and understanding that exists between the behavioral engineer and the child under treatment. Thus, while the efficacy of the technology of behavior modification may be well established, the overall success of such programs is related to the strength of the interpersonal relationship involved. In other words, despite the overall utility of a model, adults lacking in sensitivity, empathy and rapport with emotionally disturbed children will be consistently unsuccessful in the application of any intervention procedure with such youngsters. Without appropriate attention to interpersonal factors, adults charged with the management of emotionally disturbed children will meet with limited success regardless of the skill with which they apply the technology.

Finally, individuals utilizing the procedures associated with the behavioral model are expected to demonstrate knowledge of behavioral philosophy and applied behavior analysis techniques. Individuals who do not possess such background knowledge are encouraged to supplement the discussion presented in this chapter with more fundamental information.

Identifying and Operationally Defining a Behavioral Excess or Deficit

The first step in the utilization of behavioral procedures is to target and operationally characterize a response pattern considered to be excessive or deficient. While applied behavior analysis principles are extremely versatile, they are functional only to the extent that they are applied to observable and measurable behaviors that have been pinpointed for change. Further, excess and deficit patterns selected for modification must be so clearly defined that the various individuals involved with a child (e.g., teacher, psychologist, child care worker) are able to perceive and evaluate the target behavior in the same manner. For example, noncompliance to one individual might consist of a failure to turn in homework assignments; to somebody else, it might mean a child's unwillingness to abide by prescribed playground rules. Accordingly, it is essential that all participants in a behavior modification program have reached a common definition and understanding of the target response.

In addition, individuals implementing behavioral programs must attend to several other matters within the targeting domain. First, they must determine whether or not a targeted behavioral excess or deficit is under a child's control. Behaviors such as fighting with peers or professional staff, using assaulting and profane language or withdrawing from social situations are usually controllable by children; however parasympathetic functions such as sweating, hyperventilating, or similar responses may well be beyond their control. To determine whether or not a response is controllable by a child and thus, the type of behavior management procedure to be used, it is frequently helpful to judge whether or not the behavioral excess under analysis precedes or follows a controlling stimulus. Respondent behavior, or patterns developed through classical conditioning (Shoben, 1948), are elicited by stimuli; the presentation of certain environmental stimuli will cause a response. Classical conditioning involves a wide variety of involuntary behaviors, such as those involved in the functioning of bodily glands and organs. For example, a child developing heart palpitations when asked to read orally is demonstrating respondent behavior. In other words, such behaviors are a function of environmental events which take place prior to the occurrence of the target behavior. Operant behaviors, on the other hand, are developed and maintained by the environmental events which come after them (Bandura, 1969). That is, operant responses, exemplified by such common behaviors as running, talking, attending to task, fighting and having tantrums, are a function of the events which are subsequent to their occurrence. A child may be willing to demonstrate appropriate classroom or ward behavior in order to receive adult attention or tangible rewards; or children may engage in destruction of hospital or school property because they enjoy seeing the adults supposedly responsible for their behavior becoming upset.

Since the modification process involves understanding and manipulation of the controlling environmental stimuli, individuals interested in applying behavioral principles to manage the behavioral excesses and deficits of emotionally disturbed children must be able to discriminate between the two major classes of behavior. That is, the choice of treatment condition is dependent on whether or not a child has control over the behavior under scrutiny and the nature of the environmental events associated with it.

While both respondent and operant behaviors are of concern to individuals involved in the education and treatment of emotionally disturbed children, it must also be recognized that the majority of the behavioral excesses and deficits manifested by emotionally distrubed children are operant in nature and intervention with these children will be more likely to modify responses that are under a child's control. For these reasons, the present discussion centers on methods and procedures for managing behavioral excesses and deficits of an operant nature.

Behavior modification procedures are most effective (1) when applied to responses which contain movement, (2) when applied to behaviors which are repeatable and which occur on a regular basis, and (3) when the target behavior selected for change has a specific starting and ending point. Selection of behavior patterns for modification which meet these criteria increases the reliability of observations and thus, the intervener's ability to evaluate the efficacy of any treatment condition. Target behaviors such as hitting another child, screaming profanities at ward staff or failure to hand in assignments at school lend themselves to change better than sleeping or "staring at another child in a hateful manner" because they contain movements which 1) can be easily seen; 2) may be repeatable; and 3) have definite starting and stopping points. Appropriate attention to these rather elementary considerations frequently determines the success of a behavioral intervention program.

In addition to focusing on behavioral excesses and deficits, weaknesses requiring modification, professionals applying behavioral principles must also assess the strengths or positive characteristics of the children with whom the strategy is to be applied. Such a comprehensive evaluation of a child serves to establish a more realistic prespective on a child and his or her problems. Rather than viewing a child as " emotionally disturbed" or as somebody "who creates problems for everyone", (s)he must be perceived as a person displaying certain excesses and deficits as well as a variety of positive patterns. In addition to providing a thorough assessment of a child, this approach helps identify possible reinforcement contingencies. For example, if ward staff observe that an otherwise highly aggressive child tends to be very calm and involved when watching TV, use of this potentially adaptive behavior may be successfully incorporated into an intervention program.

A final matter to be considered when identifying behavioral excesses or deficits for modification is the importance of selecting a behavior with a high probability of success. While proper consideration must be given to significant problems which interfere with acceptable behavior and functioning, care should be taken to select a target response which represents a good chance for positive change. For example, a child with a history of drug abuse whose parents are unwilling to cooperate with treatment personnel to limit their offspring's opportunity to secure drugs must be considered a low-success probability if drug abuse were selected as the target behavior. In a similar manner, nonverbal, severely emotionally disturbed children would not be highly receptive to a behavioral program designed to develop functional language. At least initially, modification of behavioral excesses and deficits which have proven unresponsive to previous intervention procedures should be delayed in favor of target behaviors which present a better chance of success. Once behavioral engineers have determined a child's response to behavioral intervention techniques and have clearly established the validity and efficacy of their strategies, more challenging target behaviors can be undertaken.

Identifying Settings and Circumstances Associated with Behavioral Excesses and Deficits

As part of gaining a thorough understanding of the target response, the behavioral engineer must seek to understand the settings in which the pattern occurs and the circumstances which surround it. Bersoff and Grieger (1971) noted that "obtaining knowledge about environments and situations in which the behavior appears is a necessity" (p. 487). Specifically, it should be determined whether behavioral excesses or deficits occur primarily in certain settings or under particular conditions (e.g., on the hospital ward after dinner, in the classroom during individual seat work) or whether the response is pervasive across environments and situations. Clearly, a variety of interpersonal factors is influenced by children's behavior, an understanding of which is essential to any modification program. Therefore, the identification of settings and circumstances surrounding behavioral excess or deficit must also involve an analysis of those individuals who experience and who are associated with such response patterns. It must be determined if a child only displays the target response around a limited number of individuals (e.g., only one of his or her teachers, certain psychiatric aides) or in a more generalized manner. As suggested by Bandura (1969), "under naturalistic conditions behavior is generally regulated by the characteristics of persons toward whom responses are directed, the social setting, temporal factors, and host of verbal and symbolic cues that signify predictable response consequences" (p. 25).

Identifying Supporting Contingencies

As mentioned earlier, both the adaptive and maladaptive operant behavior of emotionally disturbed children is thought to be controlled by environmental stimuli (Skinner, 1953). Hence, the behavioral engineer is faced with the significant task of identifying and analyzing antecedent and consequent events associated with the target behavior. Even though it is unrealistic to expect to reach complete understanding of the numerous variables influencing the behavioral excesses and deficits of emotionally disturbed children, it is possible to identify major factors associated with particular patterns of behavior. Included should be attempts to understand environmental stimuli which alert a child that conditions are receptive to a display of the target response as well as those environmental events which are subsequent to the response. Since it is assumed that the operant behavioral excesses and deficits of emotionally disturbed children are a function of the consequences which follow them, a thorough analysis of the contingencies associated with a target response must be made.

Observing the Behavioral Excess or Deficit

Careful measurement and analysis are necessary for a thorough understanding of the behavioral excess or deficit and its antecedent and consequent factors. In addition, this basic component of behavior modification is the sole means of determining whether or not the consequences being applied are associated with a systematic change in the behavioral excess or deficit.

While a variety of options exist for securing baseline (a preintervention record of the behavioral excess or deficit) and experimental intervention data (a record of the behavioral excess or deficit after the application of an intervention consequence), observational procedures are typically the most functional. Hall (1970) identified five observational options—continuous, event, duration, interval and time sampling.

Continuous observation involves making anecdotal records of a child's behavior including patterns of excesses and deficits over a given period of time. Although this option provides an opportunity to observe a variety of behaviors, it typically lacks reliability while requiring an inordinate amount of time and effort. In short, continuous observations are usually not a particularly acceptable approach to observation of behavior.

Event recording consists of an analysis of the frequency with which a child engages in a particular behavioral excess or deficit. This observational approach is frequently the most efficient and simplistic means of observing and recording a response pattern.

Duration recording requires the behavioral engineer to determine the amount of time a child engages in a specified behavioral excess or deficit over a set period of time. This observational option is preferable when the length of the occurrence of the excess or deficit is the most salient consideration. For example, a determination of the number of minutes a child interacts appropriately with his or her peers is more functional than knowing the number of positive contacts.

A fourth observational approach, *interval recording*, entails the division of a predetermined period of time into equal segments. The actual measurement process involves noting whether or not the identified behavioral excess or deficit occurs during each of the intervals. Interval systems offer the advantage of allowing observers to simultaneously assess a variety of behavioral excesses and deficits.

Time sampling, a system similar to the interval method, allows the observer the advantage of not continually having to observe children. An observer records whether or not a child is engaged in a particular behavioral excess or deficit at the end of a set time interval. Thus, for example, a psychiatric aide might observe a child's fighting over the course of one hour per afternoon, noting at the end of each five-minute period whether or not the child was fighting. This alternative provides a means of securing a reliable sample of behavior while allowing observers to simultaneously engage in other activities.

Since the accurate recording of any target behavior is an integral part of effective utilization of a behavioral approach, sufficient attention must be paid to this process. In particular, care must be taken (1) to secure a well defined and universally understood operational definition of the target behavior, (2) to devise a thoroughly understood measurement method, including specific times during which recordings will be made and precise procedures and equipment to be used in securing the data (e.g., stopwatch used from 3:00–4:00 p.m. to obtain a daily duration measure for "attention to task"), (3) graphing and charting procedures to be used in displaying the data, and (4) methods for obtaining measurement reliability.

While measurement procedures may be among the most basic and tedious components of any behavior modification program, their importance to the overall accuracy and integrity of a program cannot be denied.

DESIGNING INTERVENTION PROCEDURES

The behavioral excesses and deficits of behaviorally disordered children can most functionally be modified by the systematic manipulation of consequences. While the selection of potentially efficient intervention consequences is not an easy task, neither is it overwhelming or impossible. Through observations and discussions with children, their parents, and the various individuals involved in the education and treatment of target children, potentially efficacious intervention consequences can be identified. In this connection, it is necessary to recall that the value of any intervention procedure must be empirically determined. To evaluate whether a consequence is effective, its influence on the behavior it follows must be observed and analyzed. Hence, continuous and accurate measurement must constitute an integral component of any behavior modification program.

Possible intervention alternatives include reinforcement programs, extinction procedures and punishers. In addition, antecedent events may be manipulated to effect a change in behavioral excesses or deficits.

Reinforcement Programs

Operationally, reinforcers increase the probability of the occurrence of a specific response. Such an increase may occur in one of two ways. First, behaviors which are followed by a rewarding event tend to be repeated. For example, a child who significantly increases the number of minutes (s)he remains in a seat at school as a function of receiving "ward privileges" can be assumed to be positively reinforced by the contingent application of this consequence. Second, a response may be increased by the removal of an aversive stimulus (negative reinforcement). For example, a child may be excused from participation in a particular activity if his or her classroom and therapy behavior meets certain criteria. In the event that these procedures result in a significant positive increase in school and thereapy behavior, the contingent removal of the one activity can be considered reinforcing for the child. While negative reinforcers may result in planned behavior changes, it is recommended that their use be minimized, since positive reinforcement programs can usually accomplish the same goals while also embodying obvious interpersonal advantages. Thus, negative reinforcement should be considered only if positive reinforcers prove to be ineffectual.

Specific reinforcement programs found to be successful with emotionally disturbed children include social reinforcers, tangible reinforcers, activity privileges and idiosyncratic consequences.

Social reinforcers, while taken for granted by some professionals, are among the most significant and effective reinforcement stimuli. Included among social reinforcers have been supportive verbal and nonverbal responses made contingent upon children responding in a previously determined way. Positive adult attention given contingent on specified behavior is frequently among the most powerful and efficacious of all consequences (Drabman and Labey, 1974; Madsen, Becker, and Thomas, 1968; Parks, 1976).

Tangibles have also been effectively used with behaviorally disordered children in a variety of settings (Kauffman and O'Leary, 1972; O'Leary and Becker, 1967; Walker, Hops, and Fiegenbaum, 1976). Tangibles may include edibles dispensed for specified behavior (Lovaas, Freitas, Nelson, and Whelan, 1967); token programs, whereby backup reinforces are exchanged for tokens earned for appropriate behavior (Birnbrauer, Wolf, Kidder, and Tague, 1965; O'Leary and Drabman, 1971); and other methods for rewarding children with tangible items for engaging in appropriate behavior (Walker, 1979).

Contingent activities represent another frequently employed and highly functional means of achieving specific goals. In particular, children's behavior has been successfully modified by making certain activities (e.g., recess, free time) contingent upon the display of specific types and levels of particular operant behavior (Homme, 1969; Homme, deBaca, Devine, Steinhorst, and Rickert, 1963; Peed and Pinsker, 1978).

Finally, a wide array of *idiosyncratic reinforcers* have been used to promote particular types of behavior. Since those stimulus events capable of influencing specific children and behaviors vary from individual to individual, it is not surprising that certain highly individualized reinforcers have been found to be influential. Self-charting (Mainprize and Mann, 1978), tactile stimulation (Clements and Tracy, 1978), opportunity to tutor another student (Dineen, Hewitt, and Risley, 1977), and other diverse treatment conditions have been effectively applied with individual children to bring about particular behavior changes.

Extinction

This operant conditioning procedure which is designed to decrease behavioral excesses involves the elimination of previously reinforced behaviors. That is, attempts are made to decrease the likelihood of a response by ceasing to provide whatever contingent reinforcement is thought to be maintaining the behavior. For example, based on the principles of extinction, a child who chronically talks out in class without permission, allegedly to secure teacher attention, would be denied contingent regard.

While a number of studies have unequivocally demonstrated the efficacy of extinction programs (Brown and Elliot, 1965; Williams, 1959; Zimmerman and Zimmerman, 1962), particulary in combination with praise and attention for appropriate behaviors, use of extinction involves a number of problems. First, the effectiveness of this approach to operant conditioning depends on the ability of behavioral engineers to identify and control the reinforcers that are accelerating or maintaining a given behavior. Control of these factors is not easily achieved. Not only must an accurate analysis be conducted of the sometimes numerous sources of reinforcement for a particular behavior, but virtual absolute control must be maintained over such stimuli. The fact that a child may be, at least partially, reinforced for a particular maladaptive response by his or her peer group makes the procedure all the more difficult to apply. Second, extinction programs which only gain intermittent control over the stimuli controlling a behavioral excess actually tend to make a response more immune to extinction (Mathis, Cotton, and Sechrest, 1970). Hence, behavioral engineers may further entrench a behavioral excess if they only gain intermittent control over the maintaining consequences occurring in the natural environment. Third, extinction programs often result in a short-term increase in the response excess or the manifestation of other more intense maladaptive responses. For example, if a child with a history of disruptiveness in a therapy group, ostensively for the purpose of attracting attention, is placed on an extinction schedule it can be expected that his or her initial strategy will be to increase the frequency and intensity of the disruptive responses in order to secure the contingent attention that is being denied. Behaviorally disordered children will at least sometimes, engage in such intense increases that ignoring becomes an unsuitable alternative. Fourth, extinction programs are not justifiable with certain behavioral excesses such as physical aggression, stealing, and similar responses which obviously cannot be ignored.

Punishment Techniques

Just like extinction programs, punishment techniques are designed to decelerate the occurrence of a behavioral excess by following a maladaptive response with an aversive stimulus (Mowrer, 1968). While proven to possess the capacity to influence behavior, punishers should be employed only with annoying and potentially harmful behavior, and only after other more positive alternatives have been found to be ineffective. (Lovaas and Simmons, 1969; Wood and Lakin, 1978). The reason behind such cautious use of punishers is that the decelerating influence of punishment procedures may inadvertently reduce certain desirable responses, and that individuals involved in punishment programs may actually acquire punishing properties themselves.

Yet, when used judiciously and under the right conditions, punishment techniques can serve to augment success. Of particular value are response cost systems, time out, overcorrection and reinforcing behaviors incompatible with an undesired response.

Response cost or *cost contingency* involves the removal of a reinforcer from a child contingent upon the emission of a particular maladaptive response. Thus, tokens, free time, TV watching and other privileges earned for previous appropriate behavior may be lost contingent upon emitting specific behavioral excesses. The routine use in society of cost contingency techniques is exemplified in most laws and regulations.

Response cost systems have been used successfully under a variety of conditions and with children exhibiting a number of different excesses (Iwata and Bailey, 1974; Kauffman and O'Leary, 1972; Kazdin, 1972). For example, a program of this type was responsible for almost totally eliminating the offensive playground behavior of a socially aggressive child. The boy was given one point for each of the 15 minutes of recess time he was allotted at the beginning of each period and was "fined" for aggressive behavior or breaking play ground rules. Once the child had lost all his points he was required to return to the classroom. However, he was able to exchange any points he did not lose for school and home privileges (Walker, Street, Garrett, and Crossen, 1977).

Time out, i.e., the removal of a child from reinforcement contingent upon the manifestation of a maladaptive response, has also been successfully used with emotionally disturbed children to decelerate behavioral excesses (Noll and Simpson, 1979; Wolf and Risley, 1967). While similar in some respects to the time-honored and typically ineffective practice of placing a child in the corner or outside the classroom, appropriately applied time out presents several differences. First and foremost, rather than making children the center of attention, as in the case of a child who is made to sit in a "dunce's chair," time out involves removing children from positive reinforcement for a specified period of time. For example, a child who displays disruptive behavior, particularly at times when his or her peer group is present, might be isolated from those individuals who provide the attention contingent upon the display of the maladaptive behavior. In addition to removing children from reinforcing stimuli, successful time out programs should be designed such that children understand (1) that the time out procedure is implemented contingent upon certain inappropriate behaviors, (2) that the procedure is applied only with specified behavior as opposed to globally, (3) that the removal from reinforcement is for short periods of time. One example of a time out program with noncompliant children (Wahler, 1969) involved training parents to isolate their children for five-minute periods after each instance of oppositional behavior. This consequence resulted in a significant decrease in the target behavior.

Overcorrection, a relatively new behavioral control technique, has been shown to be particularly effective with severely emotionally disturbed children for whom other forms of reinforcement and punishment have failed to decelerate responses. According to Foxx (1971) and Foxx and Azrin (1973), overcorrection includes two objectives: To overcorrect the environmental effects of a maladaptive response, and to require the disrupting child to practice a correct form of an appropriate behavior.

The procedure for achieving the first objective, termed "restitutional overcorrection", requires "the disruptor to correct the consequences of his or her misbehavior by having him or her restore the situation to a state vastly improved from that which existed before the disruption" (Foxx and Azrin, 1973, p. 2). For example, a child who smears his or her feces would be required to wash, clean, and wax the soiled area. "Positive practice overcorrection" is used to achieve the second objective. This method requires, for example, that the child who smears his or her feces practice eliminating in a toilet and then practice cleansing and bathing. It should be noted that restitutional overcorrection is applicable only when a misbehavior disrupts the environment. That is, such behaviors as self-stimulatory responses do not disrupt the environment; consequently, only positive practice overcorrection programs are implemented in such instances.

Simpson and Sasso (1978) employed an overcorrection procedure to decelerate the behavioral rumination of a ten-year-old, severely emotionally disturbed boy. This relatively rare behavior involved the voluntary regurgitation of food from the stomach into and from the oral cavity. Rumination was frequently observed during or shortly after mealtime, although it was not limited to these time periods. When the behavior was observed, the teacher would immediately approach the child, open his mouth and squirt a small quantity of lemon juice into his mouth. The subject was then told to swallow the juice. The teacher's hand would remain over the child's mouth to aid him in consuming the juice. Next, the facial area was washed with warm, soapy water and a cloth for 30 seconds. This was followed by drying the face and then applying a face lotion to the affected area for an additional 15 seconds. This restitutional overcorrection procedure completely eliminated the self-stimulatory behavior within one week after treatment was initiated.

The *differential reinforcement* of behaviors incompatible with the maladaptive response is one of the few punishment procedures which does not involve an aversive consequence. As such it should be perceived as a preferred technique within the domain of punishment techniques. The approach is based on the assumption that reinforcing an appropriate behavior which is incompatible with the inappropriate act will decrease the maladaptive response (Zabel, 1981). Hence, a differential reinforcement of other behavior (DRO) procedure used with a child who is chronically out of seat without permission might involve determining favorable reinforcers for the child and then contingently applying these consequences when the youngster is at task in his or her seat. McAllister, Stachowink, Baer, and Conderman (1969) reported the use of an intervention strategy consisting of praising appropriate behavior (not talking) and verbally disapproving of the talking out of a socially disruptive child. Results revealed the procedures to be effective in increasing adaptive behavior and decreasing maladaptive responses.

Finally, antecedent events may be manipulated to effect planned changes with behaviorally disordered children. That is, stimulus cues associated with a response may be changed in order to increase the probability of inducing certain behaviors. Almost all individuals who work with emotionally disturbed children have used these procedures, including separating certain children from one another or modifying curriculum materials to promote more adaptive behavior. Yet, in spite of the common usage of this approach, the manipulation of antecedent conditions can be effective only in combination with an accurate understanding of the antecedent stimuli controlling children's behavior, and only if these events can actually be controlled. Consequently, physical separation of two children on a psychiatric ward for fighting does not mean that they will not fight with other children; nor does placement of a student next to the teacher's desk because of failure to complete assignments necessarily facilitate positive changes when the basic issue is that the teacher is providing vague and poorly organized instructions.

One stimulus change procedure that has brought about relatively impressive results consists of providing children with appropriate models for specific behaviors (Bandura, 1969). O'Conner (1969) investigated the effects of modeling on the social behavior of preschool children. In this study, six socially withdrawn children viewed a film depicting a model child observing the social interactions of his peers and then joining the group, with pleasant consequences. The results of the study revealed that the children who viewed the film significantly increased their social interactions.

Follow-up and Maintenance Procedures

Follow-up activities are designed to evaluate the effects of intervention procedures, modify performance goals and, if necessary, make program changes. While behavioral engineers must periodically change program procedures, such modifications must not be impulsively or capriciously made. Emotionally disturbed children can periodically be slow in responding even to efficacious programs. It is important, therefore, not to discontinue an intervention too soon even if it does not initially appear effective. Any treatment must be given ample opportunities to be successful. Further, since emotionally disturbed children frequently have a history of being exposed to unpredictable and erratic conditions, it is important that intervention techniques do not further aggravate the condition.

Finally, behavioral engineers must plan to provide adequate feedback and reinforcement to other adults involved in the intervention effort. Since psychiatric aides, teachers, therapists, and other personnel working with behaviorally disordered children must be supportive and consistent in carrying out any program, plans must be made for providing these individuals with appropriate positive feedback.

CASE EXAMPLES

This section presents two examples of behavioral programs established with emotionally disturbed children for the purpose of illustrating in practice the behavioral principles discussed in previous sections.

Case Study 1

The subject was a nine-year-old, behaviorally disordered male who had been assigned to a psychiatric day treatment facility because his classroom teacher and building principal had determined that his behavior was inappropriate for the services they were capable of providing. While the child had responded adequately to the treatment routine to which he had been exposed, his teacher in the treatment program noted that he was extremely reluctant to complete his daily academic assignments, and that he had not responded well to a variety of attempts to motivate him.

As a result, the professional staff began obtaining data on the child's completion of daily classroom assignments. Specifically, the target behavior was determined to be the completion and submission of daily English, spelling, social studies and writing papers on the day these were assigned and within the appropriate class period. The measure did not include homework assignments, nor did it impose quality criteria for the material submitted.

An event measurement technique revealed that mean performance in completion of assignment was 21 percent during the first seven days of baseline. However, on the eighth day of observation, the subject made a significant gain in productivity, allegedly due to what the teacher described as "Charlie becoming aware that I was recording." Mean performance from the eighth day until the end of the baseline phase was 55.5 percent.

Following baseline, a three-part reinforcement program was agreed upon, with the goal being to increase the quantity of assignments handed in, although not necessarily the quality. The latter was considered to be a future goal. The intervention program was composed of the following components: (1) verbal praise following the submission of assignments, (2) daily self-charting of the percentage of assignments completed and submitted on time, and (3) earning the privilege of being "teacher's errand boy" on those days when at least 90 percent of the subject's assignments were completed. As errand boy the child was given the opportunity to aid the teacher in a variety of tasks in and out of the classroom.

As a result of the implementation of the treatment procedures, completion of assignments increased significantly. As depicted in Figure 1, mean performance during this phase of the program rose to 94 percent. According to subjective teacher comments, the student was described as "handing in his assignments even though they were not always well done, very regularly." The teacher also indicated that the subject was much easier to control and seemed to be enjoying school more.

A short reversal period, consisting of a withdrawal of reinforcement techniques, produced only a marginal change in classroom productivity. Mean performance during the four-day reversal was 87 percent.

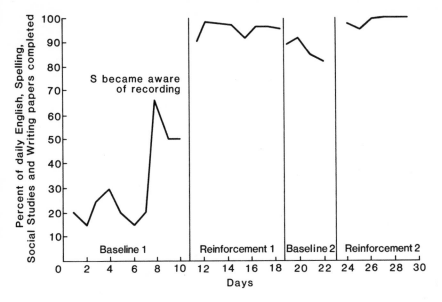

Figure 1 Effects of a reinforcement program on classroom productivity.

After reinstatement of the intervention procedures, classroom productivity again increased to a mean of 97 percent, at which level it was maintained.

Case Study 2[1]

The subject, Sydney, was a four-year-old male who was a residential patient in a state-supported psychiatric hospital located in a large midwestern city. Sydney had been admitted to the facility by his parents because, in their estimation, he was "totally out of control." This assessment had been confirmed by the personnel in the child's former preschool program, who readily admitted that they were unable to manage his many behavioral excesses. These included noncompliant responses, hyperactivity, temper tantrums and physical aggression.

As one component of the therapeutic program provided this child, he was assigned to a preschool special education classroom. The goals of this class were to extend the structure of the hospital environment into an educational setting; to develop basic preacademic skills; and to build a variety of skills that would be needed to meet the social demands of kindergarten.

[1] This program was devised and carried out by Raylene Heitman and Janice Simpson, Rainbow Mental Health Facility, Kansas City, Kansas.

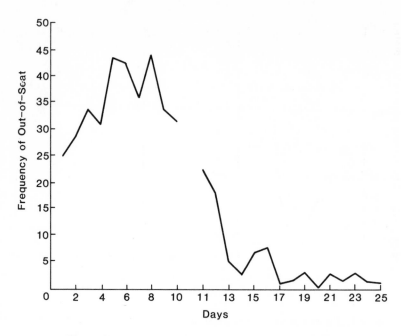

Figure 2   Response cost as a program support option.

One particular classroom problem behavior manifested by Sydney was a tendency to leave his assigned seat without permission. It was concluded by the teacher and her aide that whenever Sydney was not being attended to by an adult he would probably be out of his seat. This problem had been the subject of numerous meetings and intervention attempts. Included had been unsuccessful verbal reinforcement, token economy and reprimand programs.

As an alternative intervention strategy, Sydney was notified that the daily five-point star which he and his classmates received at the conclusion of each school day from the teacher would be modified if he failed to meet predetermined "in seat" criteria. Specifically it was explained to Sydney that each time he left his assigned seat without permission he would receive an "unhappy face." These small, adhesive backed stick-ons were attached directly to the corner of his desk. Upon the receipt of three "unhappy faces" the teacher would take a pair of scissors and cut one of the points from Sydney's star, which was prominently placed on a bulletin board in the front of the class. Sydney was required to wear his star in the hospital during the remainder of the day. While no loss of privileges were associated with the loss of segments of his star, professional and paraprofessional staff would comment on the degree to which this badge reflected upon his behavior in school that day. As shown in Figure 2, this program was extremely successful in reducing Sydney's "out-of-seat" problem.

SUMMARY

Without question, behavioral principles can be used to affect planned behavioral changes with emotionally disturbed children. As pointed out earlier, behavioral engineers must recognize, however, that the success of such intervention approaches is dependent on careful attention to the various components of the behavioral program selected for use, as well as the skillful translation of model principles into functional procedures. Finally, it should also be recognized that interpersonal relationships have a significant bearing on the outcome of the treatment program. However appropriate and well carried out, the technology used will only be as effective as the relationship between the implementer and the child under treatment.

REFERENCES

Bandura, A. *Principles of behavior modification.* New York, New York: Holt, Rinehart and Winston, 1969.

Bersoff, D. and Grieger, R. An interview model for the psycho-situational assessment of children's behavior. *American Journal of Orthopsychiatry*, 1971, *41*(3), 483–493.

Birnbrauer, J. S., Wolf, M. M., Kidder, J. D., and Tague, C. E. Classroom behavior of retarded pupils with token reinforcement. *Journal of Experimental Psychology*, 1965, *2*, 219–235.

Bower, E. M. *Early identification of emotionally handicapped children in school.* Springfield, Illinois: Charles C. Thomas, 1960.

Broden, M., Hall, R. V., Dunlap, A., and Clark, R. Effects of teacher attention and a token reinforcement system in a junior high school special education class. *Exceptional Children*, 1970, *36*, 341–349.

Brown, P. and Elliot, R. Control of aggression in a nursery school class. *Journal of Experimental Child Psychology*, 1965, *2*, 103–107.

Buell, J., Stoddard, P., Harris, F., and Baer, D. Collateral social development accompanying reinforcement of outdoor play in a preschool child. *Journal of Applied Behavior Analysis*, 1968, *1*, 167–174.

Clements, J. E. and Tracy, D. B. Effects of touch and verbal reinforcement on the classroom behavior of emotionally disturbed children. In J. Logan (Ed.), *Readings in behavior modification.* Guilford, Connecticut: Special Learning Corporation, 1978.

Copeland, R. E., Brown, R. E., and Hall, R. V. The effects of principal-implimented techniques on the behavior of pupils. *Journal of Applied Behavior Analysis*, 1974, *7*, 77–86.

Dineen, J. P., Hewitt, B. C., and Risley, T. R. Peer tutoring among elementary students: Educational benefits to the tutor. *Journal of Applied Behavior Analysis,* 1977, *10,* 231–238.

Doubros, S. G. and Daniels, G. J. An experimental approach to the reduction of overactive behavior. *Behavior Research and Therapy,* 1966, *4,* 251–258.

Drabman, R. S. and Labey, B. B. Feedback in classroom behavior modification: Effects on the target and her classmates. *Journal of Applied Behavior Analysis,* 1974, *7,* 591–598.

Foxx, R. M. *The use of overcorrection procedure in eliminating self-stimulatory behavior in a classroom for retarded children.* Unpublished doctoral dissertation, Southern Illinois University, 1971.

Foxx, R. M. and Azrin, N. H. The elimination of outside self-stimulatory behavior by overcorrection. *Journal of Applied Behavior Analysis,* 1973, *6,* 1–14.

Graubard, P. S. Children with behavioral disabilities. In L. M. Dunn (Ed.), *Exceptional children in the schools: Special education in transition* (2nd edition). New York, New York, Holt, Rinehart and Winston, 1973.

Hall, R. V. *Behavior modification: The measurement of behavior.* Merriam, Kansas: H & H Enterprises, 1970.

Hall, R. V. and Broden, M. Behavior changes in brain-injured children through social reinforcement. *Journal of Experimental Child Psychology,* 1967, *5,* 463–479.

Hall, R. V., Hawkins, R. P., and Axelrod, S. Measuring and recording student behavior: A behavior analysis approach. In R. A. Weinberg and F. H. Wood (Eds.), *Observation of pupils and teachers in mainstream and special education: Alternative strategies.* Minneapolis, Minnesota: Leadership Training Institute, 1975.

Hallahan, D. P. and Kauffman, J. M. Research on the education of distractible and hyperactive children. In W. M. Cruickshank and D. P. Hallahan (Eds.). *Perceptual and learning disabilities in children* (vol. 2). Syracuse, New York: Syracuse University Press, 1975.

Heaton, R. C., Safer, D. J., Allen, R. P., Spinnato, N. C., and Prumo, F. M. A motivational environment for behaviorally deviant junior high school students. *Journal of Abnormal Child Psychology,* 1976, *4,* 263–273.

Homme, L. E. *How to use contingency contracting in the classroom.* Champaign, Illinois: Research Press, 1969.

Homme, L. D., de Baca, D. C., Devine, J. V., Steinhorst, R., and Rickert, E. J. Use of the Premack principle in controlling the behavior of nursery school children. *Journal of the experimental analysis of behavior.* 1963, *6,* 544.

Iwata, B. and Bailey, J. Reward versus cost token systems: An analysis of the effects on students and teacher. *Journal of Applied Behavior Analysis,* 1974, *7,* 567–576.

Kauffman, J. M. *Characteristics of children's behavior disorders.* Columbus, Ohio: Charles E. Merrill, 1977.

Kauffman, J. M. and Hallahan, D. P. Control of rough physical behavior using novel contingencies and directive teaching. *Perceptual and motor skills.* 1973, *66,* 1225–1226.

Kauffman, K. E. and O'Leary, K. D. Reward, cost and self-evaluation procedures for disruptive adolescents in a psychiatric hospital school. *Journal of Applied Behavior Analysis,* 1972, *5,* 293–316.

Kazdin, A. Response cost: The removal of conditional reinforcers for therapeutic change. *Behavior Therapy*, 1972, *3*, 533–546.

Kerr, N., Meyerson, L., and Michael, J. A procedure for shaping verbalizations in a mute child. In L. P. Ullmann and L. Krasner (Eds.), *Case studies in behavior modification*. New York, New York: Holt, Rinehart and Winston, 1965.

Lovaas, O. I., Freitas, L., Nelson, K., and Whalen, C. The establishment of imitation and its use for the development of complex behavior in schizophrenic children. *Behavior Research and Therapy*, 1967, *5*, 171–181.

Lovaas, O. I. and Simmons, J. W. Manipulation of self-destruction in three retarded children. *Journal of Applied Behavior Analysis*, 1969, *2*, 143–157.

Madsen, C. H., Becker, W. C., and Thomas, D. R. Rules, praise and ignoring: Elements of elementary classroom control. *Journal of Applied Behavior Analysis*, 1968, *1*, 139–150.

Mainprize, D. and Mann, P. Educating adolescents with emotional and delinquency problems. In J. Logan (Ed.), *Readings in educational and behavioral disorders*. Guilford, Connecticut: Special Learning Corporation, 1978.

Mathis, B. C., Cotton, J. W., and Sechrest, L. *Psychological foundations of education*. New York, New York: Academic Press, 1970.

McAllister, L. W., Stachowiak, J. G., Baer, D. M., and Conderman, L. The application of operant conditioning techniques in a secondary classroom. *Journal of Applied Behavior Analysis*, 1969, *2*, 277–285.

McGrath, P., Marshall, P. G., and Prior, K. A comprehensive treatment program for a fire setting child. *Journal of Behavior Therapy and Experimental psychiatry*, 1979, *10*, 69–72.

Mowrer, O. H. *Learning theory and behavior*. New York, New York: Wiley, 1968.

Nolen, P., Kunzelmann, H., and Haring, N. Behavioral modification in a junior high learning disabilities classroom. *Exceptional Children*, 1967, *34*, 163–169.

Noll, M. B. and Simpson, R. L. The effects of physical time out on the aggressive behaviors of a severely emotionally disturbed child in a public school setting. *American Association for the Education of the Severely/Profoundly Handicapped Review*, 1979, *4*(4), 399–406.

O'Connor, R. D. Modification of social withdrawal through symbolic modeling. *Journal of Applied Behavior Analysis*, 1969, *2*, 15-22.

O'Leary, K. D. and Becker, W. C. Behavior modification of an adjustment class: Token reinforcement program. *Exceptional Children*, 1967, *33*, 637–642.

O'Leary, K. D. and Drabman, R. Token reinforcement programs in the classroom: A review. *Psychological Bulletin*, 1971, *75*, 379–398.

O'Leary, K. D. and O'Leary, S. G. Behavior modification in the school. In H. Leitenberg (Ed.), *Handbook of behavior modification and therapy*. Englewood Cliffs, New Jersey: Prentice-Hall, 1976.

Parks, A. L. *Behavior disorders: Helping children with behavioral problems*. Austin, Texas: Learning Concepts, 1976.

Patterson, G. R. A basis for identifying stimuli which control behaviors in natural settings. *Child Development*, 1974, *45*, 900–911.

Peed, S. and Pinsker, M. A. Behavior change procedures in junior and senior high school. *Education and Urban Society*, 1978, *10*, 501–520.

Reith, H. J. A behavioral approach to the management of hyperactive behavior. In M. J. Fine (Ed.), *Principles and techniques of intervention with hyperactive children.* Springfield, Illinois: Charles C. Thomas, 1976.

Risley, T. and Wolf, M. Establishing functional speech in echolatic children. *Behavioral Research and Therapy*, 1967, *5*, 73–88.

Ross. A. D. *Psychological disorders of children: A behavioral approach to theory, research and therapy.* New York, New York: McGraw-Hill, 1974.

Shoben, E. J. A learning theory interpretation of psychotherapy. *Harvard Educational Review*, 1948, *18*, 129–145.

Simpson, R. L. and Sasso, G. M. The modification of rumination in a severely emotionally disturbed child through an overcorrection procedure. *AAESPH Review*, 1978, *3*, 145–150.

Skinner, B. F. *Science and human behavior.* New York, New York: MacMillan, 1953.

Wahler, R. G. Oppositional children: A quest for parental reinforcement control. *Journal of Applied Behavior Analysis*, 1969, *2*(3), 159–170.

Walker, H. M. *The acting-out child: Coping with classroom disruption.* Boston, Massachusetts: Allyn and Bacon, 1979.

Walker, H. M., Hops, H., and Feigenbaum, E. Deviant classroom behavior as a function of combinations of social and token reinforcement and cost contingency. *Behavior Therapy*, 1976, *7*, 76–88.

Walker, H. M., Street, A., Garrett, B., and Crossen, J. *Experiments with response cost in playground and classroom settings.* Eugene, Oregon: Center at Oregon for Research in the Behavioral Education of the Handicapped, University of Oregon, 1977.

Watson, J. B. Psychology as a behaviorist views it. *Psychological Review*, 1913, *20*, 158–177.

Wheeler, A. J. and Sulzer, B. Operant training and generalization of a verbal response form in a speech-deficient child. *Journal of Applied Behavior Analysis*, 1970, *3*, 139–147.

Whelan, R. S. and Haring, N. G. Modification and maintenance of behavior through systematic application of consequences. *Exceptional Children*, 1966, *32*, 281–289.

Williams, C. D. The elimination of tantrum behavior by extinction procedures. *Journal of Abnormal and Social Psychology*, 1959, *59*, 269.

Wolf, M. and Risley, T. Application of operant conditioning procedures to the behavior problems of an autistic child: A follow up and extension. *Behavior Research and Therapy*, 1967, *5*, 103–111.

Wood, F. H. and Lakin, K. C. *Punishment and aversive stimulation in special education: Legal, theoretical and practical issues and their use with emotionally disturbed children and youth.* Minneapolis, Minnesota: University of Minnesota Advanced Training Institute, 1978.

Zabel, R. H. Behavioral approaches to behavior management. In G. Brown, R. L. McDowell, and J. Smith (Eds.), *Educating adolescents with behavior disorders.* Columbus, Ohio: Charles C. Merrill, 1981.

Zimmerman, E. H. and Zimmerman, J. The alteration of behavior in a special classroom situation. *Journal of the Experimental Analysis of Behavior*, 1962, *5*, 59-60.

6

A Psychodynamic Viewpoint on Interventions: Theory and Application

BARBARA GERSON AND MARGARET L. MARCUS

One of the basic assumptions of psychodynamic theory is that the same event and the same behavior can have a multitude of meanings which differ for each child as well as for the same child over time. In order to appreciate the idiosyncratic meaning of a particular event for a child, it is crucial not only to identify the objective behaviors, but also to understand the internal experiential world. There is no one-to-one correspondence between the actual behavior and the child's internal state, for, as has been frequently noted, behavior is multi-determined (Waelder, 1936). For example, any observer in a schoolyard at recess time could see a wide variety of reactions to what is generally assumed to be a pleasurable activity. One child may stand at the periphery of the group, closely watching the others play, but reluctant to join. Another child rushes in to the center of the activity and begins playing without regard for the rules of the game or the needs of the others. A third child seems to be ignoring the group altogether and engages in solitary play instead. However, it is not possible to appreciate, without further information, the meaning of any of the behaviors for each particular child. The child who watches but does not participate may be responding to a fear of peer rejection, a concern with bodily harm, or to a lack of knowledge of the rules. The second child may have organically based problems in impulse control, or may be acting aggressively in order to mask underlying depression. The third child might have a highly developed interest that is not commonly shared by other children of the same age, or may have a conflict similar to that of the first child.

In order for an intervention to be most effective in reducing anxiety and bringing about behavior change, it must be tailored to individual needs. A psychodynamic approach attempts to discover and explore the reason(s) underlying maladaptive behavior in order to further cognitive and emotional growth. Specifically, the focus of such intervention techniques is on strengthening "ego functions" and fostering satisfying interpersonal relationships. These two areas, ego functions and interpersonal relations, are reviewed before proceeding to a discussion of psychodynamic strategies for dealing with problems in emotional and social development.

THE FOCUS OF INTERVENTIONS

Ego Functions

The ego is a hypothetical construct referring to that part of the psychic structure which serves as a mediator between the needs of the person and the demands of the environment. In order to fulfill this function, the ego must balance the impulses of the person (the id), which are not bound by such reality-based parameters as concerns of time and space, and the rules and regulations of significant others and society, which are internalized or carried by the superego or conscience. Ego functions involve such processes as perception, thinking, language, judgment, and memory—all processes which are, in turn, crucial determinants of learning and adjustment. It is these apparatuses which "make it possible to take in information from the surroundings, to record it somehow in the brain, and to elicit and re-use it later on—in short to learn from experience" (Pine, 1974a). The ego monitors tension and anxiety aroused by stimuli from within and without by the use of unconscious defense mechanisms, such as denial (the blotting out of uncomfortable feelings or events), rationalization (giving "logical" reasons for behavior), or projection (attributing one's own anxiety-arousing thoughts or feelings to another person). Constitutional weaknesses, environmental traumas and stresses, and developmental delays or deviations may result in interference with one or more of these ego functions, which then alter not only how the individual perceives the world, but also what (s)he is able to master.

Hartmann (1958) formulated the concept of ego functions to explain the ability to adapt to the environment. These ego apparatuses are initially derived from what Hartmann has labeled "the conflict-free sphere." This means that such functions as perception, thinking, and memory originate independently of sexual and aggressive impulses. However, they may, in the course of development, become enmeshed in internal mental conflict. When this occurs, the individual's capacity for adaptation and for mastering reality is more or less impaired.

The school-age child, age seven to 11, is expected to have developed such ego functions as "secondary process thinking" (the ability to consider logical relations), "reality testing" (the ability to distinguish between what is internal and what is external in order to interpret external events accurately), and delay of gratification (Pine, 1980). The latter occurs through the increasing ability to anticipate the consequence of one's actions and to control one's impulses. The presence of a moderate degree of anxiety is essential for this process. The anxiety serves as a signal for defenses to become activated in order to avoid an overwhelming and sudden sense of panic. Behavior then becomes structured to promote mastery and learning rather than disintegrating into disorganization. Some children, who are labeled as borderline, lack this signal anxiety and are prone to panic attacks. It is assumed that a failure or arrest in development interferes with the ego's capacity to bind anxiety, to organize experience, and to relate to others (Pine, 1974).

First the family and then the school serve as resources for the child to develop ego functions and to learn from experience. The demands of each situation differ in terms of their social context and behavioral expectations. The classroom environment provides the child with an opportunity to interact with peers and adults and to have new role models for behavior outside of the family. In addition, new rules and routines are to be followed, new authority figures must be dealt with, and there is a reduction in the amount of motor activity allowed. The element of competition may emerge for the first time, as there are classmates present against whom to compare performance. The result of this comparison can lead to an increase in the motivation to succeed or to a reinforcement of feelings of failure which, in turn, influences future learning. For these reasons, the classroom may be the first place where deviations in ego functions and in behaviors, which were tolerated or consonant in the family, are noted. A youngster whose difficultes in delay of impulses result in aggressive behaviors, or one whose impaired language or poor judgment results in a passive, withdrawn orientation may be labeled as a potential problem in school, even if such conduct has been accepted or ignored by parents and caretakers. Such problems may be connected to disturbances in interpersonal relationships as well as to distortions in the sense of self.

Interpersonal Relations and Self Concept

The study of interpersonal attitudes and feelings is technically referred to as the study of "object relations", with "objects" referring to people or to internal images, fantasies or ideas that an individual may have of people. Those

aspects of interpersonal functioning which are central to understanding someone's object relations include the degree to which one is able to form "friendly
and loving bonds with others", and the "ability to sustain relationships over a
period of time" (Bellak, Hurvich, and Gediman, 1973, p. 142). Essential to these
attainments is the ability to view other people as separate from oneself, with
motivations, needs and feelings of their own, and the ability to accept both the
positive and negative aspects of another person.

The development of self concept is synonymous with the emergence of the
"self", and refers to the individual's sense of basic underlying goodness or badness. One of the prime landmarks of a stable self is the attainment of a self concept that is relatively independent of specific environmental feedback and which
is consistent over time. (Stolorow and Lachmann, 1980).

Such theorists as Mahler (1968), Fairbairn (1954), Balint (1968) and Winnicott (1965) maintain that it is the quality of care during early infancy that defines the core of the self concept and of later object relations. What must be
imparted to the infant is not just the satisfaction of needs but the feeling that
"he is a person, valued and enjoyed as such by his mother" (Sutherland, 1980,
p. 841). A failure of fit between the infant's psychological needs and the mother's care results in the development of a basic sense of having something lacking
or missing, or of having a "basic fault" within (Balint, 1968). It is necessary for
a mother to respond naturally and accurately to the infant's needs in order for
the infant to develop a sense of effectiveness and a perception of the world as
fulfilling. When a mother responds in keeping with her own needs rather than
the infant's, and thus intrudes herself on the infant, the "self" begins to become
distorted. The infant then develops a "false self", which complies externally
with what is being asked, while covering and hiding the true feelings (Winnicott,
1965). Erickson (1959) similarly speaks of the development of a sense of "basic
trust" during this earliest period.

The process of growth is a process of increasing separation from the mother.
In the earliest months of life, the infant is both totally dependent on the caretaker and unable to experience any sense of differentness between itself and the
other. Gradually, the infant begins to perceive the mother as a separate person,
a process which takes several years. During most of the first year, the infant develops only some dim awareness of the differences between itself and mother,
with the two remaining "symbiotically" fused (Mahler, 1968). It is through experiences of frustration, brought about by the mother's absence, that twinges of
separateness begin to become assimilated (Chodorow, 1979).

The "self" is consolidating simultaneously, adding an additional force to the
process of psychological separation. One of the most central and primary aspects
of the self is the sense of the physical self. Through exploration and recognition
of one's body and its sensations, and the consequences of movement, the infant

develops a recognition of the boundaries of the physical self. This reinforces the distinctions between its physical self and the physical being of others.

Somewhat ironically, it is only when some sense of separateness has emerged that a sense of dependence on another person is able to be experienced (Chodorow, 1979). Prior to that, when there is greater actual dependency, the infant's experience is that of omnipotence, or a sense of being able to bring about whatever is desired. This feeling of omnipotence is, of course, grounded on the fact of being merged with the mother, whose ego strengths are taken as the infant's own.

Later, others in the child's environment begin to exert a significant influence on the continuing process of differentiation, or development of a sense of oneself as distinct from others. The father, in particular, provides another model against which the developing child can compare himself or herself. The father also provides the toddler with a break from the intense attachment to the mother (Abelin, 1971).

Difficulties in early object relations and sense of self may lead to a wide variety of later disturbances which center around intimacy, trust, and closeness. For example, if early relationships are marked with a lack of satisfying fit and unfulfilled needs, one may come to see oneself as responsible for these disappointments, rather than understanding that the adult caretaker is deficient. Thus, the infant or young child may feel that (s)he is "bad" in a world that is essentially "good", rather than perceiving the world, or caretakers, who are indispensable, as bad (Fairbairn, 1954). Subsequently, the individual may behave in ways which perpetuate this sense of badness. Or, one may defend against the memories of unsatisfying early relationships by cutting them off from consciousness, a process which results in the splitting off of aspects of oneself. This split drains the growing child of energy and creativity and creates a sense of oneself as empty or bored.

Anxieties about relating may take forms which appear quite opposite from each other. Intense clinging to people, as well as avoiding people, both may demonstrate the same fear of involvement. Thus, the solitary isolated child as well as the child who becomes anxious whenever there is any separation from another person both are revealing difficulties in the same area. It is likely that many of the children who have deficits in social skills or who experience rejections by their peers in school are, in fact, children with anxieties about relating which stem from early disturbances in the relationship with the caretaker. Similarly, the typical pattern of immediate, intense, and indiscriminate attachment shown by abandoned children also indicates core deficiencies in object relations. The degree to which a child is able to look to teachers and to other adults as a resource in learning also reveals their sense of trust in the reliability of the world. Some children are able to accept both emotional and task-related help, while others anticipate only disapproval and punishment.

Friendship patterns similarly can reveal disturbances. Some children relate solely in order to fill an immediate need; interactions cease after a need has been gratified, or if the other person has disappointed them. The teacher who works with such a child may find the relationship even more draining than usual, since much is asked but even the expected mutuality and reciprocity between adult and child is lacking. Other children may seek exclusive and all-encompassing friendships in which the similarities are emphasized and differences are homogenized. Such friendships will be marked by possessiveness, jealousy and anger about interruptions and sharing. These children may function adequately in exclusive interactions with an adult, but will become highly anxious in group settings or when the adult indicates other interests. Thus, deviations in relationships with adults and peers, as well as distortions in self image, can stem from problems in early object relations.

INITIATING THE INTERVENTION PROCESS

The first step in the intervention process is the recognition that a child is having some difficulty coping. When the child's defenses are no longer able to manage whatever stresses are present, and the child develops some behavior or symptom that is troubling to others or to himself or herself, a parent or teacher may initiate a referral for professional assistance. At times, a child may be self-referred. Although the symptoms of the problem may be immediately apparent, frequently more detailed information needs to be collected in order to understand the meaning of the symptom and the severity of the disturbance. An individual psychological evaluation, in which projective personality assessment and intellectual and/or perceptual-motor testing is carried out, may follow. Classroom observations, physical and neurological examinations, and family interviews may also be essential.

Awareness of situations that tend to evoke difficulties can expedite the intervention process and can minimize the child's (and family's) suffering. In the process of growing up, all children are confronted by life stresses of varying degrees of severity. The child's ability to cope depends not only on the nature of the stressor, but also on the strength and flexibility of ego functions and the solidity of object relations. Such physical changes as a haircut, the loss of a tooth, the onset of menstruation, or the development of secondary sexual characteristics are common experiences which may evoke feelings of sadness, fear, or anger. Some children may view going to school or to summer camp as difficult separations. The birth of a sibling tends to elicit feelings of envy and jealousy, which may then be masked by an excessive display of attention and concern. However, there are other crises which occur less frequently, are more disruptive to the child and the family system, and require greater adjustments. Some of the more severe stressors are discussed below, with a focus on their psychological impact on the child's adaptive functioning.

Divorce

There is widespread agreement that parental separation and divorce is a crisis of major proportions in the lives of children of all ages. Kelly and Wallerstein (1980), who conducted a five year clinical research project on the effects of divorce on children, report that most children view their parents' break-up as the most stressful period of their lives and as a time filled with shock, fears and overwhelming grief. The experience of a parental divorce has been compared to the experience of a sudden death in that it involves loss, changes in family relations, and a lack of preparation (Group for the Advancement of Psychiatry, 1980). However, divorce has neither the finality nor the ritual supports of mourning. In addition, in a divorce the child must negotiate relationships with both a custodial and a noncustodial parent simultaneously, dealing with issues of divided loyalties and allegiances. Difficulties in communication with either parent about the feelings raised by the divorce may add to the strain. A divorce has potential consequences on the child's ability to master the developmental tasks of childhood by either slowing down or prematurely rushing the child's growth (Kelly and Wallerstein, 1980). Since much of development consists of mastering attachments and separations, divorce can profoundly influence the growing child's emotional and social adjustment (Group for the Advancement of Psychiatry, 1980).

The most acute symptoms in children are apparent in the first year to 18 months postdivorce, with the particular effects varying according to the age of the child. For example, preschool children become fearful, bewildered and frequently aggressive, with bizarre fantasies about the divorce being common (Kelly and Wallerstein, 1980). Their play and social relations have been found to deteriorate for up to two years postdivorce (Hetherington, Cox, and Cox, 1979). Both preschool aged children and early elementary school children feel emotionally needy and deprived. Children aged six through eight also feel a sense of pervasive sadness (Kelly and Wallerstein, 1980). Later elementary school children are more able to use their cognitive and social skills to adapt to the divorce, but feel underlying intense anger and concerns about their own identity. For adolescents, the parental break up comes at a time when separation from parents is paramount. There is a sense of role reversal for them, and a loss of the secure framework against which to test their independence.

Long term consequences of divorce persist for a large proportion of all children for at least five years postdivorce, with depression being the most prevalent and concerning symptom. The long term adjustment of a child is, however, a consequence of several features of the family, including the parents' resolution of their own anger and the family's utilization of social supports. Particularly important is the child's relationship with the noncustodial parent (Hess and Camara, 1979), the child's predivorce adjustment and the custodial parent's ability to parent (Kelly and Wallerstein, 1980). Thus, for the child who is already psychologically vulnerable or whose parents have limited capacities to cope, divorce can be intensely disruptive for a long period of time. Psychological support from a wide variety of sources is then essential for such a family to adapt.

Death of a Parent

The death of a parent is another object loss of immediate catastrophic proportions for a child which often leaves long range consequences. The specific reactions are highly dependent on the developmental level of the child, since the ability to understand death varies with the sophistication of ego capacities (Kastenbaum and Aisenberg, 1976; Wolfenstein, 1966). The consequences are also a function of the surviving parent's anxiety about death (Yalom, 1980) and his or her ability to respond to the child's reactions (Becker and Margolin, 1967). Also relevant are the availability of other supportive adults and the child's relationship with the deceased parent (Wolfenstein, 1969).

The child's typical reaction involves a sense of deep loss and perhaps guilt or concern that it was his or her own aggressive fantasies that contributed to the parent's death. Denial of the finality of the loss, and rage, often directed towards the surviving parent, combined with idealization of the deceased parent, may also be evident (Wolfenstein, 1969). Some maintain that children develop a greater "death awareness", or a greater recognition, at some level, of the possibilities of their own loss of life (Yalom, 1980). In any event, there is certainly an increase in anxiety and in vulnerability to the many stressors encountered in everyday events.

It has been suggested that it is not until adolescence that mourning, the process of grieving, "of remembering and reality testing, separating memory from hope" (Wolfenstein, 1966, p. 931) occurs, since it requires tolerating intensely painful feelings in order to accept the loss in the face of strongly opposing fantasies. Without undergoing mourning, it is more likely that the child may keep fantasies of the parent's return, which may then propel a pattern of behavior in which disappointments and losses are repeated. Adult depression (Kastenbaum and Aisenberg, 1976) and an increase in the likelihood of delinquency for boys (Rutter, 1980) are also associated with early bereavement. More symptoms of disturbance have been noted in adults who have lost a parent before age 16 than in adults with no such early losses (Langner and Michael, 1963).

Although it is frequently recommended that the surviving parent convey concrete, direct information to children about death (Furman, 1974; Grollman,

1970), many parents tend to insulate the child from confronting the pain of the loss. Professional interventions may then be appropriate to help allow the family to mourn or express whatever feelings are present.

Child Abuse

Reported cases of child abuse are on the rise and, regardless of whether this is a function of more accurate reporting or due to an actual increase in the battering of children, the physical and emotional consequences are likely to be devastating to the child. Gil (1970) conceptualizes abuse as a continuum ranging from "normal" discipline by a caretaker who has a stable personality and experiences little environmental stress, to repeated physical attacks by parents or parent surrogates who are emotionally disturbed and subject to external pressures (inadequate income, unemployment, poor housing, etc.). However, abuse is not limited to psychopathic parents or to families with a low socioeconomic status, but can occur in all types of families (Kempe, Silverman, Steele, Droegemueller, and Silver, 1962). Lack of empathy, an incomplete understanding of the developmental stages of childhood, unrealistic expectations for behavior which disregard the child's needs and abilities, low frustration tolerance, and poor impulse control, are some of the gaps and distortions which are evident in the ego functioning of abusive parents and caretakers (Steele, 1970; Spinella and Zigler, 1972).

A particular child may be selected as the target for abuse because of a physical disability or an emotional handicap. Abused children may exhibit many of the same ego deficits as their abusers and, in addition, may have difficulty in interpersonal relationships. Hospitalized abused children were found to have blunted affect and limited motor behavior, a diminished capacity for initiating interpersonal contact, and, in some instances, to have lost the ability to speak (Galston, 1965). This decrease in sensory, motor, and emotional exploration restricts the growth and development of ego functions and interpersonal relations, which are crucial for further learning.

Mental Retardation and Neurological Disturbances

Mental retardation and neurological impairment have pervasive impacts on all aspects of the child's functioning—social and interpersonal, as well as academic. The child may be deficient in one or more of the basic areas needed for learning, and may have limited intellectual potential, impaired perceptual skills or gaps in ego functions (Pine, 1980). Children who are retarded or neurologically damaged may have such ego weaknesses as inattentiveness, distractibility, hyperactivity or problems with self control, all of which can interfere with functioning with peers and at school. Thus, they will have difficulty acquiring the academic skills that are being mastered by their classmates.

The child's learning problems result in lower self esteem, since "from the child's point of view, he is smart or stupid relative to what he can or cannot do as he looks about him and sees what his age peers are accomplishing" (Benjamin, 1975, p. 19). In addition, some of the ego deficits or perceptual distortions make it difficult for the child to develop skills in interpersonal relationships, beginning at infancy and continuing through development (Buchholz, 1977). Thus, experiences of peer rejection are typical, and result in negative evaluations of social competence and social self concept.

In addition, the presence of a child with developmental delays or deviations has effects on the parents and the family system. Common parental reactions include guilt (Wolfensberger, 1967) depression and mourning (Solnit and Stark, 1961) and shame and embarrassment (Roos, 1963). The family itself is unable to undergo the typical developmental changes in the life cycle, where all members eventually become "adults" (Farber, 1968). The stresses may affect the marital relationship as well as each parent's individual role functioning (Schild, 1971; Wolfensberger, 1967).

In school, retarded or learning disabled children may become labeled as behavior problems because of their repeated frustrations over not learning. Their resistance to academic situations, disruptive behaviors and low self concept may seem, on the surface, to be similar to the behaviors of a child whose emotional conflicts are interfering with learning. However, the underlying causes of the emotionally disturbed child's inability to learn may stem from crises or changes in the family system, such as any of those discussed previously. An understanding of whether the learning disability is primary or whether it is secondary to emotional factors is crucial when planning intervention strategies (Buchholz, 1977; Redl, 1972).

In summary, these disturbances, which range from familial crises to organic impairments, affect the development of ego functions and object relations on either a temporary or a more lasting basis. The severity and duration of the impact of these stressors is, in part, dependent on how quickly the child is identified as someone in need of psychological intervention. Once a youngster has been recognized as being at risk, a wide array of psychodynamic techniques can be utilized to provide support in working through the psychic conflict with the goal of facilitating growth.

INTERVENTION STRATEGIES

In surveying a range of psychodynamic interventions, certain shared characteristics become apparent. One such characteristic is that the goal of these strategies is to help the individual to become more aware of his or her feelings and of the link between feelings and actions. Not all feelings are conscious, and some stem from early preverbal experiences, yet they continue to influence present functioning. The individual is helped to appreciate the wide range of his or her feelings and to understand the feelings underlying various kinds of behaviors. A second characteristic of psychodynamic techniques is that these explorations and insights occur within the context of a trusting relationship. It is within the safety of this relationship that thoughts, feelings and behaviors resulting from past interactions with other significant people can be more or less openly and nondefensively brought to light. Third, the relationship with the therapist is an important clue to earlier feelings, because the client comes to project onto the therapist in significant ways. Prior patterns of thinking, feeling and relating are repeated within the relationship. The client's unconscious repetition of these earlier reactions with the therapist is called the "transference." Transference reactions are present in all relationships and a therapeutic relationship allows the transferences to be noted in more detail. Finally, the content of discussions is considered on both a manifest or overt level and on a latent or hidden level. It is these hidden layers, which are communicated in symbolic ways, that provide clues to the unconscious meanings and motivations of behaviors.

Play Therapy

Play therapy is a technique which relies on the medium of play to help disturbed and, to a lesser extent, normal children to work through internal conflicts which are interfereing with adaptive functioning. It "may be thought of as a set of attitudes in and through which children may feel free to express themselves fully, in their own way, so that eventually they may achieve feelings of security, adequacy, and worthiness through emotional insight." (Moustakas, 1973, p. 2) A so-called normal child, whose behavior may be regressing as a result of a situational crisis (e.g., the birth of a sibling) approaches the play sessions in different ways than does a more emotionally vulnerable child. The former youngster establishes a relationship with the therapist more quickly and expresses feelings sooner and in a more direct manner than does the latter. However, for both groups of children, play therapy offers the opportunity to work through anxiety-arousing feelings in order to free emotional energy for ego development and for adaptive interpersonal relations.

The play therapist is the promoter of the child's emotional growth. By accepting thoughts, feelings, and actions, showing empathy and understanding, and encouraging the expression and the exploration of feelings through the use of structured and/or nonstructured materials (dolls, cars, guns versus clay, water, blocks), the therapist helps the child to improve ego functioning. Objects have different meanings and can be used to symbolize and to communicate on many levels. For example, plastic models of animals surrounded by a ring of blocks may be animals in a zoo, but may also represent a defensive effort to contain aggressive impulses. It is the task of the therapist to offer interpretations and to clarify feelings expressed in the play as well as to set limits. Parameters relating to the length of the session, the boundaries of the relationship to the therapist, and the use of the materials need to be established so that the therapist can provide acceptance rather than offer criticism or disapproval.

There are a variety of structured techniques which the play therapist may introduce in the sessions to help a child, particularly one who is emotionally inhibited or fearful, express feelings and thoughts. One of the more widely used methods is the "mutual story telling technique" (Gardner, 1975). The child is encouraged, and helped if necessary, to create a story with a moral at the end. The story may be tape recorded and an imaginary audience of listeners may be introduced as part of the dramatic setting. The therapist's job is to understand the child's latent, or underlying, message in the story and to offer the child another story with the same characters and general plot, but with changes in it which reflect more adaptive solutions or corrections in perceptions. Thus, communication between the therapist and the child is taking place indirectly and symbolically, and direct confrontations or interpretations, which may be anxiety arousing, are avoided.

Child analysis differs from psychodynamically oriented play therapy in the intensity of the relationship between the youngster and the analyst. Appointments are made three to five times a week for analysis in contrast to once or twice weekly for therapy. There is more continuity of content and less need to erect defenses against anxiety because the feelings can be dealt with in the treatment due to the frequency of the analytic sessions. Such child analysts as Klein, (1965), Freud (1946, 1965) and Winnicott (1965) emphasize the need to expand the dominance of the ego by making the unconscious conscious through interpretation, clarification, and acceptance.

Treatment generally takes place in a community agency, out-patient clinic of a hospital, or private office. However, ongoing therapy can also be offered in the schools (Nickerson, 1973), both in and out of classrooms. Such an arrangement gives the therapist easier access to a wider range of children, reduces whatever stigma there may be about seeking professional help, and can ease the communication gaps between those involved in different aspects of the child's life. When therapy is done in schools, it is important to provide transitions from the therapy back to the academic work, and to coordinate scheduling with teachers. Important questions may also arise about the confidentiality and loyality of the therapist. In schools, as anywhere else, it is essential for the therapist to be the ally of the child so that a trusting relationship and a positive transference can develop. Because being part of the school staff may blur the boundaries of the therapist's role, it is even more essential to keep the alliance with the child clearly in mind. It has even been suggested that two therapists be assigned to a single case at some times, one to work with the child and a second to be a "school consultant" (Bernstein, 1976).

Group Work

General Considerations

Group work with children is an intervention technique which has several unique characteristics. Groups provide an opportunity for direct observation of social behavior; group members are present to serve as role models and to offer support; and belonging to a group can dilute the mistrust or anxiety that may be experienced toward the leader or toward adults in general. Glass (1969) distinguishes counseling groups, where the focus is on "obvious events that occur within the group session, events that have been clearly delineated and that all the members are aware of," from therapy groups, where the emphasis is on both observable behavior and its underlying meaning and motivation. (p. 4)

Slavson (1943; 1950; 1952) describes four types of therapeutic groups. The first is play group psychotherapy, which incorporates the methods and materials of individual play therapy. Transitional groups are primarily educative, providing an arena for rehearsal and practice of interpersonal skills. Activity group psychotherapy does not have a structured program, but materials are available, and the therapist and group members are role models for appropriate behavior. The final category, which appears to represent the most common therapeutic group, is activity-interview group psychotherapy. The therapist facilitates group participation through discussion, interpretation, and insight. The emphasis is on forming new identifications and on verbalization rather than on purely actions.

Whether the group is considered to be a counseling group or a therapy group, it is important to select the members with care. The leader must be aware of the psychological make-up of the potential members as well as the phase of development. Kessler (1966), for example, recommends combining aggressive, active youngsters with more controlled youngsters since "the aggressive, active children spur the group to regressive and challenging behavior, and the more stable, socially oriented children serve as group superegos." (p. 389) A passive child may initially need a one-to-one situation with an adult to increase verbalizations and reinforce social skills before gradual introduction to a group. In contrast, a hyperactive child, whose hyperactivity is secondary to emotional problems and not organic in nature, functions best in a group of two to three members where clear limits are set and distractions in terms of available materials, noise, and activity level are minimized.

The developmental stage of the children determines, to a large extent, the type of behavior that is expected in the group. Kindergarteners and first graders have fewer social skills and a shorter attention span than eight or nine year olds and consequently need more structure and greater limits. For adolescents, group identity and concerns about body image and independence are central. These issues can be discussed in groups where social interaction is encouraged, while with younger children, problems are worked through in play and verbalizing is secondary to the activity.

Therapy Groups in Classrooms

Since children's problems frequently become explicit in the classroom setting, it is often expedient to help them to work out their difficulties where they occur (Bardon, Bennett, Bruchez, and Sanderson, 1976). The fact that other children in the class can become involved in the intervention and thereby benefit from the treatment process is also of importance. Classmates may be asked to join by the child who was initially referred for help, may invite themselves to participate, or may be solicited by the psychologist because of their involvement with the referred child (Bardon et al., 1976; Kaplan and Gerson, 1975). In this way, the children become able to assist each other to cope throughout the day, beyond the limits of a brief psychotherapy session.

Bardon et al. (1976) focus on the class for the application of "psychosituational classroom interventions". This means that the psychologist can intervene in any number of ways in classroom problems, such as quarrels, while the regular academic work is proceeding. The classroom could also be the site for on-going play therapy and activity group therapy, in which group activities are set up in order to allow for the controlled expression of feelings and for the correction of interpersonal relationships (Kaplan and Gerson, 1975). There may be puppet play, dramatics, role playing or art work as part of the therapy, and materials such as blocks and dolls, which are typically part of the therapeutic playroom, can also be used in classes. These approaches are appropriate with children whose behaviors range from withdrawn to aggressive; the only requirements are that the youngster must be able to develop a relationship with the psychologist and be controllable, since the class does not provide as safe an environment as a private office would. Consequently, a wide variety of regressive behaviors cannot be tolerated in this setting.

The specific time during which classroom interventions can be carried out depends on the structure of the particular class. Although it may be acceptable for some teachers to have psychologists present during regular activities, others may prefer that outside personnel be in the room during free play time (Kaplan and Gerson, 1975). However, as in therapy conducted anywhere, as much consistency as possible is helpful in the arrangements of the treatment. The referral of a specific child is frequently the entry point for doing therapy in classrooms. Several classroom sessions may then be spent with the referred child in order to determine the youngster's suitability for such treatment. At the same time, the willingness of the teacher to become involved can be assessed. The teacher's contribution cannot be minimized, since it is not possible to carry out any ongoing therapeutic work in the class without consistent cooperation and a trusting alliance between the mental health professional and the teacher. The teacher must feel confident that his or her work is not being evaluated and must be tolerant of having another adult present in the same territory. It has been suggested that teachers who perceive their work as concerning the mental health of children and not merely their academic learning, and who are not overly emotionally possessive of their students, are most suited for such a style of cooperation (Mumford, 1968). Once the child and the class setting are judged to be appropriate, the relationship between the psychologist and the referred student can be opened up and other children can be encouraged to join them.

Working in the classroom provides the opportunity to stimulate the natural resources of the children in the class to heal each other, given adequate models and guidance. Although many school personnel may function in the class for diagnostic or remedial purposes or for behavioral management, psychodynamic psychotherapy in a class setting is not frequently described. At this point, the effects have been described only in case studies. Clearly, more research is needed in order to pinpoint its effectiveness and to delineate the situations in which it is most beneficial.

There are a number of differences between groups conducted in a classroom setting and those which meet in a psychologist's office in the school, in a therapist's private office, or in a clinic. Both the process and content of a psychotherapy group in a class are open to public scrutiny, since nonmembers can observe their classmates who are members and may, from time to time, participate. In contrast, groups held outside the classroom are less concerned to ongoing school routines and are likely to have a more stable membership. The audience effect caused by the presence of their fellow classmates may reduce the anxiety of group participation, but may limit the expression of regressive feelings and behaviors. Transference reactions tend to be more diluted in a classroom setting due to the fluidity of the membership and to the decrease in the intensity of the interactions. The therapeutic impact of a group is influenced by the environment in which it is held.

Nontreatment Groups

Groups, particularly in schools, also provide an appropriate format for addressing typical developmental issues faced by children and adolescents. In these cases, the groups are considered nontreatment groups, do not focus on individual intrapsychic events, and are nonselective in their composition. Guidance counselors or school psychologists may, for example, run either "rap groups" or modified "sensitivity groups" for adolescents in which social and parental relationships, and current interactions and role exploration are discussed. With younger children, an equivalent group might be a "feelings groups" in which structured tasks (i.e., reading and writing stories about feelings) as well as present emotions are discussed (Buchholz, 1974). Groups may also be focused around specific themes which vary according to the needs of the population. In this category fall consciousness-raising groups which have been conducted with elementary school girls; in these groups the experiences of being a girl, a sister, and a daughter were the center of the conversations (Gerson, 1974). Groups have been conducted with early adolescents concerning their attitudes to and experiences of their schooling—that is, their relationship to their peers, teachers and their schoolwork itself (Hill, 1978). Groups may also be set up to encourage creative self expression and may use techniques of theatre games, imaginative exercises, art, music, or dance to expand the ordinary limits of the child (Buchholz, 1974; Newman, 1974).

Limit Setting in the Classroom

In order to establish effective, nonpunitive discipline so that learning can proceed, several psychodynamic principles can be helpful. First, the differences between the expression of feelings and actions must be clarified, since feelings and wishes are to be identified and explored, while actions may have to be limited and redirected. Second, an awareness of underlying meanings of behaviors is important when deciding which actions are to be regulated. Thus, some conduct may be tolerated if it is typical of a developmental stage or symptomatic of a personality problem or a current environmental stress, such as a divorce, illness, or a recent move (Long and Newman, 1976). However, it is necessary to intervene to stop behaviors that are physically dangerous, psychologically maladaptive, destructive to property or to a group activity, or which have the potential to escalate so that the child or group will soon lose control.

Setting limits provides a child who has inadequate control of impulses (an ego function) with external, auxiliary ego supports. The techniques used to attain this goal range from the removal of distracting objects, to planning structured activities with a minimum of stimulation, to firm, but not rough, physical restraint of a child who is in a state of panic or having a tantrum. One of the outcomes of this intervention is to reassure all children of the safety of their environment, while at the same time helping the ego deficient child to develop more adequate control. Additional techniques that involve different aspects of limit setting follow.

Life Space Interviewing

Life space interviewing is a method developed by Fritz Redl (1959) for on-the-spot crisis intervention, although it is applicable to noncrisis situations as well. The goals of this strategy are to aid the child to regain control and/or to learn from the event so that future situations are approached differently. The youngster is first asked to describe what happened and is then sympathetically questioned about it. Alternate perceptions from other students may also be explored (Morse, 1976). Through this process, it is assumed that the child's initial emotional reaction and perceptions will become more rational and controlled. In addition, the teacher attempts to assess what the major underlying (latent) issues are for the child. When these issues seem central and pervasive for the child, the discussion may continue and the youngster will be asked for possible solutions to the problem. If the child is unable to provide any acceptable solutions, the teacher may have to present some realistic procedures and define a way of following through on the problem. In other words, the adult provides the skills that the child lacks, after helping the child to control the troubling feelings. Solutions are not attempted while the youngster is in a state of high anxiety, since it is not possible for an individual to focus clearly and to problem-solve when in an agitated state.

The adult who uses this technique needs to be nonmoralistic and empathic, just as in any affective interactions. Teachers of special education classes may find this method of dealing with problems to be essential in their work, and may be able to use it most effectively if there is another adult present to continue working with the other class members while they talk individually with the child in crisis (Newman, 1974). Regular classroom teachers can also use this style in handling the conflicts they face, although it may be more difficult for them to be free to deal with an individual child in the depth necessary for full resolution.

Time Out Room

Another intervention strategy for containing behavior before dealing with the underlying feelings or motivation is the time out or quiet room. This is a place where a child can go in order to calm down and restore emotional equilibrium when impulses are out of control. It may not be a separate room, but rather a sectioned off corner of the classroom where visual and auditory stimulation is minimized, and there is an opportunity for privacy. Such reactions as temper tantrums or aggressive behaviors may warrant removal from the setting in which they occur as well as from the individual who may be the source of the frustration or the target of the attack. In addition, the attention to be gained from misbehaving in the presence of peers may be reinforcing and outweigh the costs of negative behavior. Isolation from the audience eliminates this source of gratification and support.

A time out room provides the child's ego with a chance to re-establish inner controls against maladaptive behaviors. An adult may be available to facilitate this process through discussion of the sequence of events which results in the exclusion and to help formulate alternative strategies for behaving. However, such discussion should take place after the child is calm and able to listen and

and to problem-solve; this is an important consideration with both this intervention and the life space interviewing technique. Children may request to go to the quiet room when they feel the need for concrete external limits to prevent an explosive situation. In these cases, the time out room serves a preventive function to avoid a confrontation or an outburst. In conclusion, it must be emphasized that the purpose of the time out room is not to punish a child, but instead to offer a safe place for working through potential crises and for strengthening ego defenses in order to better contain impulses and bind anxiety.

Mental Health Education

The interventions described thus far tended to focus on working with children who are already functioning maladaptively. A comprehensive intervention program also includes services directed towards preventing problems before they occur, insuring the continued health of well-functioning children, and helping children cope with normal developmental conflicts. The general goals of such programs are to help increase ego strengths, develop self-awareness, and improve interpersonal relationships. In such programs, children's affective states are considered as appropriate for classroom discussions as cognitive material typically is (Buchholz, 1974).

Affective education may be part of the regular curriculum, such that any educational material or classroom event becomes an impetus for spontaneous explorations of emotions and feelings. Thus, stories in English classes, art projects or historical studies may all stimulate discussions of values, judgments, feelings, and interactions. Problems in the classroom may become the basis for group discussions or for role-playing ways of problem solving. Some teachers may have hesitations about conducting such impromptu discussions, due to their reluctance to evoke unconscious or anxiety provoking material or to their view of their role as one in which cultural values are to be reflected (Clarizio, 1979). Affective education, on the other hand, involves value free explorations of alternatives and tolerance of individual and social differences. Therefore, many teachers find it helpful to consult with guidance counselors or school psychologists about affective education, both for support as well as for training.

There are also many structured programs through which affective education may be conducted (Baskin and Hess, 1980; Clarizio, 1979; Medway and Smith, 1978). One such program is the Human Development Program, also known as the "Magic Circle" because of the fact that children sit in circles for the groups (Besell and Palomares, 1970). There are daily lesson plans for 10 to 30 minute groups with specific curriculum for each grade. Generally, they focus in on helping students understand their attitudes, values and emotions. Similarities and differences between people and each person's input into social relationships are stressed. Typical topics for young children include such things as "Something I do that makes people unhappy (or happy)," and "Something that makes me feel good and bad at the same time." The leader's role is to help children communicate their ideas, to further their ability to listen and to be tolerant, and eventually to promote leadership skills.

Another common elementary school program is one known as "DUSO", Developing Understanding of Self and Other (Dinkmeyer, 1970). The program consists of materials—books, records, cassettes, posters, puppets—which illustrate typical problems children have. Daily discussions using the materials are focused on helping students verbalize their feelings, understand the relationships between feelings and behavior, and speak about their feelings and behavior more easily (Clarizio, 1979). The materials are appealing to children and the curriculum is easy to follow.

A third program is the cognitive problem solving approach of Spivak and Shure (1974). In this program, skills that are basic to interpersonal problem solving are systematically taught. The training focuses first on "pro-problem solving skills" such as knowing the concepts of *same* and *different*, and then teaches students to be sensitive to the nature of interpersonal problems, to come up with several solutions to any problem, to understand the relationship between means and ends, and to be aware of the consequences of actions.

Research on affective education has been marked with inconsistent results. Some research, for example, has found that both Magic Circle and DUSO resulted in changes in self-evaluation and attitudes towards schools, and that the Spivak and Shure approach resulted in improvements in peer relations. Other studies have found no changes (Baskin and Hess, 1980; Medway and Smith, 1978). Methodological difficulties abound in such studies and include difficulties in setting up equivalent control groups, accounting for the effects of teacher (leadership) styles, and problems objectifying "internal emotional" goals (Baskin and Hess, 1980). Despite the inconsistencies, however, the general conclusion of the bulk of the studies is that consistent and long term use of affective education materials can improve self concept, attitudes to school and cognitive growth. Some progress has been made in specifying the particular outcomes of particular programs, but further research is still necessary.

CONCLUSIONS

The decision of which strategy or strategies to implement is a complex one, with no rigid set of guidelines. Some practical considerations, such as the degree to which the parents can be involved, must be taken into account. Some types of interventions (therapy outside of the school) require a good deal of parental assistance, since they usually must provide transportation and must plan the family's schedule systematically in order to accommodate the treatment. If this seems unlikely, it may be preferable to initiate an intervention in the school setting, where the child's help can be more independent of the parents' involvement. Immediate crises also require different handling than chronic difficulties in that they present the necessity for some alleviation before ongoing depth-oriented work can proceed. Depending on the circumstance, removal of the child from the home to a hospital, group residence, or foster care placement may be required. In other cases, reduction of particularly distressing symptoms, such as encopresis or school phobia, may be accomplished through behavioral management programs.

Qualitites of the individual also influence the choice of intervention strategy. The capacity to tolerate intimacy, the need for social support and the degree of social awareness all must be evaluated. Some children may profit most from an individual relationship and others from a group. Some may need a relationship with an adult before being able to tolerate the presence of peers, while others may need peer support before being able to trust an adult. Finally, the nature of the problem must be considered. A child whose difficulty stems from recent family crises, such as a divorce or birth of a sibling, may benefit from classroom affective education and a nontreatment group, while a child with underlying difficulties which were merely exacerbated by the crises may also need individual therapy.

The ultimate success of any intervention strategy depends on a number of factors discussed in this chapter. These include the accuracy of the assessment of the child's problems, the fit between this assessment and the thrust of the intervention, the ability of the therapist and the child to develop a trusting bond with each other, and the degree to which the parents support the child's treatment. The entrance of a therapist into the life of a family can elicit intense emotional reactions from the parents, which may include fear, anger, or feelings of helplessness and dependency, as well as a sense of relief. The therapist may also find equally strong feelings being elicited by contact with the parents; these may include competitiveness with the parent or an over-identification with the child. It is essential for these feelings to be worked through so that an alliance can be established between therapist and parents which will maximize the effectiveness of the treatment plan.

REFERENCES

Abelin, E. L. The role of the father in the separation-individuation phase. In J. B. McDevitt and C. F. Settlage (Eds.), *Separation-individuation: Essays in honor of Margaret S. Mahler.* New York, New York: International Universities Press, 1971.

Balint, M. *The basic fault.* London: Tavistock, 1968.

Bardon, J., Bennett, V., Bruchez, P. and Sanderson, R. Psychosituational classroom intervention: Rationale and description. *Journal of School Psychology.* 1976, *14* (2), 97–104.

Baskin, E. and Hess, R. Does affective education work? A review of seven programs. *Journal of School Psychology,* 1980, *18* (1), 40-50.

Becker, D. and Margolin, F. How surviving parents handled their young children's adaptation to the crisis of loss. *American Journal of Orthopsychiatry,* 1967, *37,* 753–757.

Bellak, L., Hurvich, M., and Gediman, H. *Ego functions in schizophrenics, neurotics, and normals: A systematic study of the conceptual, diagnostic, and therapeutic aspects.* New York, New York: Wiley, 1973.

Benjamin, L. H. *Learning disorders in children.* Unpublished manuscript, Albert Einstein College of Medicine, 1975.

Bernstein, M. Psychotherapy in the schools: Promise and perplexity. *Journal of School Psychology,* 1976, *14* (4), 314-321.

Bessell, H. and Palomares, U. *Methods in human development: Theory manual and curriculum activity guide.* San Diego, California: Human Development Training Institute, 1970.

Buchholz, E. The proper study for children: Children and their feelings. *Psychology in the Schools,* 1974, *11,* 10–15.

Buchholz, E. *Emotional development and controls in learning disabled children.* Paper presented at the annual meeting of The New York Orton Society, April 1977.

Chodorow, N. *The reproduction of mothering: Psychoanalysis and the sociology of gender.* Berkeley, Califonia: University of California Press, 1979.

Clarizio, H. School psychologists and the mental health needs of the students. In G. Phye and D. Reschly (Eds.), *School psychology: Perspectives and issues.* New York, New York: Academic Press, 1979.

Dinkmeyer, D. *Developing understanding of self and others.* Circle Pines, Minnesota: American Guidance Service, 1970.

Erikson, E. Growth and crises of the healthy personality. *Psychological Issues,* 1959, *1* (1), 50–100.

Fairbairn, W. R. D. *An object-relations theory of the personality.* New York, New York: Basic Books, 1954.

Farber, G. *Mental retardation: Its social context and social implications.* Boston, Massachusetts: Houghton Mifflin, 1968.

Freud, A. *The psychoanalytical treatment of children.* New York, New York: Schocken Books, 1946.

Freud, A. *Normality and pathology in childhood: Assessments of development.* New York, New York: International Universities Press, Inc., 1965.

Fromm, E. *Man for himself.* New York, New York: Rinehart, 1947.

Furman, E. *A child's parent dies.* New Haven, Connecticut: Yale University Press, 1974.

Galston, R. Observations on children who have been physically abused and their parents. *American Journal of Psychiatry,* 1965, *122,* 440–443.

Gardner, R. *Psychotherapeutic approaches to the resistant child.* New York, New York: Aronson, 1975.

Gerson, B. Consciousness-raising groups with elementary school girls: A case study. *Psychotherapy: Theory, Research and Practice,* 1974, *11* (1), 30-35.

Gil, D. W. *Violence against children.* Cambridge, Massachusetts: Harvard University Press, 1970.

Glass, S. D. *The practical handbook of group counseling.* Baltimore, Maryland: B C S Publishing Co., 1969.

Grollman, E. *Talking about death: A dialogue between parent and child.* Boston, Massachusetts: Beacon Press, 1970.

Group for the Advancement of Psychiatry. *Divorce, child custody and the family.* New York, New York: Mental Health Materials Center, 1980.

Hartmann, H. *Ego psychology and the problem of adaptation.* New York, New York: International Universities Press, Inc., 1958.

Hess, R. and Camara, K. Post-divorce family relationships as mediating factors in the consequences of divorce for children. *Journal of Social Issues,* 1979, *35,* (4), 79–96.

Hetherington, E. M., Cox, M. and Cox, R. Play and social interaction in children following divorce. *Journal of Social Issues,* 1979, *35* (4), 26–49.

Hill, D. *Student supervision groups: An example of the participant model of school psychology.* Unpublished manuscript, New York, New York, 1978.

Kaplan, R. and Gerson, B. *Therapy in the classroom: A model.* Unpublished manuscript, Queens College Educational Clinic, 1975.

Kastenbaum, R. and Aisenberg, R. Death as a thought. In E. S. Shneidman (Ed.) *Death: Current perspectives.* New York, New York: Jason Aronson Inc., 1976, 369–422.

Kelly, J. B. and Wallerstein, J. S. *Surviving the breakup.* New York, New York: Basic Books, 1980.

Kempe, C. H., Silverman, F. N., Steele, B. F., Droegemuller, W., and Silver, H. K. The battered-child syndrome. *Journal of the American Medical Association,* 1962, *181,* 17–24.

Kessler, J. W. *Psychopathology of childhood.* Englewood Cliffs, New Jersey: Prentice-Hall, Inc., 1966.

Klein, M. *The psychoanalysis of children.* New York, New York, Dell Publishing Co., Inc., 1975.

Langner, T. S. and Michael, S. *Life stress and mental health.* New York, New York: Free Press, 1963.

Long, N. and Newman, R. Managing surface behavior of children in school. In N. Long, W. Morse, and R. Newman (Eds.), *Conflict in the classroom: The education of emotionally disturbed children.* Belmont, California: Wadsworth, 1976.

Mahler, M. *On human symbiosis and the vicissitudes of individuation, Volume I: Infantile psychosis.* New York, New York: International Universities Press, 1968.

Medway, F. and Smith, R. Jr. An examination of contemporary elementary school affective education programs. *Psychology in the Schools,* 1978, *15* (2), 260–269.

Morse, W. C. Worksheet on life space interviewing for teachers. In N. J. Long, W. C. Morse, and R. G. Newman (Eds.), *Conflict in the classroom: The education of emotionally disturbed children.* Belmont, California: Wadsworth, 1976.   1976.

Moustakas, C. *Children in play therapy.* New York, New York: Jason Aronson, Inc., 1973.

Mumford, E. Teacher response to mental health programs. *American Journal of Psychiatry*, 1968, *125* (1), 113-119.

Newman, R. *Groups in schools.* New York, New York: Simon and Schuster, 1974.

Nickerson, E. The application of play therapy to a school setting. *Psychology in the Schools,* 1973, *10* (3), 361-365.

Pine, F. On the concept "borderline" in children. *Psychoanalytic Study of the Child,* 1974, *19*, 341-368.

Pine, F. *Workshop on developmental aspects of perception and congition.* Paper presented at the meeting of the American Psychoanalytic Association, New York, December 1974a.

Pine, F. On phase-characteristic pathology of the school-age child: Disturbances of personality development and organization (borderline conditions), of learning, and of behavior. In S. Greenspan and G. Pollock (Eds.), *The course of life: Psychoanalytic contributions toward understanding personality development.* Adelphi, Maryland: NIMH, 1980.

Redl, F. The concept of the life space interview. *American Journal of Orthopsychiatry,* 1959, *29* (1), 1-18.

Redl, F. Ego disturbances. In S. Harrison and J. McDermott (Eds.), *Childhood psychopathology: An anthology.* New York, New York: International Universities Press, Inc. 1972.

Roos, P. Psychological counseling with parents of retarded children. *Mental Retardation,* 1963, *1*, 345-350.

Rutter, M. Parent-child separation: Psychological effects on the children. In S. I. Harrison and J. F. McDermott (Eds.), *New directions in childhood psychopathology, Volume I.* New York, New York: International Universities Press, 1980.

Schild, S. The family of the retarded child. In R. Koch and J. C. Dobson (Eds.) *The mentally retarded child and his family: A multidisciplinary handbook.* New York, New York: Bruner Mazel, 1971.

Slavson, S. R. *An introduction to group therapy.* New York, New York: The Commonwealth Fund, 1943.

Slavson, S. R. *Analytic group psychotherapy.* New York, New York: Columbia University Press, 1950.

Slavson, S. R. *Child psychotherapy.* New York, New York: Columbia University Press, 1952.

Solnit, A. J. and Stark, M. H. Mourning and the birth of a defective child. *Psychoanalytic Study of the Child,* 1961, *16*, 523-527.

Spinella, J. J. and Rigler, D. The child-abusing parent: a psychological review. *Psychological Bulletin,* 1972, *77*, 296-304.

Spivak, G. and Shure, M. *Social adjustment in young children.* San Francisco, California: Jossey Bass, 1974.

Steele, B. F. Parental abuse of infants and small children. In E. J. Anthony and T. Benedek (Eds.), *Parenthood.* Boston: Little, Brown & Co., 1970.

Stolorow, R. and Lachmann, F. *Psychoanalysis of development arrests.* New York, New York: International Universities Press, 1980.

Sullivan, H. S. *The interpersonal theory of psychiatry.* New York, New York: Norton, 1953.

Sutherland, J. D. The British object relations theorists: Balint, Winnicott, Fairbairn, Guntrip. *Journal of the American Psychoanalytic Association,* 1980, *28* (4), 829–860.

Waelder, R. The principle of multiple function: Observations on overdetermination. *Psychoanalytic Quarterly,* 1936, *5,* 45–62.

Winnicott, D. W. *The maturational process and the facilitating environment.* New York, New York: International Universities Press, 1965.

Wolfensberger, W. Counseling parents of the retarded. In A. A. Baumeister (Ed.), *Mental Retardation.* Chicago, Illinois: Aldine Co., 1967.

Wolfenstein, M. How is mourning possible? *Psychoanalytic Study of the Child,* 1966, *21,* 93–123.

Wolfenstein, M. Loss, rage and repetition. *Psychoanalytic Study of the Child,* 1969, *24* (2), 432–460.

Yalom, I. D. *Existential psychotherapy.* New York, New York: Basic Books, 1980.

7

Family Systems Therapy

Ramon G. Corrales and Laurence G. Ro-Trock

SYSTEMS THEORY: BASIC ASSUMPTIONS

One of the basic contributions of systems theory has been to make explicit the link between *person* and *context* or between *behavior* and *organization*. The systems therapist sees a child's behavior, not simply as a product of intrapersonal processes, but as an individual expression of the interpersonal organization. To put it simplistically, in order to have a son who behaves "delinquently" one must also assume a certain organizational pattern in the family-peer-school system that elicits, accomodates, and even invites such behavior. Thus, behavior and system are viewed as two levels of the same reality.

For the systems therapist, labels like hyperactive, depressed, schoolphobic, delinquent, or sociopathic are conceptually inadequate because these terms presuppose the locus of the problem to be within the individual. Thus, diagnosis and treatment will most likely revolve around influencing the child's behavioral, emotional, and cognitive processes. The behavior is assumed to exist out of context of the child's surroundings. If a "hyperactive" child suddenly behaves in a particular situation, the conclusion might be that (s)he is hiding the hyperactivity but that it is still there. In the systemic view, however, behavior is always seen within the context of his relationship system.

Systemic thinking is a view of the human world so different from traditional psychotherapy that it merits the designation of a paradigm shift. So radical is the shift that in comparing other forms of psychotherapy with family systems therapy, we find a fundamental difference both in the unit of analysis and in the model of causality. These differences have a profound impact on the manner of providing therapeutic change.

Causality: Linear or Circular

Linear causality carries the form: A causes B. This thinking presupposes a unidirectional flow of impact or influence. Only A is the cause; B is the effect and only the effect in relation to A. In this model of the world, B cannot be simultaneously the cause and effect of A. This causal view is in fact deeply embedded in the epistemology of most traditional and modern theories of personality and of therapeutic change.

Linear thinking, in our view, is not a useful way to map complex human systems like marriage and family relationships. We can illustrate the outcome of linear mapping in the following ways:

Let us assume a situation in which the husband nags and the wife withdraws. If one asks the husband to explain his behavior, he will most likely say: "I nag because my wife doesn't want to be with me." She, in turn, will likely say: "I withdraw because he nags all the time." Their linguistic pattern is characterized by the form: A causes B. A parent who shows hostility in response to his son's lying could say: "I'm mad because my son keeps on lying." The son could say: "I'm afraid to tell the truth because my parents get so hostile." Again the form A causes B.

There are some very pernicious presuppositions deeply embedded in the linear causal approach. One is that someone or something is to blame. Another is that impact or influence is a one way street. Even more deeply embedded is the presupposition that there is *one* cause and if one can ferret out this one cause, everything will be fine. In the medical model, this view is well celebrated in the concept of etiology: "The cause of a disease." All of these presuppositions are captured in the form: "I nag (withdraw) because my wife (husband) withdraws (nags)." They are also expressed in the sentence: "It's all my fault."

In systemic thinking, we jump to an Einsteinian model of the universe—a world of relativity. In lieu of linear causality, we propose *circular causality*— a view of the world as a related (relative) set of mutually interacting, impacting parts or components. Diagrammatically, we go from A→B to A⟳B. This is a universe where "causes and effects" are interchangeable and thus we talk of "circular chains" of interaction. In this view, nagging is related to withdrawing is related to nagging. Another way to put it is to say that nagging and withdrawing attract each other. Similarly, hostility and deception are related and attracted to each other.

When one asks the question, "Which came first, the chicken or the egg?" one presupposes a unidirectional (linear) chain of events. In the systemic view, it is more useful to recognize that chicken and egg are vitally related.

Unit of Analysis

Most traditional as well as most modern theories of human functioning and principles of change view the individual person as the site or unit of health or pathology. What is "right" or "wrong" with a person or his behavior is contained within the skin or the individual brain. What logically follows from this model is that if you want to intervene educationally or therapeutically, all you need to do is to intervene intrapersonally. The organization of the interpersonal world—the context of the person—becomes simply a matter of curiosity or, at best, simply the effect of the intrapersonal.

Systemic thinking, on the other hand, makes no rigid boundary between the intrapersonal and the interpersonal, between the individual and the context. Systems theory holds the tenet that person and context are vitally and dynamically related, almost like mirrors of each other. To think that one unidirectionally causes the other is a fundamental, epistemological error.

In the systemic view, the individual's behavior is a comment on the whole system (family, school, business) and the whole system is involved in the individual's behavior. No longer is the dancer isolated from the dance: The essence of systemic thinking is to look at the *patterns* of the dance of which the dancer is a part. Thus the family is seen not as a collection of individuals but an organization of interacting human beings.

The essence of systemic thinking is the view that the most useful unit of analysis is the organization of parts (human beings). Organization refers to patterns or rules of interaction among the parts. Systems theory is not essentially about the level of social organization (two, three, or more people); it has to do with the *interaction patterns* within a given level of social organization (marriage, family, peer, school, church). The essence is the dance, not the number of dancers. This is the meaning of system.

Rules

Another way to conceptualize the dynamics in interpersonal relationships is to think in terms of rules. The concept of *rule* helps one to think about the way the members of a communication process are defining their relationship. Rules tend to be the product of continuing interaction sequences between two or more people. Rules have to do with such issues as who can say what to whom and in what manner and when. One can say then that rules are the dynamic fibers of the construct of *boundary*. Just as every interaction is a push or a definition of the relationship so every interaction confirms or pushes for a change in rules. Patterns are recurring interaction sequences based on rules governing the relationship.

A very important distinction in systems theory is between verbal (digital) and analogic rules. Verbal rules are those that are most explicit in the conscious functioning of the family. An example of a verbal rule would be the explicit statement of the curfew hours for the children. Most families have a verbalized representation of those rules. Verbalized rules form only a very small proportion of family rules and do not constitute the major source of influence in family functioning. For this major rule, we turn to analogic rules.

Analogic rules are those implicit, recurring, and precise nonverbal patterns of interaction that become to the system what the network of highways are to a city. Analogic rules are the systemic pathways that link and shape the interaction among the components of the system. An example of an analogic rule may be verbalized as follows: mother and son are to provide the main form of intimacy to each other, with father distant emotionally from both; this is so in order to preserve the marital dyad while protecting the marital pair from facing their issues as a couple.

Let us suppose, for the sake of discussion, that this rule is temporarily broken. Father and son spend a whole day together on a fishing trip and are able to experience a significant sense of emotional closeness. They come home smiling, joking, and verbally effusive. Chances are that homeostatic[1] mechanisms in the system will be activated to restore the current analogic rule. It could conceivably proceed as follows.

Son and father see a certain look on mother's face and hear a certain sound in her voice. Son drops his fishing gear on the floor. Mother scolds son. Son answers back. Father reprimands son for answering back disrespectfully. Mother experiences dad's reprimand as too harsh and so proceeds to defend the son. Mother and son are once again close and dad is pushed out.

It is important to realize that *all* members cooperate in the creating, maintaining, and changing of analogic rules. No one member is the cause of a rule or totally responsible for it. Symptomatic behavior, then, is a comment on the whole system. It is simultaneously an attempt to challenge and to preserve the analogic rules of a system. The aim of family therapy, then, in the words of Selvini-Palazzoli and her associates is to:

---

[1] *Homeostasis* is the tendency of a system to maintain a given structure (deviation-counteracting processes). A related concept is morphogenesis: the tendency of a system to elaborate or to change structures (deviation-amplifying processes).

1. To detect quickly the rule or the rules which generate and perpetuate the dysfunction.

2. To devise prescriptions instead of interpretations aimed at breaking the rules which perpetuate the dysfunction. (Selvini-Palazzoli, Boscolo, Cecchin, and Prata, 1978, p. 3).

Patterns in the Well-Functioning Family

Every therapeutic approach has, at least implicitly, a set of assumptions or generalizations about the characteristics of the well-functioning person or, as we would put it, the well-functioning family system.[1] Our therapeutic maneuvers presuppose goals aiming at structures of family interaction that we consider more useful and effective than others. We now offer a summary of these generalizations.[2]

Clear Subsystem Boundaries

A family system is composed of at least three major subsystems—the marital, the sibling or child, and parental subsystem. In well-functioning families, the marital unit has an identity and life of its own, able to experience intimacy and conflict resolution with the dyad, and able to periodically separate itself from the rest of the family in order to attend to marital needs. In the role of parents, the dyad has a clear identification as a team in relation to its children, the extended family, and those agencies outside the family that relate to the children (e.g. school, church, clinic). Finally, the children, as a sibling unit, have an identity as a subgroup within the larger family system.

Correct Hierarchies

In well-functioning families, the hierarchies are clear and in the rank-order prescribed by the sociocultural system. In blunt language, the parents are in charge as responsible executives, and the children are the followers and recipients of this strong, benevolent leadership. Whenever there are conflicts between parents and children, the parents make the final decisions following some input from the children consistent with their age and development.

---

[1] For brevity, we will refer to these families simply as well families.

[2] For those who want to pursue the basis of these ideas, I refer them to the following works: Barnard and Corrales, 1979; Haley, 1976, 1980; Minuchin, 1974; Minuchin, et al., 1975; Madanes, 1981; Beavers, 1966.

Children's Birth Order Is Respected

In healthy families, the first born is treated and is expected to act like the first born. Each child, according to age and birth order, is given a set of duties and privileges. Through these means, the family acknowledges that each member has a unique position and a unique set of roles. Position is sociologically defined as a location within a social structure (e.g., husband-father, wife-mother, and second-born daughter). Role (e.g., breadwinner, disciplinarian) is defined as a set of expected behaviors attached to a position. Roles are much more fluid than positions; the specific content of roles can change from one day to the next. Position, on the other hand, remain unchanged unless there is an addition or subtraction of family members.

Person to Person Communication and Closeness

Communication in well-functioning families is direct and can occur between any two members. If there is an issue between husband and wife, they talk to each other; if there is an issue between the parents and a child, the parents talk to that child directly, rather than to or through a sibling. In other words, gossip systems are generally avoided, or if they exist, they are shortlived. With this kind of communication, closeness can be expressed and experienced between any two family members without a third party being unduly jealous. It is important to state that even in the healthiest families, some sibling jealousy occurs; however, these are handled swiftly and fairly. Also this way, persistent, unhealthy coalitions (two against one) are bypassed.

Wide Range of Feelings and Opinions Expressed

In these families, members are able to express a wide range of unique feelings and opinions. This, we believe, is facilitated by the existence of a clear structure of leadership and a clear definition of positions and age-appropriate roles.

Cognitive Map Is Systemic

The family's implicit way of looking at the world and thinking about it is not black and white, either/or. The family's way of mapping the world, allows for shades, degrees, and especially the existence of mixed motives and multicausal possibilities. If a child expresses anger, this is not seen as evidence that the child is bad, disloyal, or seeking to end a relationship. Since the family can accommodate a wide range of feelings, the child can be regarded as very loving and yet capable of feeling somewhat irritated and perhaps a little jealous at times. Furthermore, there is, at least implicitly, the recognition that "my actions affect yours and yours affect mine." Parents, for example, might acknowledge the possibility that their harsh handling of a situation might have influenced their son to withdraw emotionally from them.

Affective Map Is Cooperative

The feeling map among these families is based on a sense that people are generally well intentioned and that it is better to help one another than to "cut each other's throats." Although not naive about physical and social hazards, these families encourage and support a cooperative, rather than fiercely oppositional, approach to each other and to people outside the family.

THERAPY: CREATING NEW REALITIES

Family systems therapists generally agree that the main task of therapy is to help create new experiences or new realities for their clients. The main goal for a systemic therapist is to intervene at the level of the system sᴖ that clearer and more flexible patterns of interaction become possible. When ᾿s happens, the family members have a much better chance of expressing (verbally and nonverbally) the unique, varied aspects of their personalities.

From Diagnosis to Hypothesis

The concept of set personality syndromes with lifelong diagnostic labels (e.g., schizophrenic, manic-depressive) runs counter to the very grain of systemic thinking. If the system is subject to radical change, then personality patterns also have that capacity. We think it is more useful to view the personality as "unlimited potential," capable of displaying and expressing a vast array of behavioral patterns. Which patterns will be expressed at any given time is the result of the mix between person and system.

Such a fluid view of action and interaction leads the therapist to drop traditional diagnostic categories in search of more specific sensory-based descriptions of current behavioral sequences in the system (e.g., family, school, peer). Such descriptions of how the family members relate and how the problem behaviors fit in the system are usually put in the form of hypotheses. An hypothesis might take the following expression; "The twelve-year old boy is bedwetting three or four times a week; this elicits from the mother words of frustration and inability to help the boy overcome this habit. Since at this point the bedwetting ceases for a few days and the father gets verbally involved with the son, we hypothesize that the symptom has two major functions: a) it is an analogic expression of the boy's autonomy, and b) it functions as a systemic mechanism to get the father involved in a more direct, emotional way with the boy and the other family members."

The above hypothesis is offered in brief form only as an illustration. For it to be therapeutically useful, many more sensory descriptions will be needed to refine and to elaborate upon its implications. The hypothesis may change from one session to the next, depending upon the information that emerges. It would, therefore, be useful at this point to present a case in greater detail in order to illustrate how a systems therapist conceptualizes a child's behavior in systemic terms and how a hypothesis is developed in such a manner as to lead directly to a treatment plan.

THE JOHNSON FAMILY

The Johnson family[1] contacted a member of the cotherapy team[2] asking for help for their sixteen-year-old daughter, Theresa. Although the Johnsons have a seven-year-old, multi-handicapped son, David, it was their daughter about whom they were most concerned. Their other child Eric, is eleven, and is reported to be very athletic and to "not have a worry in the world."

During the initial interview with the team, Joe and Betty Johnson said they had been increasingly worried about Theresa since the beginning of her junior year in high school. Her eleventh year was almost completed and she had barely passed to her senior year. The parents felt that if she had not been a straight A student up to this point her teachers would not have passed her at all since she had done no homework for the past six months and was frequently absent due to illness. They also reported that Theresa spent a lot of time in her room and lately had refused to eat with the family. Joe and Betty had taken Theresa to a physician numerous times the past year when she complained of stomachaches, headaches, severe cramps, breathing difficulties, and lack of appetite. Since no organic problems were found, the family was referred for therapy.

Prior to coming for family therapy, the Johnsons had sought help from a local psychiatrist who wanted to hospitalize Theresa for ninety days until he could discern the exact nature of her disease. His preliminary diagnosis was that she was psychotically depressed and needed intensive treatment. The parents agreed that Theresa was "a very sick girl," but they said they could not stand the thought of her being out of the home for an extended period. Therefore, after ten visits in a four-week period with no discernable improvement, the family decided to try another approach.

---

[1] Not their real name.

[2] The authors conduct most of their private practice as cotherapists. Quite often, they have staff members and trainees observing behind a one-way mirror. The use of the word "team" will refer primarily to the cotherapists and secondarily to those behind the mirror.

In order to understand the organization of the Johnson family, the Team noted the relative role positions of each family member. Theresa, as the oldest daughter, has a history of being very responsible beyond her years. Her responsible nature was particularly evident in terms of her ability to care for David, her handicapped brother. Mrs. Johnson reported that Theresa had always been a like a "second mother to David." Since both parents worked outside the home they have been particularly appreciative of Theresa's ability to perform complex mothering tasks even at the early age of ten. The team observed that during the initial interview when the parents praised Theresa's maternal skills, she very politely asked to be excused to go to the rest room and returned some minutes later when another topic was being discussed.

David has been severely and profoundly retarded since birth. The parents said that, although David had many problems, they had been able to adjust well to his condition. They reported that he was a "blessing to the family," and further said, jokingly, that in many ways he was a perfect child since he could never grow up and leave them.

Eric wore a letter sweater to the interview and was obviously proud of his athletic ability. He frequently made humorous comments during the session. He said he was probably closest to his mother in the family, but that he and his Dad attended sporting events and sometimes went fishing together.

Betty has worked as a receptionist since David was six months old and saw herself as closest to Theresa in the family although they rarely did anything together that was not focused around tasks. She said that she was the family member most upset about the problem with Theresa.

Joe was a construction foreman who worked long hours and loved sports and beer. He mentioned, in an off-handed way, that Betty had been worried about his drinking earlier in the marriage, but the problem was corrected when he switched to drinking beer only. Like Betty, he was very worried about Theresa. He also reported that it was sometimes easier for Theresa to talk to him about her problems rather than talk with her mother. Joe also commented that since Theresa had been "laid up" the past few months, Betty had been saddled with the care of David as well as work full time. Therefore, Joe mentioned that Betty had been very irritable and difficult to be around. He said, however, that this situation was not as bad as it could have been had Eric not been present to console his mother when he (the father) was forced to work late. The team observed that Eric had a unique gift of being able to cheer up mother with a slight gesture or comment.

Hypothesis and Therapeutic Goals

The team carefully avoided diagnosing Theresa's behavior in terms of individual categories such as depression, anger, psychosis, and so on. Rather, they

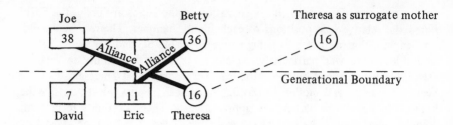

Figure 1.   Johnson family dynamics.

found it most useful to describe Theresa's behavior in terms of relationship principles. With this in mind, the Team made an hypothesis as to the organization of the Johnson family which was responsible for maintaining Theresa's problem behavior.

Although the major dynamics within the Johnson family are complicated, the Team has found it most beneficial to focus only on those aspects of the family which need to be changed in order to help the family improve. First of all it was noted that the generational boundaries were not clear in the Johnson family. This confusion was especially evident in terms of Theresa's position. It appeared that at times Theresa was indeed functioning as a second mother to David. Moreover, this position was historically very familiar to her and that, until recently, she had managed successfully to carry the burden. Their situation was, of course, exacerbated by David's problems since he required more than an average amount of care.

In more technical family systems language, Theresa was parentified, i.e., occupying a position in the executive rather than the sibling subsystem (Minuchin,

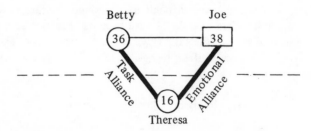

Figure 2.   Johnson family: major triangle.

1974). The Team also observed that a major ingredient of the problem was the presence of overlapping *triangles* created by cross generational emotional alliances between the parents and the nonhandicapped siblings of the opposite sex. A diagram of the Johnson family is shown in Figures 1 and 2.

For the purposes of simplicity and therapeutic economy, the Team chose to focus on creating a change in the triangle of father, mother, and Theresa as the most elegant and least painful avenue for change. It should be mentioned that the Team was convinced that the problem in the Johnson family could be corrected by working with the nuclear unit only, since the issue seemed to be relatively uncontaminated by extended family members.

The therapeutic goal, simply stated, was to unburden Theresa of the excessive worry and care of her handicapped brother and to shift this responsibility to her parents in a way that would not unduly stress their marriage. An important secondary goal was to build a stronger emotional bond between the parents. If this goal could be achieved, the parents would serve as more effective leaders of the family and would no longer relate emotionally through their children.

BEGINNING PHASE OF THE THERAPY

We see the beginning phase of the therapy as setting the tone and laying the foundation for the entire therapeutic process. We think of this phase in terms of three general areas: (1) family system information, (2) dynamics of the therapeutic system, and (3) framing of the problem by the therapist.

Family System Information

This area refers to the gathering and organizing of information about the problem and desired outcome as seen from the eyes of the family members. At this stage, we recommend the Brief Therapy format utilized by the Palo Alto group (Watzlawick, Weakland, and Fisch, 1974). The following steps represent a slight modification of their format.

Family Definition of the Problem/Symptom

The basic question to be asked is: "What is the problem?" Each family is given an opportunity to respond. We require specific, sensory descriptions of the problem and the behavioral sequences involved. We discover the major complainant by asking questions like : "Who is most upset by the problem?" We also elicit the family's theory or explanation about why the problem exists. The answer to this latter question may or may not be inherently useful. Nevertheless, it provides useful information about the family's perception of the situation.

Solutions Previously Attempted

A major principle of Brief Therapy is captured in the phrase: "the solution is the problem." Translated, this means that the parental response to a child's behavior maintains the problem as much as the child's behavior itself. Further, answers to the question "How have you tried to solve this problem?" will offer the therapist information about how the family is organized, as well as offer clues about the major interaction patterns and behavioral sequences which maintain the problem.

Goals and Indicators of Change

We also ask each family member what they want to have happen as a result of the therapy. Again we require very specific descriptions. A related and very important question is: "How would you know when the first, small but significant step has taken place?" Family members will often give us internal, kinesthetic indicators like "I'll feel better." Although we respectfully accept these answers, we press further with a question like this: "And if you were already feeling a little better, what would we see or hear on the outside that is not now occurring?" In other words, we elicit external indicators of change—especially minimal or "first-step" criteria.

Dynamics of the Therapeutic System

The phase *therapeutic system* refers to the relationship system that is created when therapist and family interact. There are three characteristic dynamics of this system that we consider crucial to the therapeutic process: (a) joining, (b) initiative, and (c) therapeutic structural decisions.

Joining

The concept of joining is more popularly referred to as rapport. Other terms utilized are trust, understanding, or connectedness. Carl Whitaker (1970) refers to this quality as a sense of caring that provides the anesthesia that is necessary before the surgery. We like the way that Bandler and Grinder (1975; Grinder and Bandler, 1976; Grinder, DeLozier, and Bandler, 1977) think about rapport: they see it as a process of matching the clients' realities. Joining family members basically involves entering (at least perceptually) the clients' map or model of the world. One can join by matching the client's posture and tonal qualities (e.g., tempo, timber, volume). One can join by matching the client's belief systems about therapy, their child, or the world in general. Another way is to respect and utilize the analogic rules governing the family system. We were once interviewing a family which had a rule that mother was the "central switchboard."

All communication from inside and outside the family went through her and had to meet with her approval. After we detected this rule, we simply asked mother if it was all right to talk to her daughter. She graciously allowed us direct access to her twelve year old child.

Joining is a characteristic that must not only be established at the beginning; it is a quality that must be maintained throughout the therapeutic process so that the family will continue to come for therapy until the desired outcome is achieved.

Initiative

The issue of initiative is captured in the following question: "Who wants the change more, the therapist or the family?" It is our very strong conviction that the balance of the initiative question must be in favor of the family. They must desire the change more strongly than the therapist. If it were the other way around, the family members would lose the motivation for change, and allow the therapist to do most of the work. This latter situation constitutes an effective formula for therapist burnout, psychosomatic illness, and acute episodes of "clientphobia." Needless to say, it also leads to poor outcomes.

It requires a great level of artistry to elicit a strong sense of initiative in clients. The technique of mild paradox is often effective. If a young boy is having problems with grades and behavior at school, we will often ask him why he wants good grades. As he defends the desirability of getting good grades, we escalate the questions to cast challenging doubts about his stamina to act upon his verbalized goal. This defense and declaration of his ability to follow through subtly shifts the initiative from the therapist to the client.

Structural Decisions

The question here is: Who makes the decision about where and when sessions take place and who is to be involved? We believe these decisions ought to be the domain of the therapist. The therapist is being asked to be an agent of change for the family. He should then have the authority and leverage to decide about the important ingredients of the change process. The family decides on the goal and, hopefully, provides the initiative toward achieving that goal. However, the therapist is the process expert.

Framing of the Problem

The therapist will do well to examine the following question: "Is the problem solvable as perceived and formulated by the family? A problem framed as one of "low self-esteem" is potentially unsolvable if it is seen as a feeling "inside" the person that he does not count. One could argue that all human beings have this problem to some degree. If on the other hand, the problem is defined by way of example, as a child's not going to school three days out of each week, then the problem is solvable. One can demonstrate if the problem is being resolved or getting worse.

Another important question to raise is, "What is the function of the particular symptom?" Since the symptom is a form of communication, an analogic message, we assume that it has an intended purpose or function. Otherwise, how would one explain the repetitive, recurring nature of a symptom.

Another way to look at a symptom is to regard it as an attempt to solve a crisis. A female adolescent, for example, who is afraid to leave home (implying a complementary parental reluctance to let go), but yet wants to preserve her sense of personal autonomy, could develop the behaviors usually attached to the syndrome known as *anorexia nervosa.* Such behaviors ordinarily lead to an unhealthy, excessively thin and undernourished body; hence, the dependency on parents. However, the rebellious aspects of the behavioral manifestations (e.g., refusal to eat) allow the young girl to experience a kind of independence. Thus, anorexia, in this case, could be conceptualized as an attempted solution to the developmental crisis of leaving home.

INTERVENTION TECHNIQUES

In this section, we offer a brief description of the major intervention techniques that we utilize in family therapy with troubled children. These techniques are also representative of two related approaches in family therapy: strategic and structural.

Reframing

It is important to realize that in our normal states of consciousness, we do not experience the world directly; we only deal with our subjective map or experience of the world. The anorectic girl to whom we referred earlier most likely did not view her symptomatic behavior in the way we did. She had her own interpretations. Each situation, problematic or not, is viewed or "framed" by a person or group in a certain way. The art of *reframing* involves the process of introducing a more useful view or map of the situation than the one currently used by the individual or family.

Reframing presupposes that every behavior/symptom/communication is useful and meaningful in some way. In other words, behind every behavior, there is a useful intention if not a useful effect. The existence of a problem or symptom implies, however, that despite this intention, the client's framing or view of the situation is faulty and permits a very narrow range (usually only one) of possible solutions. Reframing, therefore, introduces a view that permits new, more effective solutions to the problem. It is important that the view be presented in such a way that it is at least as convincing as the one originally held by the client.

Often a problem situation can be changed by helping the involved members to view or perceive the situation in a different light. In his classic tale, Mark Twain describes how the young Tom Sawyer managed to convince the neighborhood boys that the job of whitewashing a fence was actually a privilege reserved for only a few careful painters. Tom Sawyer very skillfully succeeded in reframing drudgery as a special privilege, thus causing the neighborhood boys to view the event in a different way.

Watzlawick, et al. (1974) describe a situation in which a man with a very bad stammer had no alternative but to try his luck as a salesman. Quite understandably this deepened his life long concern over his speech defect. The situation was reframed for him as follows: Salesmen are generally disliked for their slick, clever ways of trying to talk people into buying something they do not want. Surely, he knew that salesmen are trained to deliver an almost uninterrupted sales talk, but had he ever really experienced how annoying it is to be exposed to that insistent, almost offensive barrage of words? On the other hand, had he ever noticed how carefully and patiently people will listen to somebody with a handicap like his? Was he able to imagine what an unusual advantage his handicap could become in his new occupation? As he gradually began to see his problem in this totally new—and, at first blush, almost ludicrous—perspective, he was especially instructed to maintain a high level of stammering, even if in the course of his work, for reasons quite unknown to him, he should begin to feel a little more at ease and therefore less and less likely to stammer spontaneously.

To reframe, then, means to change the conceptual or emotional viewpoint of a situation and place it in another framework. What is actually changed as a result of reframing is the *meaning* attributed to a situation, but not the concrete facts—or as the philosopher Epictetus expressed it as early as the first century A.D., "It is not the things themselves which trouble us, but the opinions that we have about these things" (cited in Watslawick, et al., 1974).

Restructuring Tasks

Strategic family therapy is undeniably directive. The family therapist, in conjunction with the family, is actively engaged in creating an evolving context, setting goals, planning interventions, evaluating the group's responses to his directives and modifying these if necessary, and working toward the disengagement of the family at the termination of the therapeutic process.

One avenue by which a family therapist can be directive is through the creation of tasks for the family to accomplish. Tasks can be assigned to the entire family or to only select members of the family; they can be carried out in the sessions or they may be assigned to be accomplished during the interval between sessions.

Andolfi (1979) describes different types of tasks which are intended to restructure the family system. The term *restructuring* is used to denote a process in which the habitual transactional patterns of the family are modified by using elements and energies present (at least potentially) in the family system. The system thereby takes on new characteristics; it changes, although the elements of which it is composed remain the same.

Contextual Tasks

The therapist may develop a contextual task to be carried out during the sessions with the intention of promoting a better therapeutic context during the sessions. For example, the therapist can request silence when one family member tries to interrupt another, or (s)he can actively engage a member who remains in a marginal position in the therapeutic process, or (s)he might ask an overly intrusive member to observe from behind the one-way mirror. (S)he could also solicit particular interactions by directing two or more persons to discuss or do something together during the session.

System-Restructuring Tasks

The goal of these tasks is to restructure the models of communication habitually used by the family. Restructuring is achieved by substituting new and more functional communication patterns arrived at through an exploration of elements and energies existing in the system. For example, a father and son may become engaged in daily efforts to accomplish a task assigned by the therapist. The consequence of the fact that they are spending time together helps to create a new bond between father and son while simultaneously lessening the extreme bond between mother and son.

Reinforcing Tasks

These types of tasks are used to strengthen movements that are already under way in the family system. They serve to consolidate changes that have already taken place and to promote further change. They are frequently utilized during the last phase of therapy.

Paradoxical Interventions

Occasionally families will change their rules and patterns simply by means of advice and coaching from the therapist. For example, families may be instructed on how to promote better communication, how to control and discipline their children, or how to achieve a balance between togetherness and separateness. However many families are resistant to changing long-standing patterns of interaction regardless of how much it would improve home life. It is in an attempt to reshuffle interactional patterns that paradoxical interventions are given.

A paradoxical intervention can be understood only by first defining the meaning of paradox as it is used within the family therapy field. A paradox exists when two messages that are pragmatically incompatible are transmitted simultaneously. The message that an unhealthy parent might give to his child—"grow up and become an independent person, but yet don't ever leave me"—has components that are pragmatically incompatible. Within the practice of family therapy, the creation of a paradoxical intervention is done with the intention of reshuffling relational forces operating in a family, shaking the family out of its destructive clinches, and trying to give all members a new chance to pursue their own growth and separateness. A paradoxical intervention is successful only if it accomplishes the opposite of what it is seemingly intended to accomplish. The intervention is considered successful if the family defies the therapist's instructions or follows them to the point of absurdity and then recoils and disobeys them.

Papp (1981) describes three approaches used in delivering a paradoxical intervention.

Defining the Symptom as Benignly Motivated to Preserve the Family Stability

Families often interpret symptoms in ways that make for continuing difficulty. If the meaning or implication of the symptom is redefined in a positive way, the redefining itself may have a powerful effect on attitudes and relationships. For example, redefining anger as caring, suffering as self-sacrifice or hostile behavior as concerned interest helps toward promoting more harmony within the family.

Prescribing the Symptom-Producing Cycle of Interaction

Once the therapist has an accurate knowledge of the relation between the symptom and the family interactional patterns, and more specifically, the manner in which they activate one another, (s)he might choose to make the process explicit. The therapist would carefully and directly request the family to continue doing what they do so well, specifically to continue the cycle of interaction that produces the symptom. When the family begins to consciously act out the sequence, the secret rules are exposed and the family becomes less capable of producing a symptom. Instead the family will move toward abandoning their endless game and will try to discover new ways of relating.

Restraining the Family Whenever They Show Signs of Changing

Whenever a symptom has been used to regulate a dysfunctional family system, the disappearance of a symptom will cause the system to become off balance and family members will then become uncomfortable with the changes. As a way of preventing the family from reverting back to their destructive, yet familiar and comfortable patterns of interaction, the therapist skillfully prepares the family for the changes. (S)he might accomplish this by predicting their desire to revert back, by making the rules of the destructive interaction explicit again, or by enumerating the pleasant and unpleasant consequences of the change. The family will then unite together and consolidate their improvements in an effort to "correct" the therapist's erroneous notions about their ability to handle new changes.

Metaphorical Tasks

When families communicate to each other or to a therapist, they send multiple-messages at different levels of abstraction. For example, when a therapist is listening to someone talking about a problem, (s)he keeps in mind that on a literal level, the speaker is communicating facts or opinions, but that on another level, the speaker is communicating something that cannot be stated explicitly. For example, if a mother says that her son is insecure and frightened, she may mean, on another level, that her husband is insecure and frightened and that their marital relationship is precarious. If a father states that the son threatens to run away from him, it may actually be the wife who is threatening to leave him.

Andolfi (1979) describes how a family therapist can utilize metaphorical language in a variety of ways. (S)he can speak metaphorically about a sensitive topic, thereby avoiding direct reference to the problem topic, or (s)he can activate the family by assigning metaphorical tasks. Some families are more willing to accept tasks if they do not consciously recognize them as such, or if the task does not directly involve the problem situation. A young couple who did not feel competent about disciplining their two, small, overly active boys were given the metaphorical task of purchasing a small playhouse and specifically teaching the boys how to organize the rooms and keep the furnishings in order. The successful experience of getting the boys to follow their directions regarding the playhouse gave the couple confidence in their ability to discipline the boys in other aspects of their daily lives.

THE BENSON FAMILY

We shall offer the highlights of a case we had a year and a half ago in order to illustrate the way we conceptualize the problem, the hypothesis, and goals, as well as our method of beginning and intervening.

Sara Benson, the mother, was 37. She had been separated from her husband, Jerry, for about three months. Jerry was 38. They had two children: Linda, 17, was a junior and Mark, 15, was a sophomore.

Family System Information

Mother was the major complainant and Mark was the problem being presented. After some probing, Sara listed her complaints in order of importance: (1) poor grades (3 Fs, 2 Ds, according to progress reports), (2) discipline problems in school (e.g., suspension), (3) showing anger by arguing disrespectfully with his mother before finally carrying out her orders.

The family, especially Sara, tried the following solutions: arguing, reasoning, grounding, coaxing, encouraging, and threatening unspecified consequences. None of these solutions was effective in influencing study habits or grades in a positive direction. Sometimes, Sara would call Jerry to come in and discipline Mark. The boy would settle down for a week or two, but then would revert back to old habits—such as not bringing books home. Linda was very pessimistic that Mark would ever change his habits. She also directed a number of critical remarks toward her dad (who was not present in the first two sessions).

The major therapeutic goal was to help Mark get grades good enough to pass the school year. There were seven weeks left. Two Fs would result in his having to repeat the entire sophomore year. As a general rule, Sara would be satisfied with a C average, as long as there were no Fs.

The minimal indicators of change (small, but significant signs) were: if Mark brought books home (even if he didn't actually study them); studying for fifteen minutes—even once. Neither of these indicators were seen as sufficient but simply as possible indicators of the beginning of the change process.

Therapeutic System Process

Joining was accomplished by matching the family belief systems, especially the following: (a) that this was a serious and important problem; (b) that Mark was not a bad boy, just confused and perhaps suffering from low self-esteem; (c) that change is difficult, and, therefore, we, the therapists, shared the family's pessimism about passing the year. We also supported the hierarchy by asking Sara primarily to shape the definition of the problem. Further, we matched the family members' body posture and tonal qualities through the first two sessions.

Initiative was elicited by gently questioning Mark's motivation to get good grades. A series of questions about why he wanted good grades found Mark defending the desirability of such a goal. When told that we would respect his right to go down the tubes, he insisted that that was not what he really wanted.

Structurally, we determined who was to be included and how many sessions we wanted as a minimum. We decided on one evaluation session and four treatment sessions. We had the three members of the household in each session, with Jerry, the father, joining us for the third session.

Framing of the Problem

We accepted the family's framing of the problem as one involving poor grades because it was relevant and solvable. The report cards would show whether Mark passed or not. We developed the following hypothesis about the functions of the symptom:

1. Mark was worried about adjustment to the divorcing process and especially about father's new position in the family as an "outsider." His dysfunctioning served a call to bring Jerry into the picture and to imply Mark's dependency on his dad's input.

2. When Mark was in trouble, the alliance between Sara and Linda was calm and strong, when Mark was doing well, Sara and Linda would get into very vocal fights, these occasionally became physical. Therefore, the symptom served to strengthen the alliance between mother and daughter.

We diagrammed the major family dynamics as shown in Figure 3.

With respect to the presenting problem, we saw two major triangles: (a) Sara and Linda versus Mark; (b) Jerry and Mark versus Sara. The latter was the more covert of the two.

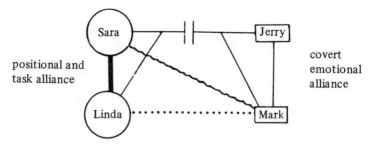

Figure 3.   Benson family dynamics.

Major Intervention

At the end of session two, we delivered the following interventions:

1. We told the family that Mark's low motivation to study was related to his worrying about his father. Mark's way of being loving and loyal to his father came by way of dysfunctioning and thus allowing father to feel needed and useful.

2. We then suggested that every evening, Mark was to report to Sara and to make two choices: (a) which one-hour block he was to use for a task we would suggest, and (b) whether he was going to use that hour to study or to worry about his father.

During the third session (two weeks later), with Jerry present, we found that Mark chose to study every night except for the first night. After reiterating the importance of giving himself permission to worry about his father, we went on to explore alternative ways that father and son could make contact and still respect Sara as the major parent in the family system. The final two sessions (without Jerry) involved streamlining these directions, as well as jokingly urging Mark to get into trouble just to cover up for Linda's shortcomings and thus assure peace for the mother-daughter relationship.

Results

Mark continued to study every night for one to two hours. He passed—"by the skin of his teeth," to use his mother's words. Six months after the last interview, a follow-up phone call revealed that Mark was continuing to do relatively well (C average) with no major discipline problems at home or in school. Sara mentioned that Linda had become somewhat more difficult to control at home. We asked her if she would want an additional session or two to deal with Linda. Sara said that she thought she could handle this phase of Linda's behavior and that if she couldn't do it successfully, she would call us. A year has passed since that phone conversation.

REFERENCES AND SUGGESTED READINGS

Andolfi, M. *Family therapy: An interactional approach.* New York, New York: Plenum Press, 1979.

Auerswald, E. H. Interdisciplinary versus ecological approach. *Family Process,* Sept. 1968, 7, 202-215. Reprinted in S. Sager and M. Kaplan (Eds.), *Progress in group and family therapy.* New York, New York: Brunner/ Mazel, 1972, 309-321.

Bandler, R. and Grinder, J. *The structure of magic* (Vol. 1). Palo Alto, California: Science and Behavior Books, Inc., 1975.

Barnard, C. and Corrales, R. *The theory and technique of family therapy.* Springfield, Illinois: Charles C. Thomas, 1979.

Bateson, G. *Steps to an ecology of mind.* New York: Ballantine Books, 1972.

Bateson, G. *Mind and nature: A necessary unity.* New York, New York: E. P. Dutton, 1979.

Beavers, W. and Robert, M. D. *Psychotherapy and growth.* New York: Basic Books, 1966.

Bertalanffy, L. V. General system theory and psychiatry. In S. Arieti (Ed.) *American handbook of psychiatry,* New York: Basic Books, 1966.

Boszormenyi-Nagy, I. and Spark, G. *Invisible loyalties.* New York: Harper & Row, 1973.

Buckley, W. *Sociology and modern systems theory.* Englewood Cliffs, New Jersey: Prentice-Hall, 1967.

Cameron-Bandler, L. *They lived happily ever after.* Cupertino, California: Meta Publications, 1979.

DeMeyer, M. K. *Parents and children in autism.* Washington, D.C.: V.H. Winston & Sons, 1979.

Ferreira, A. J. Decision-making in normal and pathologic families. *Archives of General Psychiatry,* 1963, *8,* 68–73.

Fullmer, D. W. Family group consultation. *Elementary School Guidance and Counseling,* 1972, *7,* 130–136.

Gath, A. The impact of an abnormal child upon the parents. *American Journal of Psychiatry,* 1977, *130,* 405–410.

Grinder, J. and Bandler, R. *The Structure of magic* (Vol. 2). Palo Alto, California: Science and Behavior Books, Inc., 1976.

Grinder, P., Delozier, J., and Bandler, R. *Patterns of the hypnotic techniques of Milton Erickson* (Vol. 2). Cupertino, California: Meta Publications, 1977.

Guerin, P. and Pendergast, E. Evaluation of family system and genogram. In Guerin, P. (Ed.), *Family therapy: Theory and practice.* New York, New York: Gardner Press, Inc., 1976.

Haley, J. An Interactional description of schizophrenia. *Psychiatry,* 1959, *22,* 321–322.

Haley, J. *Problem solving therapy.* San Francisco, California: Jossey-Bass, 1976.

Haley, J. *Leaving home: The therapy of disturbed young people.* New York, New York, McGraw-Hill, 1980.

Holt, K. S. *The Impact of mentally retarded children on their families.* Unpublished thesis. University of Manchester, Manchester, England, 1957.

Keeney, B. *Ecosystemic epistemology: An alternative paradigm for diagnosis.* Unpublished paper, 1978.

Lewis, J. M., Beavers, W. R., Gosset, J. T., and Phillips, V. A. *No single thread.* New York, New York: Brunner/Mazel, 1976.

Madanes, C. *Strategic family therapy.* San Francisco, California: Jossey-Bass, Inc., 1981.

Minuchin, S., Baker, L., Rosman, B., Liebman, R., Milman, L., and Todd, T. A conceptual model of psychosomatic illness in children. *The Archives of General Psychiatry,* 1975, *32,* 1031-1038.

Minuchin, S. *Families and family therapy.* Cambridge, Ma.: Harvard University Press, 1974.

Minuchin, S., Rossman, B., and Baker, L. *Psychosomatic families.* Cambridge, Massachusetts: Harvard University Press, 1974.

Napier, A. and Whitaker, C. *The Family crucible.* New York, New York: Harper & Row, 1978.

Papp, P. Pradoxes. in S. Minuchin and H. Fishman (Eds.), *Family therapy techniques.* Cambridge, Massachusetts: Harvard University Press, 1981.

Ruesch, J. and Bateson, G. *Communication: The social matrix of psychiatry.* New York, New York: W. W. Norton & Co., 1951.

Satir, V. *Conjoint family therapy.* (2nd edition). Palo Alto, California: Science and Behavior Books, 1967.

Satir, V. *Peoplemaking.* Palo Alto, California: Science and Behavior Books, 1973.

Selvini-Palazzoli, M., Boscolo, L., Cecchin, G., and Guiliana, P. *Paradox and counterparadox.* New York, New York: Jason Aronson, Inc., 1978.

Selvini-Palazzoli, M., Boscolo, L., Cecchin, G., and Prata, G. A Ritualized prescription in family therapy: Odd days and even days. *Journal of Marriage and Family Counseling,* July 1978, 3-9.

Torrie, C. A preliminary report on parent observations and needs as they relate to programs for deaf-blind children in the south central region, unpublished paper, 1973.

Watzlawick, P., Beavin, J. H., and Jackson, D. *Pragmatics of human communication.* New York, New York: W. W. Norton, 1967.

Watzlawick, P., Weakland, J. H., and Fisch, R. *Change. Principles of Problem Formation and Problem Resolution.* New York: W. W. Norton, 1974.

Whitaker, C. *Marital and family therapy.* Cassette audiotapes. Chicago, Illinois: Instructional Dynamics, 1970.

Wilden, A. and Wilson, T. The double bind: logic, magic, and economics. In C. Sluzki and D. Ransom (Eds.) *Double bind: The foundation of the communicational approach to the family.* New York, New York: Grune and Stratton, 1976.

8

Intervention with Disturbed Children: The Ecological Viewpoint

VALERIE J. COOK AND JEANNE M. PLAS

This chapter is focused on the ways that psychologists have used the concept of "ecology" to bring about an understanding of the complexity of human development and relationships, and emotional disturbance and intervention. First we attend to the theory of ecological psychology and the concept of emotional disturbance. Implications for intervention then are drawn, followed by descriptions of ecological intervention programs.

ECOLOGICAL PSYCHOLOGY

We begin by adopting the Kurt Lewin maxim that "there is nothing so practical as a good theory," since "it is theory which provides for our ways of looking at the world and guides action toward a vision of the ways things could be" (Plas, 1981, p. 73). Ecological views are comparatively new and, as yet, do not have a strong identity as a unified school of thought (Rhodes and Paul, 1978). The word ecology has its origins in the Greek *oikos*, meaning "house." The first ecologists were biological scientists who studied the balance of organisms and their environments. Giving attention to the work of Egon Brunswick on "ecological validity," Roger Barker, in the 1950s, was among the first to apply the concept of ecology to human behavior, and popularized the term "ecological psychology." Others have since expanded or modified his basic theories to include the concept of ecosystem (Hobbs, 1965-1980; Rhodes, 1967; Sarason, 1972), ecoenvironmental psychology (Scott, 1976) and transactional-ecological psychology (Plas and Dokecki, 1982). While this chapter is written from an eco-systems and transactional-ecological psychology viewpoint, it is important to begin by discussing the background of ecological psychology.

Carlson, Scott, and Eklund (1980, p. 76) identified four basic assumptions shared by ecologists, regardless of discipline:

(1) Organisms (including humans) do not exist or act in isolation but rather are linked in a complex net work of relationships; (2) all organisms are affected by both internal and external forces; (3) Organisms adapt, i.e., they act selectively toward their environment to achieve a harmonious working relationship with it (Wilker, 1979); (4) Methods of examining organisms seek to discover the relationships between organisms and their environment by unobtrusively recording the natural course of events . . . .

Ecological psychology is concerned with both the ecological environment (i.e., the physical context of behavior; the real-life settings within which people behave) and the psychological environment (i.e., as Kurt Lewin puts it, the life-space; the world as a particular person perceives it and is otherwise affected by it) (Barker, 1968, p. 1). This dual concern leads us to a discussion of two concepts that are integral to the ecological viewpoint, behavior settings and ecosystems.

Behavior Settings

Barker (1968, p. 27) defined a behavior setting as "a standing behavior pattern *together with* the part of the milieu to which the behavior is attached and with which it has a synomorphic relationship." His classic example is: when in church, people act "church." A combination of individual behavior and milieu is unique to each behavior setting. Barker and Gump (1964) conducted an encompassing study of the behavior settings of big high schools and little high schools. The conglomerate of the behavior settings found there defined the nature of the two ecologies, which were found to be substantially different, and, at a molar level, related to the development of different competencies in the students. Rhodes and Paul (1978) used the term "niche" to describe the unique functional role of the individual within the ecology. Applying this concept to Barker and Gump's findings, one might suggest that the same student attending a big school would develop a different niche than he or she would if attending a small school.

The individual's niche, however, is not developed solely by the environment. Barker (1968, p. 205) notes that the same environmental unit provides different inputs to different persons, and even different inputs to the same person should his or her behavior change.

The behavior setting is the simplest unit of analysis within ecological psychology. Yet it goes beyond the behaviorist's conceptualization of behavior as a stimulus-response relationship to that of an inextricably interwoven relationship of the physical setting, time, people, and individual behavior. It is a conglomerate of behavior settings that forms an ecology.

The Ecosystem

Any given individual functions in more than one ecology. The interrelationships and conglomeration of these ecologies form the individual's ecosystem. The child's ecosystem consists of the self, the family, the school, and the community (see Figure 1). The child in the context of his or her ecology or environment is not a particularly novel idea. But, as Hobbs (1979, p. 27) noted: "What is powerful in the concept of ecology is the idea that the child or adolescent cannot be juxtaposed with the environment, that he or she is an inextricable part of an ecological system." Thus, the child becomes the defining member of the ecosystem which is composed of the overlapping subsystems of family, school, and community.

Psychological and emotional development and adjustment are viewed as a result of the transaction between the child and environment (Neuhaus, Mowrey, and Glenwick, 1982, p. 152). The ecological psychologist, then, sees a bidirectional and cyclic impact between child and environment; the environment contributes to the development of the child, the child's behaviors create responses within the environment, and the changed environment thereupon exerts a different effect on the child (Salzinger, Antrobus, and Glick, 1980). Ecological psychologists agree that this process is one of mutual influence, however some describe it as a sequential mutual influence (e.g., A affects B which in turn affects A), while others, notably transactional-ecological psychologists, describe it as simultaneous mutual influence (e.g., A and B form a unity which defines the situation).

The ecological viewpoint shifts the focus from the child and his or her personality, psychic make-up, and behavior, to the relationships between the child and his or her family, school, and community (Plas, 1981; Rhodes and Paul, 1978). "Most normal children are operating in a social ecology that may be defined as adaptive or congruent; that is, the child is in harmony with the social norms of his or her environmental context" (Swanson and Reinert, 1979).

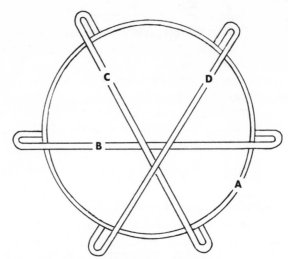

Figure 1   Representation of the ecosystem defined by the child (A = Child, B = Family, C = School, D = Community) (Plas, 1981).

Defining Emotional Disturbance

Traditional viewpoints focus on the individual child, and the deviant child is labeled as emotionally disturbed or behavior disordered. In contrast, the ecological psychologist does see symptoms of individual pathology, but of a malfunctioning ecosystem (Apter, 1982; Hobbs, 1979).

[T] he ecological point of view treats emotional disturbance as a comprehensive problem of ongoing adaptation between organism and environment, with any maladaption being conceptualized as residing as much in the environmental activity upon the child as the child's activity upon the environment. The disturbance is a pattern of maladaptive interactions. . . (Rhodes and Paul, 1978, p. 222).

The child is not likely to be identified as "disturbed" until "some consequential member of the ecosystem can no longer tolerate the discord in the system" (Hobbs, 1979, p. 25). Thus, emotional disturbance is viewed as an interactive, reciprocal, and dynamic set of forces operating between the child and the ecosystem.

The connection between the ecology and emotional disturbance has been documented in the relationships between differences in social organization of communities and suicide rates (Durkheim, 1951), between social class and psychiatric hospitalization (Hollingshead and Redlich, 1958), and between the spatial pattern of a community and the probability of certain kinds of mental illness (Faris and Dunham, 1965). Szasz (1961) concluded that society labels people mentally ill when they violate the ethical, political, or social norms of the society. Thus, emotional disturbance arises not when persons commit certain acts, but when that act becomes known to some other person(s) who then defines (or labels) that act as disturbed (Swanson and Reinert, 1979). Newbrough (1971) adds that this labeling occurs with clear reference to ecological contexts.

The early connections between ecology and emotional disturbance were conceptualized within a "main effects" framework (bad environments cause emotional disturbance) or within an "interactional" framework (the interaction of bad environments and personal characteristics cause emotional disturbance). Sameroff and his colleagues have advanced our understanding of the relationship between ecology and emotional disturbance by adopting a transactional framework. (See Sameroff, 1975 and Sameroff and Chandler, 1975 for a discussion of the three frameworks.) "The underlying assumptions of the transactional model are that the contract between organism and environment is a transaction in which each is altered by the other" (Sameroff, 1975, p. 67). Sameroff provides the following example:

> The mother who comes to label her infant as "difficult" may come to treat the child as difficult irrespective of his actual behavior. . . . [T] he child . . . will come to accept "difficulty" as one of the central elements in his self-image; thereby, indeed becoming the "difficult" child for all time (p. 73).

The transactional model has been applied to the understanding of the relationship between child abuse/neglect and childhood emotional disturbance and to the development of schizophrenia. Sameroff and Chandler (1975) concluded, following a review of the literature, that attempts to isolate linear cause-effect relationships between child abuse/neglect and emotional disturbance in children have been largely futile. They point out that while abused/neglected children have been presumed to be passive recipients of negative environmental influences, these children have been shown to exhibit a variety of negative behaviors (e.g., decreased sucking vigor) that in some cases influence the processes of abuse/neglect. Thus, they emphasize the mutual influence that the parent-child partners in transaction seem to possess. Sameroff and Zax (1978) conducted a longitudinal study of schizophrenic women and their young children. They found no evidence that schizophrenia had been transmitted linearly during the first 30 months of the child's life. This led them to suggest that "the intellectual incompetence of the young infant makes it highly unlikely that he can learn the schizophrenic facts of life. As he grows in cognitive and linguistic skill, he becomes increasingly competent at identifying and adapting to the craziness of his social environment" (p. 439).

As the child learns to make increasingly more significant contributions to the schizophrenic transaction with the mother, evidence of disturbed behavior in the child begins to manifest itself across increasingly larger numbers of ecological contexts. Furthermore, the child judged to be the most disturbed is the one who uniformly arouses disturbed reactions in those around him or her in more than one setting (Rhodes, 1967, 1970).

In summary, the ecological viewpoint requires a shift of thought when considering emotional disturbance; a shift away from the individual toward an understanding of a unit defined as individual-in-the-ecology. Disturbing behaviors are viewed as learned patterns (Hobbs, 1966) that may be understandable responses to a maladaptive system (Salzinger et al., 1980; Sameroff and Zax, 1978). Ecological psychologists are, therefore, concerned by the traditional labeling of the child as emotionally disturbed. We will use the alternate label of "disturbing children" to better communicate the transactional nature of the reciprocity between child and ecology.

IMPLICATIONS FOR INTERVENTION

We began this chapter with an affirmation that theory guides action toward a vision of the way things could be. The ecological psychologist's understanding of the disturbing child guides intervention away from the "cure" of the child. The goal becomes one of enabling the child's ecosystem to function reasonably well (not perfectly—no system, as no individual, is perfect) (Hobbs, 1966; 1979; 1980).

The locus of emotional disturbance in the relationship of child and ecology leads to a dual focus on the child and ecology in intervention (Samuels, 1981), and to the simultaneous implementation of what Hobbs (1979) has termed psychological and ecological strategies. There is no prescribed ecological intervention plan, so we take a global look at the strategies consistent with ecological theory and their implications for service delivery.

Psychological Strategies

Psychological strategies are "ways of working with individual children" (Hobbs, 1979, p. 18) and encompass the direct intervention services provided children (Apter, 1982). A variety of strategies are used in child-focused intervention, many of which are described in other chapters of this book. The ecological psychologist's selection of specific strategies will be governed by two principles:

(1) the strategy should serve to emphasize the natural *strengths* of childhood, i.e., growth and development of competencies, and (2) the strategy should take the whole child into consideration. Rather than focus on specific psychological strategies, we describe the ecological psychologist's organization of strategies in the intervention program.

One of the major developmental tasks of childhood is achievement in the greatest sense of the word, i.e., attainment of competence (Erickson, 1963; Thomas and Chess, 1980). The curriculum as a planned environment (i.e., "the composite of designed opportunities for learning and development") is a major tool of intervention (Rhodes, 1970). The organized structuring of the curriculum provides an opportunity for the child to attain current success while preparing him or her for successful adaptation to the world and providing him or her the skills to influence the world. The term curriculum is used to designate the planned nature of the psychological strategies to be employed.

An ecologically oriented curriculum is designed to promote the child's development educationally, socially, and in living skills. The individual educational program is organized around group "units" or "enterprises" in order to consider the child's interests as well as the child's educational achievement level (Rhodes, 1970). Competence is also encouraged in arts, crafts, drama, sports, and life skills such as cooking and camping.

It is likely that it was the social behavior of the child that cast him or her as disturbing. Thus, the curriculum includes use of behavior management techniques to help the child learn to control "symptoms" and engage in more socially appropriate behavior (Hobbs, 1979; Rhodes, 1970). Exclusive reliance on behavior modification strategies, however, "pays insufficient attention to the evocative power of identification with an admired adult, to the rigorous demands of expectancies stated and implicit in situations, and to the fulfillment that comes with the exercise of competence" (Hobbs, 1979, p. 21). Additionally, the child's natural orientation to groups and peers is used as a strength from which to develop group process interventions that provide feedback to the child (Rhodes, 1970).

This all-encompassing curriculum demands a variety of teacher competencies, including (but not limited to): Individual educational programming, behavior management, and group dynamics. While such competencies are important, it may be that belief in the child and his or her ability to develop a full range of competencies is the most basic characteristic needed by teachers who work with disturbing children.

Ecological Strategies

Ecological strategies are "ways of working with child, family, neighborhood, school, and community" (Hobbs, 1979, p. 18) and include a variety of indirect services (Apter, 1982). Salzinger et al. (1980) identified two guiding principles for ecological strategies: (1) they should take place, at least in part, in the child's everyday environment, and (2) significant people within the child's network should be thought of as both agents of change and as targets of change. The primary intervention techniques are consultation and the development of networks and covenants (Rhodes and Paul, 1978). These techniques will be discussed in the context of their use in the child's ecosystem.

"The family is probably the most important factor in the success or failure of the child's adaptive process" (Swanson and Reinert, 1979, p. 148). Parent involvement in the intervention process, from planning through implementation and maintenance, is integral to ecological intervention. At a minimum, family involvement includes the commitment to work with school staff and to participate in goal setting. If the intervention program is residential, continued contact with the family is accomplished by returning the child home on weekends. "During the weekend it is hoped that the child and parents can interact with new found skills and attitudes" (Alwes, 1978, p. 69). Parent consultation serves the purposes of developing an increased understanding of the problem situation and a repertoire of adapative coping strategies. The latter may be enhanced by the development of covenants focused on direct intervention with the parents, and may include techniques such as: parent groups, parent training, family therapy, and/or individual therapy (e.g., for alcohol/drug abuse) (Apter, 1982). The goal is to bring the family to a level of competence and flexibility so that it may assume the coordination of intervention efforts as soon as possible. Though the term parents has been used here, family intervention may include significant others in the family network.

In the case of extremely disruptive systems, it may be necessary to develop a residential intervention program (Hobbs, 1966) or an alternative day-school probram (Neuhaus et al., 1982). These placements are considered temporary and the goal is the timely return of the child to the home school. The coordination of the intervention program with the home school is essential to the development of the intervention plan and the preparation for the return of the child. Consultation is focused on the development of an appropriate educational program and placement in the home school, attending to the specific needs of the child with regard to curriculum, management, and family involvement.

Ecological intervention requires the involvement of community agencies (Swanson and Reinert, 1979) such as mental health centers, children's organizations (e.g., Boy/Girl Scouts), community recreation centers (for children and families), health care providers, social services (e.g., day care for younger siblings) and churches. Should the family lack community network support, the first step is to assist in networking. Covenants are often made with mental health centers to provide or assist in supportive service delivery.

Organizing Ecological Strategies

While one goal of the ecological intervention program is to bring each of the subsystems "to threshold" (Hobbs, 1966), the linkage and coordination of agencies, services, and individuals of the ecosystem is a "necessary condition" for optimal functioning (Dokecki, 1977). Thus, a primary function of ecological intervention is to coordinate the efforts of the subsystems (Neuhaus et al., 1982). This coordination effort is best achieved when it is the responsibility of a staff member who may be a teacher, school psychologist, or social worker. Though this individual has been described as a "case manager," Hobbs (1979, p. 30) criticizes that term as "semantically infelicitous. No one wants to be a 'case,' and no one wants to be 'managed.' " Hobbs and others (cf., Dokecki, 1977; Plas, 1981; Rhodes, 1970) prefer the term "liaison specialist." "The liaison specialist may best be thought of as a facilitator, a gatherer of information, a mobilizer of other people, an enabler of other people, but not as an expert who takes over responsibility from the parents or the child or the adolescent" (Hobbs, 1980, p. 283).

The single most important intervention tool of the liaison specialist is consultation (Apter, 1982; Rhodes, 1970). Broadly speaking, consultation is a "change-oriented relationship focusing upon problems of adaptation between individuals and environment" (Rhodes, 1970, p. 52). The consultation process may be based in a mental health, behavioral, or organizational framework. A detailed description of the consultation process is beyond the scope of this chapter, thus the reader is referred to Apter (1982), Caplan (1970), and Gallessich (1982).

A necessary prerequisite for the development of an ecological intervention program is the ecological assessment, also to be coordinated by the liaison specialist. Ecological assessment involves: "(a) identifying sources of discord in the ecosystem as well as sources of strengths that can be used to improve the goodness of fit between the individual and important people and places in his life and (b) specifying what services are required to enable the child to make reasonable progress toward achieveable developmental goals" (Hobbs, 1980, p. 276). The shortcomings of the traditional psychological assessment of the child for this purpose are obvious. The liaison specialist uses a variety of interview and observation techniques in ecological assessment (cf., Apter, 1982; Barker, 1968; Barker and Wright, 1955, 1971; Hobbs, 1979; Plas, 1981; Prieto and Rutherford, 1980; Wallace and Larsen, 1978).

Ecological assessment is differentiated from traditional assessment not so much by the specific techniques used, but by the way that the assessor conceptualizes and organizes the assessment-intervention process. Plas (1981) described seven stages of the ecosystems-oriented assessment-intervention process that can be employed once a disturbing child has been referred for psychological services.

1. *Entering the system* of relationships that comprise the child's world. This entry should be attempted at a natural point of system fracture, e.g., an already scheduled parent conference, inviting relevant persons (e.g., grandmother, socialworker) to attend.

2. *Mapping* and

3. *assessing the ecology* utilize system analysis strategies and result in the production of tentative diagnostic and intervention-oriented hypotheses.

4. *Creating a vision of change* by coalescing the persons in the child's ecosystem and orienting the group toward the naturally occurring strengths that have been identified within the child's world to effect an initial intervention plan.

5. *Coordinating-communicating,*

6. *re-assessing* and

7. *evaluating* are geared primarily toward implementation of the change strategies that are in continual process of formulation throughout this type of intervention process. [See Plas (1981) for a full description of this process and Hobbs (1979) or Williams (1977) for descriptive case studies.]

While a detailed description of the liaison specialist's attitudes and behaviors throughout this process is beyond the scope of this discussion, it is obvious that this approach does not separate the processes of assessment from the processes of intervention. Rather, assessment and intervention are seen as interdependent phases of action (Cook and Plas, 1980). Finally, rather than focusing on the child, the assessment-intervention process is geared toward the set of relationships that compose the ecosystem of the disturbing child. Throughout the assessment-intervention process, the liaison specialist models behaviors and approaches for the parents to adopt when assuming the coordination and maintenance function.

Summary

While there are no prescribed guidelines, ecological intervention programs are likely to have a combination of the following characteristics:

1. Emphasis is placed on both the child and the ecology, including family, school, and community.

2. Intervention is based on the natural strengths of the child and the ecosystem.

3. Consultation is of high value.

4. Specially trained personnel are required.

5. The goal of the program is to "fade out the professional and to turn over the responsibility for maintenance, continuation, and enhancement of treatment effects to caretakers in the child's everyday environment and to the child" (Salzinger et al., 1980, p. 5).

ECOLOGICAL INTERVENTION PROGRAMS

Project Re-ED, "a project for the re-education of emotionally disturbed children" (Hobbs, 1966), has served as a model ecological program, and it will serve as our central example. The description of Re-ED presented here is based on the numerous writings of Hobbs (1965, 1966, 1970, 1974, 1977, 1978, 1979, 1980), as well as Hermann (1979) and Rhodes (1967).

Development of Re-ED

The first White House Conference on Children in 1909 called attention to the paucity of services for emotionally disturbed children. In the following years, several shortcomings of the existing traditional programs were identified: (a) Insufficient allocation of resources, (b) ineffectiveness, (c) alienation of children from their homes, schools, and communities, and (d) the costly expense, which limited services to a relatively small number of children. While influenced by the development of ecological thought, Hobbs became impressed by the *educateur* professional role developed in France in response to the needs of thousands of children following World War II, when there was a shortage of mental health service providers.

Nicholas Hobbs and his colleagues at George Peabody College for Teachers had all of the above considerations in mind when they collaborated with mental health officials in Tennessee and North Carolina, the Southern Regional Education Board, and the National Institute of Mental Health in the development of the initial Re-ED proposal. "Just what re-education meant was not at all clear at the outset" (Hobbs, 1979, p. 6). Theory was nonexistent and the developers worked from their clear preferences for educational rather than psychiatric concepts, placing heavy emphasis on improving the transactions between child and environment through appropriate changes in each and in mobilizing existing resources to restore the child's ecosystem to effective functioning (Hobbs, 1980, p. 287). These preferences also formed the basis for the principles or processes of re-education on which the school programs are structured:

1. *Life is to be lived, now.* Each day should be designed so that the probability of success outweighs the probability of failure.

2. *Time is an ally.* "Several studies suggest that therapeutic intervention is not demonstrably superior to the passage of time without treatment in the subsequent adjustment of children diagnosed emotionally disturbed . . . in Re-ED we . . . try to avoid getting in the way of the normal restorative processes of life" (Hobbs, 1966, p. 1110).

3. *Trust is essential,* and the first step in the re-education of the disturbing child who has generally lost trust in adults.

4. *Competence makes a difference,* and results in self respect and respect from others.

5. *Symptoms can and should be controlled* as such behaviors alienate the child from others and stand in the way of normal development.

6. *Cognitive control can be taught.* The discussion of immediate personal problems and experiences assists in the resolution of the problem as well as establishing a habit of talking things over that may be generalized to the home situation.

7. *Feelings should be nurtured,* and expressed in socially appropriate ways.

8. *The group is important to children* as a souce of motivation, instruction, and control. Children's groups are kept intact for nearly all activities. Group techniques are used to discuss difficulties, plan activities, and share experiences.

9. *Ceremony and ritual give order, stability, and confidence* to otherwise chaotic lives.

10. *The body is the armature of the self* and is to be known and developed through physical education, sports, and crafts.

11. *Communities are important,* thus children are involved in community activities, e.g., field trips, YMCA memberships.

12. *A child should know joy* in each day and look forward with eagerness to tomorrow.

The Original Re-ED Schools

The two schools established in the demonstration grant were Cumberland House Elementary School in Nashville, TN (opened November, 1962) and Wright School in Durham, NC (opened January, 1963). They were designed to serve a small number of children, ages 6 to 12, who had been diagnosed as moderately to severely disturbed. Over the years the Re-ED schools have served more and more seriously-disturbed (including autistic) children and youth.

Three teacher-counselors are assigned to each group of approximately eight children. One teacher-counselor is responsible for the day program, the second for the night program, and the third for the liaison program (thus one-third of the professional resources are invested in making the ecosystem work well). The teacher-counselors are the heart of Re-ED and are selected for their commitment to children. The teacher-counselor is not a psychotherapist; rather (s)he is the implementer of the total curriculum. The liaison teacher-counselor is responsible for the implementation of the ecological strategies.

Though Cumberland House and Wright School were established on the same principles, shared similar structures, and were founded at approximately the same time, differences in the programs have emerged. Cumberland House has emphasized individualized instruction, goal achievement, enterprise teaching, outdoor programming, art, and family and community agency participation. Wright School has expanded admissions to include physically handicapped, mentally retarded, and homeless children. Wright School has emphasized educational diagnosis and remediation while developing a highly successful outreach program in a local public school, providing consultation regarding the management of moderately-to-severely disturbed children.

The Re-ED program includes all of the intervention strategies described in the "Implications" section of this chapter. In doing so, several conspicuous differences become apparent when comparing Re-ED with traditional residential intervention programs.

1. The length of residence in the Re-ED Program is four to six months as compared to an average of 18 months in a traditional program.

2. The family is fully involved and the child returns home each weekend, as compared to the isolation of the child in traditional programs.

3. The Re-ED child is involved in regular community activities.

4. The cost-per-child in Re-ED is approximately one-half that of the traditional treatment program.

A variety of evaluation strategies have been employed to assess the effectiveness of the Re-ED model. An 80 percent success rate was noted in comparing the six-month post-discharge observations with the enrollment observations of approximately 100 children (Hobbs, 1966). Weinstein (1969, 1974) compared Re-ED children with a group of equally disturbed children receiving a variety of available interventions (e.g., within-the-school, mental health center). Re-ED children showed higher academic performance, better adjustment (as reported by staff, parents, regular teachers, and agency representatives), more positive self-concepts, and greater confidence in their ability to control their environment. The final statistical support for the effectiveness of the program is that of the 223 "graduated" students, 87 percent returned to their homes and regular classrooms (Hermann, 1979).

The qualitative evidence for the effectiveness of Re-ED is reflected in the reports of a 1969 NIMH "Panel of Visitors" and the 1970 Joint Commission on Mental Health of Children. Both concluded that Re-ED was sound, effective, and economically feasible, and strongly recommended national dissemination of the model. [See Hobbs (1979) or Herman (1979) for a summary of these reports.]

Additionally, the Re-ED Project has stood the test of time (over 20 years) and the discontinuance of federal funds (1968). In 1965 the North Carolina legislature "through a misunderstanding" withdrew the funding of Wright School, creating a state-wide reaction from parents and teachers, leading to the re-establishment of state funding (Hobbs, 1979). The Tennessee State Department of Mental Health assumed responsibility for Cumberland House in 1968. The Tennessee Re-ED program has been expanded to include schools in Memphis, Chattanooga, Knoxville, and most recently Crockett Academy for adolescents in Nashville. Currently, 200 of the 225 children and adolescents in Tennessee public residential care are in Re-ED Programs, and all but two traditional treatment wards in state mental hospitals have been closed (Hobbs, 1979). The additional dissemination of the Re-ED model throughout the United States provides further testimony for its success.

Dissemination of the Re-ED Model

The Re-ED model has been disseminated nationwide under the "Re-ED School Dissemination Contract" with the United States Office of Education (Alwes, 1978). Hobbs (1978, 1979) has noted that while certain theories and practices make it easy to distinguish Re-ED Programs from other mental health programs for children, no Re-ED "orthodoxy" has been established and each of the 20 schools now using Re-ED principles has unique components.[1] We will highlight some of these unique features here.

Pine Breeze School, Chattanooga, was the first Re-ED program for adolescents. The extension of the program to adolescents brings additional "problems" associated with the natural developmental period of adolescence (e.g., identity crises, drug and alcohol attraction) as well as altering of the ecosystem to place greater focus on peers and opposite sex relationships (Hobbs, 1979). Thus, they: (1) increased opportunities for personal counseling by the teacher-counselor, (2) shifted the focus of the ecological intervention from family to community and peers, and (3) extended the concept of enterprise learning to true adult-like enterprise, including work experience.

In 1969, psychiatrists at Marshall I. Pickens Hospital in Greenville, South Carolina, established the *Children's Program*. The staffing patterns are typical of Re-ED, though teacher-counselors are called therapists. Perhaps the most striking feature of this program is that it was developed and is maintained by the medical system.

Serving 150 children and adolescents, the *Pressley Ridge School*, Pittsburgh, maintains the original Re-ED model for its residential program, and has expanded the concept to include a night program for children who attend public schools, a day school for children who live at home, and a year-round wilderness camping program for older boys.

The *Kentucky Re-ED School*, Louisville, is a public school residential program, serving approximately 32 disturbing children, ages 6 to 12, from a seven county area (Alwes and Montgomery, 1978; Hermann, 1979; Hobbs, 1979).

---

[1] Re-ED schools are located in Nashville, Memphis, Knoxville, and Chattanooga, TN; Durham, NC; Greenville, SC; Lexington and Louisville, KY; Pittsburgh, PA; Elkhart and Fort Wayne, IN; Cleveland, OH; East Granby, CT; and Sacramento, CA.

Each group of eight students is served by a team of a teacher-counselor (for academic development), a program specialist (for social and physical development), aides, and a liaison teacher-counselor. The Kentucky School uses all of the psychological and ecological strategies described earlier in this chapter.

In 1973 the Kentucky Re-ED School was identified as one of the top twelve Title III projects in the nation, boasting a return of 80 percent of its 116 students to the regular classroom with satisfactory adjustment. Montgomery and Van Fleet (1978) conducted an evaluation of 138 students who spent an average of 19 weeks in the program. They found positive changes in each individual, significant growth in targeted academic areas, and consistent significant changes in behavior ratings by self, peers, and adults in the school, home, and neighborhood.

The *Central Kentucky Re-ED Program,* Lexington, has the core Re-ED residential component, plus a summer program and ten additional liaison workers assigned to a ten county prevention-outreach program. The liaison worker enters a child's or adolescent's ecosystem when disruption occurs in the family, school, or community. An ecological assessment is conducted and an enablement plan is developed. The goal is to prevent residential placements in the Re-ED Program. "The program is working very well and at a cost considerably less than residential placement" (Hobbs, 1980, p. 288).

The *Positive Education Program* (PEP), Cleveland, is a day program conducted by community mental health centers under contract with the Board of Education (Hobbs, 1979; PEP 1980). PEP serves 300 disturbing children, ages 18 months to 18 years. The primary intervention strategies include contingency management, group process, individualized academic instruction, and parent training in child management and communication skills, including a Parent Training Parents Program. PEP (1980) reports an 80 percent success rate of students returning to home schools. In addition to the day program, PEP collaborates with a local psychiatric hospital to provide acute care for adolescents and offers a preschool program.

The *Regional Intervention Program* (RIP) is a downward extension of Re-ED for disturbing children ages one to five (Hobbs, 1979). The preschool child's ecosystem differs substantially from that of the school-aged child, therefore the focus of intervention becomes the parent, particularly the mother. The mother and child are coparticipants in the day treatment program which focuses simultaneously on the enhancement of (a) the child's behavioral and developmental competencies and (b) the mother's understanding of and ability to deal with her child's disturbing behaviors and/or developmental disorders (Fields, 1975). When the mothers "graduate" from the program, they in turn teach other mothers.

Comments On Re-ED

In reviewing his twenty-plus years experience with Re-ED, Hobbs (1980) concluded: "By any criterion, the schools have been remarkably successful." However, Re-ED has not been without its problems. The high tension levels associated with working with disturbing children are exacerbated in Re-ED, a system that eschews locks and drugs, and sends children home on the weekends. This tension has taken its toll on the young, idealistic teacher-counselor, especially when disappointment is encountered (Hobbs, 1979). Furthermore,

> ... the irony of treatment insitutions is that they often reinforce the aberrations they are designed to cure ... Re-ED schools are no exception. When programs are going poorly, expectations of failure generate failure. But when programs are going well the schools are so positive, so alive ... And the affirmative expectations are contagious; they often spread to families, to regular schools, and to cooperating social agencies (Hobbs, 1979, p. 12).

Division TEACCH

The Program for the Treatment and Education of Autistic and related Communications Handicapped Children (Division TEACCH) grew out of the research of Eric Schopler and his colleagues in North Carolina (Apter, 1982; Schopler, 1978). Through the first statewide program for severely disturbed (autistic and psychotic) youngsters, Division TEACCH has been decentralized to three centers and 18 classrooms all over North Carolina. Each class is staffed by one teacher and aide, serving six to eight children. These "therapists", who are generalists trained on the job, write individual developmental curriculum for school and home. Parents are viewed as allies and cotherapists, thus emphasis is placed on parent involvement in the planning and implementation of the curriculum. Home programs are first demonstrated by the therapists, then parents demonstrate their implementation of the program while the therapists observe. The parents and therapists work together to develop an individualized, personalized program that works for all concerned.

The efforts of the Division TEACCH staff have been reflected in the development of innovative assessment procedures for use with severely disturbed children as well as in the success of the parent cotherapists. Perhaps the ultimate test of this model has been met in that parents and professionals combined to push for legislation mandating this kind of service on a statewide basis (Apter, 1982).

Cooperative Learning Program

The Cooperative Learning Program (CLP) in Portage County, Ohio is a collaborative effort of the County Children's Services Center, the County Board of Education, and ten participating school districts (Neuhaus et al., 1982). CLP is a day school program that serves very disturbing six to eighteen year olds who have demonstrated an inability to function within regular public schools, even with the support of special education classes, in-school counseling, or traditional mental health services.

Each student has a multi-factored evaluation prior to placement in CLP, and an individual educational plan which includes both academic and behavioral goals is developed. Groups of six to eight students are organized around four classes: primary, intermediate, junior high, and senior high. Each class has two teachers who have the roles of instructor, behavior manager, counselor, and liaison worker. Psychological and educational consultants assist in the liaison function and two part-time clinical psychologists assist with the individual, group, and parent counseling. Though all of the psychological intervention strategies discussed earlier in this chapter are used in CLP, an emphasis is placed on the liaison-consultation activities within the ecological strategies.

In the first five years, CLP served over 80 children having an average stay of 9.5 months. An increase of 1.0 grade level in math and 1.2 grade levels in reading was accomplished in the nine month school year. At least 61 percent of the junior high and senior high students made a successful transition to the home, school or work setting; 14 percent were committed to a mental health or juvenile court facility; data were missing for the remaining 25 percent due to moves out of the county. In contrast, 86 percent of the primary and intermediate students made a successful return to their home schools, underscoring the efficacy of early intervention.

Prevention Programs

The ecological viewpoint provides a unique orientation to the organization of intervention strategies, moreover, it is in harmony with the concept of prevention. Though several of the intervention programs described above include prevention components, there is one prevention program that merits specific attention.

The *Primary Mental Health Project* (PMHP), "begun approximately 20 years ago by Emory Cowen and colleagues in Rochester, New York, has served as the model for a great variety of early secondary prevention programs" (Apter, 1982, p. 217). Cowen and his associates (Cowen, 1978; Cowen, Trost, Lorion, Door, Izzo, and Isaacson, 1975) have described the PMHP in detail. The central elements of the program are: (1) implementation of a brief, objective, standardized screening program for early identification, (2) the addition of aides in the school for children needing assistance, (3) building intervention around regular contacts between the child, the teacher, and the aide, (4) frequent exchange of information among adults in the child's ecosystem, and (5) the role of the school psychologist as trainer and consultant. The PMHP is located in more than 25 schools in the Rochester area, serving approximately 12,000 children, and has been disseminated in a variety of geographic locations around the United States (Apter, 1982). Though the success of this program has been amply documented, Cowen would be among the first to point out that the PMHP is a secondary prevention program and that there is an urgent need to develop primary prevention programs in order to promote health and growth from the start.

HIGHLIGHTING THE ECOLOGICAL VIEWPOINT

Ecological psychologists view persons and their behaviors as inextricably linked in the complex network of their environments which are composed of both persons and settings. Behavior, whether adaptive or disturbing, is a function of the reciprocal and cyclic relationship of person and ecology. Thus intervention from an ecological view is focused on both the person and the ecology. Hobbs (1966) has summarized the underlying philosophy of ecological intervention:

> ... We assume that the child is an inseparable part of a small social system, of an ecological unit made up of the child, his family, his school, his neighborhood and community ... The effort is to get each component of the system above threshold with respect to the requirements of the other components. The Re-ED schools become a part of the ecological unit for as brief a period of time as possible, withdrawing when the probability that the system will function appears to exceed the probability that it will not. We used to speak of putting the child back into the system but we have come to recognize the erroneous assumption involved; the child defines the system and all we can do is withdraw from it at a propitious moment (p. 1108).

Though the ecological model is not as organized or systematized as the behavior or psychodynamic model, it suggests a "bridge of conceptions and actions between the more established models" (Rhodes, 1970, p. 41). The effectiveness of this bridging between child and ecology and across a variety of intervention strategies was demonstrated in the review of the Re-ED Programs, Division TEACCH, the Cooperative Learning Program, and the Primary Mental Health

Project. Indeed, it may be concluded that "the strength of the ecological approach is its all-inclusive emphasis" (Samuels, 1981).

ACKNOWLEDGMENT

The authors wish to thank Vicki Newman, a student in the Transactional-Ecological Psychology Program, for her assistance in the literature review necessary to the development of this chapter.

REFERENCES

Alwes, D. R., Sr. Re-ED School: A model for serving emotionally disturbed children. Behavioral Disorders, 1978, 3, 67–79.

Alwes, D. R. and Montgomery, P. A. Guest Co-editors of special issue of Behavior Disorders, Journal for the Council for Children with Behavior Disorders, 1978, 3(2).

Apter, S. J. Troubled children: Troubled systems. New York, New York: Pergamon Press, 1982.

Barker, R. G. Ecological psychology: Concepts and methods for studying the environment of human behavior. Stanford, California: Stanford University Press, 1968.

Barker, R. G. and Gump, P. V. Big school, small school. Stanford, California: Stanford University Press, 1964.

Barker, R. G. and Wright, J. F. Midwest and its children. Hamden, Connecticut: Arihon Books, 1955/1971.

Caplan, G. The theory of practice of mental health consultation. New York, New York: Basic Books, 1970.

Carlson, C. I., Scott, M., and Eklund, S. J. Ecological theory and method for behavioral assessment. School Psychology Review, 1980, 9, 75–82.

Cook, V. J., and Plas, J. M. Making the relationship primary: Transactional-ecological psychology. A paper presented at the annual convention of the American Psychological Association, Montreal, Canada, 1980.

Cowen, E. Prevention in the public schools: Strategies for dealing with school adjustment problems. In S. J. Apter (Ed.), Focus on prevention: The education of children labeled emotionally disturbed. Syracuse, New York: Syracuse University, 1978.

Cowen, E. L., Trost, M. A., Lorion, R. P., Dorr, D., Izza, L. D., and Isaacson, R. V. New ways in school mental health: Early detection and prevention of school maladaptation. New York, New York: Human Sciences Press, 1975.

Dokecki, P. R. The liaison perspective on the enhancement of human development: Theoretical, historical, and experiential background. Journal of Community Psychology, 1977, 5, 13–17.

Durkheim, E. Suicide: A study in sociology. Translated by John A. Spaulding, Glencoe, Illinois: The Free Press, 1951.

Erickson, E. H. Childhood and society. (2nd edition). New York, New York: W. W. Norton & Co., 1963.

Faris, R. E. and Dunham, H. W. *Mental disorders in urban areas: An ecological study of schizophrenia and other psychoses.* Chicago, Illinois: University of Chicago Press, 1965.

Fields, S. Parents as therapists. *Innovations,* 1975, *2,* 3–8.

Gallessich, J. *The profession and practice of consultation.* San Francisco, California: Jossey-Bass, 1982.

Helm, J. The ecological approach in anthropology. *American Journal of Sociology,* 1962, *67,* 630–639.

Hermann, A. *An analysis of public policies affecting project Re-ED: An educationally-oriented program for emotionally disturbed children.* Nashville, Tennessee: Vanderbilt Institute for Public Policy Studies, 1979.

Hobbs, N. How the Re-ED plan developed. In N. J. Long, W. C. Morse, and R. G. Newman (Eds.), *Conflict in the classroom.* Belmont, California: Wadsworth Publishing, 1965.

Hobbs, N. Helping disturbed children: Psychological and ecological strategies. *American Psychologist,* 1966, *21,* 1105–1115.

Hobbs, N. Project Re-Ed: New ways of helping emotionally disturbed children. In Joint Commission on Mental Health of Children, *Crisis in child mental health: Challenge for the 1970's.* New York, New York: Harper & Row, 1970.

Hobbs, N. Nicholas Hobbs. In J. M. Kauffman and C. D. Lewis (Eds.), *Teaching children with behavior disorders: Personal perspectives.* Columbus, Ohio: Charles E. Merrill Publishing, 1974.

Hobbs, N. *The futures of children.* San Francisco, California: Jossey-Bass, Inc. 1977.

Hobbs, N. Perspectives on Re-Education. *Behavioral Disorders,* 1978, *3,* 65–66.

Hobbs, N. *Helping disturbed children: Psychological and ecological strategies, II: Project Re-ED, twenty years later.* Nashville, Tennessee: Vanderbilt University Institute for Public Policy Studies, 1979.

Hobbs, N. An ecologically oriented, service-based system for the classification of handicapped children. In S. Salzinger, J. Antrobus, and J. Glick (Eds.), *The ecosystem of the "sick" child: Implications for classification and intervention for disturbed and mentally retarded children.* New York, New York: Academic Press, 1980.

Hobbs, N., Bartel, N., Dokecki, P. R., Gallagher, J. J., and Reynolds, M. C. *Exceptional teaching for exceptional learners.* New York, New York: The Ford Foundation, 1979.

Hollingshead, A. B. and Redlich, F. C. *Social class and mental illness: A community study.* New York, New York: John Wiley & Sons, 1958.

Montgomery, P. A. and Von Fleet, D. S. Evaluation of behavioral and academic changes through the Re-ED process. *Behavioral Disorders,* 1978, *3,* 136–146.

Neuhaus, S. M., Mowrey, J. D., and Glenwick, D. S. The Cooperative Learning Program: Implementing an ecological approach to the development of alternative psychoeducational programs. *Journal of Clinical Child Psychology,* 1982, *11,* 151–156.

Newbrough, J. R. Behavioral perspectives on psychosocial classification. *American Journal of Orthopsychiatry,* 1971, *41,* 843–845.

Plas, J. M. The psychologist in the school community: A liaison role. *School Psychology Review,* 1981, *10,* 72–81.

Plas, J. M. and Dokecki, P. Philosophy-based education: A transactional approach. *Professional Psychology*, 1982, *13*, 278–282.

Positive Education Program. *Helping disturbed children: A model for systematic treatment.* Cleveland, Ohio: Positive Education Program, 1980.

Prieto, A. G. and Rutherford, R. B., Jr. An ecological assessment technique for behaviorally disordered and learning disabled children. In N. L. Long, W. C. Morse and R. G. Neroman (Eds.), *Conflict in the classroom: The education of emotionally disturbed children* (4th edition). Belmont, California: Wadsworth Publishing, 1980.

Reinert, H. R. *Children in conflict: Educational strategies for the emotionally disturbed and behavior disordered.* St. Louis, Missouri: C. V. Mosby Co., 1976.

Rhodes, W. C. The disturbing child: A problem of ecological management. *Exceptional Children*, 1967, *33*, 449–455.

Rhodes, W. *The emotionally disturbed student and guidance.* New York, New York: Houghton Mifflin Co., 1970.

Rhodes, W. C. and Paul, J. L. *Emotionally disturbed and deviant children: New views and approaches.* Englewood Cliffs, New Jersey: Prentice-Hall, 1978.

Salzinger, S., Antrobus, J., and Glick, J. The ecosystem of the "sick" kid. In S. Salzinger, J. Antrobus and J. Glick (Eds.), *The ecosystem of the "sick" child: Implications for classification for intervention for disturbed and mentally retarded children.* New York, New York: Academic Press, 1980.

Sameroff, A. J. Transactional models in early social relations. *Human Development*, 1975, *18*, 65–79.

Sameroff, A. J. and Chandler, M. J. Reproductive risk and the continuum of caretaking casuality. In D. Horowitz, E. M. Hetherington, S. Scarr-Slapstek, and G. M. Siegel (Eds.), *Review of Child Development Research, Volume 4.* Chicago, Illinois: University of Chicago Press, 1975.

Sameroff, A., and Zax, A. In search of schizophrenia: Young offspring of schizophrenic women. In L. C. Wynn (Ed.), *The nature of schizophrenia.* New York, New York: Wiley, 1978, 430–441.

Samuels, S. C. *Disturbed exceptional children: An integrated approach.* New York, New York: Human Sciences Press, 1981.

Sarason, S. B. *The creation of settings and the future societies.* San Francisco, California: Jossey-Bass, Inc., 1972.

Schopler, E. Prevention of psychosis through alternate education. In S. J. Apter (Ed.), *Focus on prevention: The education of children labeled emotionally disturbed.* Syracuse, New York: Syracuse University, 1978.

Scott, M. *Ecoenvironmental psychology: A critical period.* Unpublished manuscript, Indiana University, 1976.

Swanson, H. L. and Reinert, H. R. *Teaching strategies for children in conflict: Curriculum, methods, and materials.* St. Louis, Missouri: C. V. Mosby Co., 1979.

Szasz, T. S. *The myth of mental illness: Foundations of a theory of personal conduct.* New York, New York: Hoeher-Harper, 1961.

Thomas, A. and Chess, S. *The dynamics of psychological development.* New York, New York: Burner/Mazel, 1980.

Wallace, G. and Larsen, S. C. *Educational assessment of learning problems: Testing for teaching.* Boston, Massachusetts: Allyn & Bacon, 1978.

Weinstein, L. Project Re-ED schools for emotionally disturbed children: Effectiveness as viewed by referring agencies, parents, and teachers. *Exceptional Children*, 1969, *35*, 703–711.

Weinstein, L. *Evaluation of a program for re-educating disturbed children: A follow-up comparison with untreated children.* Washington, DC: U.S. Department of Health, Education, and Welfare, 1974, (ERIC ED-141-966).

Wilker, A. W. *An introduction to ecological psychology.* Monterrey, California: Brooks/Cole, 1979.

Williams, J. S. Liaison functions as reflected in a case study. *Journal of Community Psychology*, 1977, *5*, 18–23.

9

Transactional Analysis as a Frame of Reference for Therapeutic Intervention

STEPHEN T. SIRRIDGE

Disorders of childhood or adolescence may encompass a wide variety of behavioral problems, ranging from bizarre symptoms exhibited by psychotic children to less severe emotional disturbances of a developmental nature. The Joint Commission on the Mental Health of Children (1969) estimated that of the 95 million persons under the age of 25 in the U.S. in 1969, ten million, or about 10%, had major psychological problems and needed help. Studies of normal children have shown that on the average, 50% have temper tantrums or many fears; about 30% experience nightmares or bite their nails; 10% to 20% wet their beds, suck their thumbs, or show tics or other evidence of tension; five to ten percent have adjustment difficulties sufficient to warrant professional attention; and another 30% show mild adjustment problems (Anthony, 1967; Newbrough, 1972). A reasonable total estimate is that all, or almost all children show at least some disturbing or abnormal behavior at some time, and that the average child or adolescent has at least one such problem at any one time (Mussen, Conger, and Kagan, 1974).

These statistics on the trends of adjustment in children and adolescents underscore the continuing need for written material available for lay and professional audiences which orients itself toward understanding childhood problem behaviors. To meet this growing need for information and direction, a large number of books have been written for parents and mental health practitioners (Axline, 1947; Moustakis, 1959; Dreikurs and Grey, 1968; Becker, 1971; James, 1974). Each of these books tends toward a specific orientation and seeks to help the reader develop a frame of reference from which to analyze and intervene in problem situations. The interpersonal theory of Eric Berne called Transactional Analysis (TA) is a specific model for systematically intervening with disturbed children. TA is a viable psychological orientation toward understanding behavior, thinking and feeling, and outlining the pattern of growth in the human personality. As such, TA provides a workable and realistic set of intervention strategies for working with children and adolescents.

The aim of this chapter is to present professionals with the basic concepts of Transactional Analysis and a discussion of these principles as they may be applied to children in a clinical setting.

BASIC TRANSACTIONAL ANALYSIS THEORY

Transactional Analysis (TA) is an interpersonal theory; that is, it is a theory that defines as its primary focus the social relations between people and the development of personality within a social environment. As the name implies, TA is the complex analysis or study of transactions and how these social interchanges shape an individual's personality and determine an overall pattern or style of life.

Strokes

The concept in TA that embodies or defines the need for stimulation is "Strokes." A stroke, in its broadest context, is a unit of recognition. A stroke is a pat on the back or a word of recognition. A verbal insult or a kick in the shins is also a stroke. The stroke that feels good and helps a person feel OK about himself or herself is called a positive stroke. The other type of recognition that is painful or leaves a person feeling bad and not OK is labeled a negative stroke. Each person needs strokes to survive, whether the strokes are pleasant or unpleasant. A child who does not obtain the necessary positive stroke (s)he needs, will set things up to acquire negative strokes rather than receive no attention at all.

Positive and negative strokes come in all shapes, sizes, and intensities. Basically, they fall into two broad categories: recognition based on doing, and recognition based on *being*. A stroke given to a person for what he or she does and how that person performs is called a conditional stroke. For example, when a mother says to a child, "I like you when you make your bed and clean up your room," she is paying attention to him or her based on the condition that something is done in return.

A stroke given to a person for *being* has been named an unconditional stroke. This recognition is based on the person being alive and existing, and not on any act or performance. For example, when a father says to his daughter, "I like you and I care for you because you are you," he is telling her that she is liked because she exists. Unconditional strokes are given with no strings attached.

Both types of strokes are necessary for developing positive feelings about self and appropriate social skills for adjusting to a world with other people. Conditional strokes, positive and negative, label for the child the thing (s)he must do to get attention from significant adult figures. This process earmarks to the child the things other people like and do not like. Alternately, positive, unconditional strokes help the child to define his or her sense of self, the internal boundary, that allows the child to perform with the certainty that (s)he is good and important. A balance in the child's stroke economy is necessary so that the child does not define feelings about self based on doing and achieving, nor should the child be overwhelmed with suffocating strokes for being, which neglect to define what the child does that is important.

Basic Life Position

The dynamic interplay of giving and getting strokes defines for children their feelings about themselves and other people in the world. How a person feels about himself or herself and others is called a basic position. There are four basic life positions that denote the relationship of self to the world (Harris, 1969).

1. I'm OK—You're OK. This is a healthy position that says that "on the whole" the person is satisfied with himself or herself and comfortable with other people. The statement implies that the person can feel all feelings and be OK in being aware and expressing them. This position is a winning position, and motivates the person to "moving on" and "growing."

2. I'm Not OK—You're OK. This is a position of the person who feels inadequate and inferior in comparison to others. The person's sense of self lies in the hands of others who must bestow the give of OKness to him or her. It is a depressed and unworthy position.

3. I'm OK—You're Not OK. This is a position of a person who defines others as inadequate and unworthy. Although the person is scared, insecure, and distrustful of others, the basic life stance is being one-up on other people. It is an angry, ignoring, condescending position.

4. I'm Not OK—You're Not OK. This is the "nowhere" position because the person does not trust anyone, including himself or herself. It is a position of someone who feels (s)he cannot win, and life is bleak and not worth it.

The life positions of people are in part determined by the strokes they give and receive. If children feel OK about themselves and others, then they will probably draw upon reserves of positive strokes, enabling them to give and enjoy themselves. A winning person has the energy and stroke support to carry out the activities of a fully functioning personality structure—the functions of feeling, thinking, and doing.

Personality Structure

The personality of each individual is composed of several parts called ego states. "Ego states are organized ways of defining reality, processing information, and reacting to the world (Babcock and Keepers, 1976, p. 30)." Stated in another way, ego states are a definable collection of behaviors, values and feelings that are visible and focused in conscious awareness. The building blocks of TA are three observable ego states: the Parent, the Adult, and the Child.

A person operates in one of three distinct ego states at any one time. The diagnosis of ego states is made by observing visible and audible characteristics of a person's appearance. The ego states are distinguishable on the basis of body movement, paraverbal voice features, and the content of verbal utterances.

The three ego states can be diagrammed by three circles (see Figure 1). The three circles signify that each of the three ego states is separate and discrete and can be identified by different contents and actions. The Child ego state is present from birth (probably is functioning prenatally); the Parent and the Adult ego

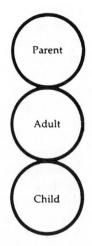

Figure 1   Ego states.

states are adaptations to a social world that requires each person to think and take care of himself or herself.

Child Ego State

Eric Berne (1964) states that "the Child is in many ways the most valuable part of the personality and contributes to the individual's life exactly what an actual child contributes to family life: charm, pleasure and creativity. In the child reside intuition, creativity and spontaneous drive and enjoyment (p. 25)."

The Child ego state is the repository of the person's biological needs and basic feelings. It provides for the person a sense of who (s)he is and, as such, is often experienced as the most real part of the person. The Child part of each person has recorded all the significant emotional events of a person's life, even from infancy. Thus, the Child ego state in an adult has the same feelings and ways of behaving that he or she had as a child. The Child can be natural; that is, act on its own, connected only to internal needs and wants. The Child can also be adapted, which is the response of a person in a pleasing or rebellious fashion.

The Child ego state tends to make fleeting appearances in grownups because of sanctions against acting "childish or childlike." Situations of great pain or joy and less inhibited activities (sporting events or playing with children) allow for the spontaneous emission of childlike expressions of delight, anger, fear, and sadness. The childlike behavior also is accompanied by the corresponding perceptions, thoughts, and feelings of a three-to-five-year-old.

Adult Ego State

The Adult part of the personality gathers and processes data, follows the rules of logic, and arrives at conclusions. The Adult is considered an impassionate organ, computer-like in the absence of feeling because of its function of observation and prediction of external reality.

The Adult ego state is first operative in the infant at a sensori-motor level, and moves to a more symbolic level with the child's use of word combinations at two years of age. Throughout the development of the individual child, his or her information levels increase and the structure of cognitions become more complex and mature. The Adult's most mature level of functioning begins at the age of 12 and rounds our more fully at 16, with the onset of a child's ability to deal with abstract, hypothetico-deductive ideas. Each person possesses a functional Adult ego state, but it may vary in level of sophistication.

Parent Ego State

The Parent ego state is the part of us that has recorded the behavior of significant others in a person's life. It contains the rules a person has learned about things he or she should or should not do—manners, traditions, values—and has recorded what is important. Thus, the Parent ego state is a videotape of instructions about all the things a person needs to know to get along in the society and culture in which (s)he lives. The Parent ego state, because it is a copy of the behavior of the mother and the father, can be critical and controlling, or helping and nurturing.

The Parent ego state of the child will reflect the values and how-to's of the parents. No one set of parents has all the needed information to get along in the world. In addition, the parents' perspectives of the world are limited and distorted by prejudice and singular experiences being generalized to "that is the way things are." As the child acquires more data about the world and attaches to other significant authority figures, (s)he updates (adds and subtracts) the Parent ego state repertoire.

Games

A game is an "ongoing series of complementary ulterior transactions progressing to a well-defined, predictable outcome (Berne, 1964, p. 48)." Clearly, a game includes three important elements, (a) a behavioral sequence with a defined beginning and end, (b) an ulterior motive, and (c) a payoff for the players involved. According to Berne, every game is basically dishonest and the outcome has a dramatic, exciting quality. Although the game seems to move in a predictable direction and apparently has been repeated on other occasions, a person will generally experience a lack of awareness that he or she is involved in a game.

Here is a list of common games:

Ain't It Awful	Yes, But . . .
Schlemiel	Kick Me
See What You Made Me Do	Stupid
Cops and Robbers	Do Me Something
If It Weren't for You	Wooden Leg
Rapo	Harried
Debtor	Let's You and Him Fight
Courtroom	Blemish
Now I've Got You Son of	Uproar
a Bitch (NIGYSOB)	Poor Me

In general, there are two types of games: NIGYSOB and Kick Me. The former usually entails a persecuting position with the objective of one person winning and the other person losing. When people feel put down, but sense that they asked for it, they know they are playing a self-defeating (victim) game like Kick Me.

Such games are played at varying degrees of intensity or hardness. A first-

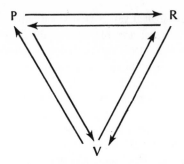

Figure 2   Karpman Drama Triangle. Reproduced through courtesy
of S. Karpman.

degree game involves a payoff of hurt feelings, so the payoff will generally occur
at the psychological level. Second-degree games receive some sort of social payoff or consequences, as when the student gets suspended or dismissed from
school for selling drugs or stealing. Some games, however, are dangerous and the
outcomes result in physical damage. A real life game of Cops and Robbers may
result in a shootout where the person is killed or injured.

A game of NIGYSOB ends with a feeling of winning or putting down the
other person. A game of Kick Me may end with the feeling of being victimized.
Players can switch places, or roles, while playing games; however, each person
plays the games that best fits his or her life decisions, and that person plays them
from a favorite position. The positions in a game, and the switches that may occur in a series of transactions, can best be understood in a schematic called the
Karpman Drama Triangle (Karpman, 1968; see Figure 2).

The NIGYSOB player plays the Persecutor (P) when feeling superior and
critizing the Victim (V). The Victim may unwittingly play the patsy for this
righteous individual. However, when the Persecutor, in a state of guilt over his
or her insulting treatment shifts to Rescuer and attempts to mollify and comfort the Victim, (s)he may end up the Victim if (s)he is told by the other player
"to forget it." The switches go in either direction around the triangle, and a
player may find himself playing as many as three positions in a full-handed
game.

Script

The way an individual lives life and how it turns out is her or his script. It
is a pattern, theme, or story line that threads its way in repetitive form throughout a person's lifetime. When a person makes a life script, (s)he incorporates
present and future events with previous life experience. The script includes all
that a person has learned about acquiring strokes in the family, preferred ways

of transacting, the psychological games that (s)he has learned, the chosen basic life position, and the cultural and historical influences that (s)he has experienced. Babcock and Keepers (1976) state that script decisions are often phrased like resolutions—"Well, if this is the way things are, then from now on I'll (never) do . . . " For example, an individual makes decisions about getting close to others, whether men or women are trustworthy, adequacy and trust in self, and the individual then sets out in life to collect data to support these script decisions, which were made early in childhood with limited information about the world. By updating these early decisions and by obtaining additional new information about intimacy, trust, and adequacy, the person can change the course or theme of his or her life.

Scripts can be categorized according to their course and outcome. Some scripts are tragic (also called hamartic), and their course is characterized by a string of third-degree games, ending in injury, illness, imprisonment, disgrace, or death. Other scripts call for a person to be a "loser" by setting goals and never reaching them. The course of the latter's life pattern is a series of setbacks and disappointments, ending with the person "not making it." Another series of life patterns, although not as destructive and disappointing, are dull and humdrum, without much happening or going on. These scripts are called "banal scripts," and refer to a drab story line where a person never reaches his or her potential.

Some scripts call for the person "to make it" and be a "winner." This story line contains many chapters where goals are set and achieved. The winner sees himself or herself as OK, and thrives on interacting with an OK world.

Everyone has a life script. A person can determine what many of his or her script decisions are by examining parent messages and child feelings. Some messages from parents are spoken and out front; these give the child directions as to what is expected if (s)he is going to make it in the world and get strokes in the family. Another series of messages, largely nonverbal and unspoken, dictate a heavy dose of "don'ts" on the child. Some injunctions may be alluded to verbally and may include only simple restrictions on the free behavior of the child (don't sing, don't laugh too loudly), whereas other injunctions can be passed on with great intensity, which can bring on severe repercussions.

Script injunctions may also be passed to children before the onset of language and, because of their preverbal content, will be experienced by the person as a bodily or physical sense that something is bad/wrong with them or that the world is a scary and distressing place to live. The preverbal injunctions may be the result of particularly traumatic events such as physical abuse, isolation and neglect (especially the lack of touching), inconsistency in meeting the basic needs of the infant, and the transfer to the infant of the mother's anxiety and tension. The end product of this parenting is that the child fails to incorporate a pattern of satisfaction and contentment, and moves to rage or passivity in order to avoid the hurt of unmet, survival-level needs.

Extending further the notion that script injunctions can be passed prever-bally and experienced as a body sense is the idea that at the moment of script decision the child's repressed feelings and script beliefs are accompanied by corresponding physiological inhibiting reactions. In effect, script formation is a product not only of the unexpressed feelings and corresponding beliefs (such as "I am not lovable"), but also a muscular/chemical reaction or defense against what the child experiences as threatening (Erskine, 1980). For example, an adolescent who inhibits expression of angry feelings may make up that her mother will reject and leave her if she is open and spontaneous with her angry feelings. The repression of feelings causes a simultaneous muscular defense manifested in a soft voice, which at time is barely audible. Similar body constriction in other children holding back anger may be evident in their rigid body posture and tight jaws. This protective armoring of the body keeps painful feelings and memories from conscious awareness. Treatment interventions (deep muscle massage, expressive dance, physical exercise) oriented toward the letting go of tension and the more natural flow of body movement permits children to live life more fully and easily within their own body.

Though the parenting influence can be potent and pervasive in determining a child's script, other events in the life of a growing child may contribute to the formation of child's outlook of himself, others, and the quality of life. One particular influence upon script decisions is the interpretation the child makes about his or her adjustment to the environment outside the home. The inevitable disparity between the home environment and that of the neighborhood and school may be such that the child may make some long lasting decisions about his or her problems in making it and fitting in with others. For example, a boy who is overprotected, pampered, naive and perhaps physically underdeveloped may find that he is picked on, excluded from games, and called a "sissy." From these negative experiences he may conclude that he will never belong (except to his mother), people are mean, and being a boy is painful and nonrewarding. The discrepancy between home and the outer world is so great and the adjustment pains so real, that constrictive life decisions are a likely result.

Additionally, script decisions can be made as a reaction to traumatic life events such as severe accidents, sickness, death of a family member and hospitalization. The pain and isolation fostered by recurrent middle ear infections, the fear of surgical operations (big people in white coats hurt you) or the untimely death of a favorite sister may be familiar examples of trauma which lead a child to make a premature decision about how life will turn out.

A child's fantasy of trauma or injury may also lead to a script decision. A girl who watches her brother punished on a consistent basis, may internalize a vision of that hurt and conclude that the pain is unbearable and that she must adapt and be very certain not to break the rules. Or a boy who observes another friend being beaten up may fantasize about the pain, though never himself experience it, that he would be killed if hurt that badly. The fear of being killed may lead to his pleasing and passive ways and his avoidance of all confrontation.

The ongoing problems for individuals who make fantasy-based decisions of hurt and pain is that they never really know the realistic limits of that pain and forever magnify it. In essence, the hurt in the imagination has no bounds and it never seems to be over or finished.

STRATEGIC INTERVENTIONS USING TRANSACTIONAL ANALYSIS

An inevitable extension of basic Transactional Analysis theory is the translation of theoretical concepts into useful intervention strategies for practicing mental health professionals. These strategies must be usable, replicable, and be securely linked to a proper conceptual-philosophical base. The purpose of this section is to review some general considerations with regard to the treatment process and present several techniques commonly employed in TA therapy.

General Treatment Considerations

TA as a treatment approach may be used in either individual or group therapy. By its very nature, however, TA is a therapy oriented toward interaction by and among people. Thus, the natural medium for analyzing how interpersonal dynamics emerge and unfold is through the process of group interaction. What will become evident among the individual group members is the manner in which they mingle before and after group (how they structure time) and how they react to others during the group process. One can discern the primary ego state used in relating with others, the type of transactions that occur between group members, and the psychological games which emerge as consistent patterns with specific individuals. In essence, the group is an excellent vehicle for the therapist to diagnose the internal psychological system learned at home and how that same system is then projected to the outside world. The group will operate as a microcosm of the larger outside world and an accurate barometer of how well the child adapts to the frames of reference of others and the social system of which (s)he is a part. One such family dynamic, competition, is easily projected into a group setting and underlines the options available to individuals about how to share time, how to get and receive strokes, and how to obtain the attention and involvement of the group leaders (the surrogate parents). Each child will have learned and decided something about competition (i.e., that strokes are scarce and parents need to make the initial contact) and (s)he brings these beliefs to group (and the school classroom), waiting and watching to see how his or her view of life will be confirmed and upheld.

As to the process that occurs in group, the therapist will need to determine how active or passive (s)he will be in directing group flow, and whether that flow will be centered upon individuals or the group as a whole. At times the focus will need to center on a single individual where the primary energy exchange is between the therapist and the child. If the nature of the work is intrapsychic and an attempt to redo or correct old unresolved scenes in a child's life, then the agent directing the work most prominently will need to be the group leader. Also, the therapist may be the object onto which the child projects unresolved fantasies, psychological games, family script, and basic life position. If this is so, the therapist will need to respond with behavior which is not script reinforcing and which invites the child to exercise new options and view himself or herself and others in a more healthy manner.

Because personal issues are both intrapsychic and interpersonal, the process of group interaction is important in facilitating productive group therapy. As such, the focus of energy will be the feedback and input among members of the group. A child may present a problem of being picked on at school, whereupon the response of the group may bring to his or her attention different options for taking care of himself or herself. Alternately, the child may also be faced with feedback which states that (s)he encourages being a victim by acting goofy, cyring or throwing fits. Contributions from peers often have more power than those offered by the therapist, and are a potent influence for challenging a child's frame of reference and producing change.

In summary, the balance of a group is dependent upon the subtle shifts from individual therapy within a group setting to the use of group process. The group leader will need to apply his or her significant bag of skills in sensing whether to center attention upon the individual or the group interaction.

Contracting

TA therapy requires specific and discrete contracts for change. A contract is a negotiation between a helping figure and a child which concerns at least one mutually agreed upon goal for change. Some goals are more global (I want to be more outgoing) while others are specific statements of what a child wishes to focus and change (I want to ask a girl out for a date). Global contacts often represent eventual and long-range plans while the more discretely defined goals are weekly, working contracts which eventually lead to major changes. Henry (1979) effectively used contracting as a means of shifting responsibility to inner city students referred for undesirable behavior. His process required written contract to clarify behavior that needed to be changed and consequences if the contract was not honored or carried out.

Contracts are obtained through the process of having the child review current problem areas. In this review several areas of importance by the child are chosen and if mutually agreed upon by the therapist or teacher become the focus of his or her change process. Even young elementary age children can identify problem areas and negotiate contracts for change.

Contracts may require the energy of another person, especially in the form of information, feedback or reward. For example, if a boy is contracting to change his nighttime wetting, then his negotiation with the therapist may entail verbal strokes as well as material rewards. Similarly, an adolescent boy who contracts to express angry feelings toward his parents may ask other group members for options in order to choose an acceptable alternative to meet his contract.

Some contracts will focus upon the here-and-now process of the group while others will pertain to home and school. Contracts in group may include bragging about self, speaking up and contributing in group, taking a risk and telling a secret about self, or asking for a physical stroke from someone. Contracts for school may involve academic (assignment completion) or social behavior (not hitting in line). Home contracts often pertain to chore responsibilities, curfews and relations among family members.

The individual nature of the contracting process allows each person to identify his or her own needs and goals. As such, contracts meet the idiosyncratic needs of each person and provide an external framework so that the contracting person and group can clearly observe what is the plan and what, if any, changes have occurred.

Stroking

A stroke is any act that recognizes the presence of another person. Our need to be stroked is the primary psychological motivation behind all behavior. The stroking, then, of child and adolescent clients is an important therapeutic strategy because strokes internally gratify the recipient and serve to reinforce behavior. A child who brings a grade card to group or who wishes to have his or her drawing posted on the board is asking to be recognized for something (s)he has accomplished. Also, the adolescent girl who asks you to comb her hair or sign a birthday card is inviting attention based on her being and existing, irrespective of anything she does to please or displease.

Positive stroking is a vital process of increasing appropriate academic and social behavior, and consolidating a child's self-esteem and sense of well-being with the world. For example, a group leader who systematically strokes the verbal contributions of group members adds greatly to the activity level and quality of input into the group. This feedback leads to greater interest and cohesion among group members.

Similarly, negative stroking based on performance and doing appears necessary at times. A confrontation about being late, teasing others and a forceful position about an adolescent's self-injurious drug intake or careless driving point out and set limits as to what is acceptable behavior. Though used more infrequently, a strongly stated parent position, which identfifies what the therapist is not satisfied with, or what the therapist is greatly concerned about, may be the "stopper" required to halt the unhealthy pattern of behavior.

A balance of strokes for doing and existing allows the therapist to shape and mold a child's behavioral repertoire of what (s)he must do to make it in the world, and shape a child's inner sense of worth and importance. For the latter, a therapy style which incorporates a varied amount of physical stroking (such as wrestling, tickling, holding, hugging and massage) signals to the child that (s)he is lovable and touchable. Touching also meets a child's needs for physical contact and develops a sense of how his or her body moves through space. Children are touchy/feely beings whose natural energy flow is to touch and be touched by others.

A child who must survive on external strokes from others alone may suffer some uncomfortable, insecure, not OK feelings when the flow of strokes is diluted or shut off. This dilemma, which faces all people, can be solved when the child uses his or her ability to self stroke and draw on his or her internal backlog (a bank account) of strokes. Thus, directives from the therapist which push the child or adolescent to become aware of his or her own strengths and accomplishments, help develop a child who can stroke himself or herself in the absence of external feedback. Similarly, a child who can use mental images of important people or recordings of strokes that sounded and felt good in the past, can bolster and shore up feelings about self.

Somewhat related to the idea of self-stroking is "asking" for strokes. Most children have deficits in asking for what they want, and children in group are particularly susceptible to the problem of passivity and noninitiation in asking for and defining the strokes they want to receive. A group process which expects a child to ask how and what they want and rewards them for doing so, builds a pattern of autonomy, independence, and self-sufficiency. A child or adolescent who consistently asks for what (s)he needs, develops a clear sense of mastery in his or her ability to make the world work for him or her.

Identification of Feelings

One of the primary strategies in working with children is to teach and shape an introspective process which allows them to think about feelings and behavior. A major requirement of growing up is learning how to name and identify feelings inside self, and correctly assessing feeling states in others (Babcock and Keepers, 1976). A child gradually integrates how an emotion feels internally, the word that goes with it, and how that feeling is manifested externally. The appropriate integration of these components permits a child to present himself or herself in a congruent fashion. In many families, however, children are not expected to think about their feelings nor is congruent expression of feelings modeled by the parents. A major task, then, in the classroom and in therapy is to teach children to think and feel at the same time. Various studies have reported (Bloomfield and Goodman, 1976; Hansen, 1978; Bendell and Fine, 1979; Edwards, 1979) success in teaching children which feelings correspond with a particular ego state, especially the importance of a strong Adult ego monitoring the feeling activities of the Child ego state.

Successful attempts at teaching children about their feelings involve a labeling process whereby names begin to be associated with both external behavior and internal body sensations. Anger may be identified by loudness or terseness of voice tones, fear with voice hesitancy and sensitivity in the pit of the stomach. In any case, common verbal and nonverbal behaviors are pointed out as signals for certain feelings, signals for each child to think about which sensations are occurring internally. Finally, stroking a straight and congruent presentation of feelings further cements the sequence of feeling, thinking, and doing simultaneously.

Children regularly take the position that they "won't" or "can't" think, especially about what they are feeling or what they need. Such episodes are reminiscent of the two to three year old era when children often say "no" and refuse to think about how they are going to fit in or negotiate a socially acceptable position in the family. To facilitate a child giving up this egocentric and withholding stance, (s)he may be sent to the "corner" in order to cathect his Adult. The corner may be any location (though most often a corner of a room) where the child temporarily separates from others and is forced to think about how to solve a problem. The problem may entail a refusal to perform a task or a hidden feeling translated into obnoxious behavior. Occasionally, the corner strategy will require actual physical placement and maintenance of the child in the corner. For example, seven year old Jimmy may arrive at group fidgety, distracted, and overactive. If he continues to interrupt conversations and hit and poke other children after several warnings, he may be sent to the corner to think about what he needs. He is also directed to think of the feelings he is avoiding and how he can interact with others in a desirable manner. Jimmy can return to the group only after a short period of isolation and evidence of solutions to solve the problem.

An Adult awareness of emotions will permit the child to identify more repetitive and predictable feeling payoffs, and the sanctioning of certain feelings and exclusion of other feelings in the family. Additionally, a child's awareness of which feelings are most uncomfortable to feel and the easiest feeling to escalate under stress will be significant factors in a child gaining awareness of his or her life. Thus, the utilization of further therapeutic strategies is dependent upon a foundation of a thinking position about basic human feelings and needs.

Game Analysis

Because we are social beings, considerable amounts of time and energy are related to how we interact with other people. One part of our time structure involves the use of psychological games and how people use these non-straight transactions not only to fill time, but to gain strokes and reinforce our existential life position. Games, then, become an inevitable part of how children structure their time at home, school and therapy.

The analysis of what games a child plays and his or her roles in those games may be a significant exercise in gaining personal awareness (Chapman, 1971). A therapist may take several approaches in his or her use of game analysis—allowing the game to reach its conclusion, confronting a game early in its formulation stage, or providing a series or crossed transactions which successfully stop the game from concluding with bad feeling payoffs for the participants (Dusay, 1966). The first strategy, analyzing a game at its completion, permits the therapist an opportunity to ask the game players the question "What has just happened and what is your role in it?" Using the Karpman Drama Triangle as a simple way to structure the transactions, each child can begin to identify the name of the game and to see his or her part in the game. For example, Shannon says she wants to get out from between her divorced parents, but counters each suggestion from the group with reasons why she must remain in the middle. After a period of time some of the kids have given up and become silent, others are offering solutions, while others are saying she cannot be helped. Stopping the action and asking the group to focus on the past series of transactions shows the group how each member has moved in to help and after having had their suggestions rejected either withdraw or became angry. Using the drama triangle, the children are quick to see their role as a rescuer or persecutor, and Shannon's role as the misunderstood victim. Through the analysis of game transactions, an awareness arises as to how helpers can become frustrated, how victims fail to solve problems, and how both parties pull away feeling bad.

Confronting a game before it moves to its predictable conclusion is also an acceptable strategy. Most games begin with an identifiable stimulus (some signal or sign) which tip off that a game transaction has been initiated. A confrontation of the intent of the game before it occurs focuses awareness upon the behavior and foregoes the painful negative payoff. A child who plays a game of "Now I've Got You—Kick Me" may say nasty things to evoke a negative and punishing response and thus reinforce his or her own not-OKness (nobody likes me) and his or her view that parent figures are authoritarian and do not understand. A response which fails to produce the intended kick, but instead confronts the child with information that a game has just been initiated stops the negative flow and allows for other alternative responses and options. Also, a sharp parental confrontation which says, "Stop! You are being nasty and provocative!" may shut down the game before it gets off the ground.

Somewhat related to the confrontation approach of game analysis, is the therapeutic use of crossed transactions. Because psychological games are built upon a predictable series of transactions, a response which is not expected may divert the anticipated flow or direction. A child who yells at a teacher "I hate you. You don't care about me," may expect a denial or defensiveness from the teacher. A response which says, "It sounds like you are angry and scared" may disarm the indignation of the child and permit the teacher to quietly touch the real need of the child (which in this case may be his or her need to express anger and be heard without rejection). Similarly, an adolescent boy who complains that nothing goes right for him may be playing a game of "Poor me." An exaggerated response from group members which says "Sounds like things will never work out," or "I agree that the problem is unsolvable" may jam the game signals such that he throws his arms up exclaiming that "he gets the message."

An effective therapeutic plan will utilize all game analysis approaches. Each strategy allows for its own separate level of awareness. Also, one cannot deny the importance of variability and unpredictability which, in itself, is a solution to games set up by children learning how to read and psyche out the system (Hansen, 1978). A therapist or teacher who can spontaneously interject a wide range of appropriate options, models the flexibility he is attempting to teach and lessens his own vulnerability in being invited and trapped into games.

Potency, Permission, and Protection

In its broadest sense, therapeutic potency is the ability of the therapist to bring about speedy improvement (Steiner, 1974). Potency is the power of the therapist to overcome the negative and self-limiting injunctions that the child has incorporated in his interactions with significant others. At times, it is imperative that the teacher or therapist confront the child or adolescent and exert pressure when necessary and appropriate.

This sense of therapeutic potency may be demonstrated by a command or stopper transaction issued from the therapist in order to arrest or interfere in a dangerous situation for the child. A child who head bangs will need to be restrained and given verbal commands to stop hurting himself. A suicidal adolescent will need the force of "don't kill yourself" in order to inhibit the temptation to commit suicide.

Potency is also evidenced in a helping person by his use of therapeutic permission and protection. Permission refers to giving the child the license to disobey an injunction and choose instead to behave autonomously (Crossman, 1966). By aligning himself or herself with the natural and spontaneous part of the person, the therapist sanctions or stamps OK the child engaging in a healthy behavior or disobeying an order which restricts the child from feeling or think-ing his or her own thoughts and emotions. A child who hangs back in group and rarely draws attention to himself or herself, may need for the therapist to stroke the child for any contribution while telling the child that it is OK and good to express what (s)he believes and be center stage while doing it. In so doing, the child experiences a permission to be important and belong. Similarly, a helping person who laughs and has fun, models congruence and spontaneity, thus giving group members a permission to be and enjoy themselves.

Protection, another of the three Ps of therapy, is that part of the helping person's potency which gives to a vulnerable child a sense of security and safety. The therapist's Parent provides for the client's Child protection, especially if the child has rejected a parental injunction and feels the fear and panic of being alone and abandoned. The presence and strength of therapeutic protection allows the child to feel more secure in the new choices (s)he has made to become script free.

Mary, age 16, used promiscuous sexual behavior as a way to get strokes and reinforce her fragile concept of self as lovable and desirable. At times she felt like calling someone up and going out but called the therapist instead, expressing her fear and vulnerability and need to make contact. The therapist responded by telling her that he cared about her and it was important that she hang tough about her decision to stop having casual and unhealthy sexual encounters. In this case, the vacuum created by her new decision was scary and unpredictable, and Mary needed the protection and caring from her therapist to bolster her sense of goodness and OKness and to caringly provide appropriate limits for her behavior.

Potency, permission, and protection are as much a product of the helping person's own health as it is a series of techniques and strategies. The power of these strategies comes from their integration in the personal life of the person. A therapist or teacher must have more permissions than his or her clients in the area in which he is treating them or (s)he is bound to fail (Klein, 1980). The protection, power, and safety needed to cure is inexplicably wedded to the inte-gration of these issues in the helping person.

Energy Work

The child or adolescent comes into therapy having already made decisions about self, others, and the quality of life. The narrowing and constricting de-cisions are a product of uncompleted or unfinished episodes in his or her life where a significant need was not met or a feeling not expressed. Over the years, these unresolved scenes led to a backlog of feelings which are pent up or stored somewhere in the child's mind and body. In some cases, the feelings are ex-pressed indirectly through physical pain and illness, some are displaced onto other objects (drugs and vandalism), while others are manifested in the muscu-lature of the body through posture or rigidity of certain muscles.

Secondly, in the process of game playing, a discount of self, others, or situ-ation occurs which leads to a psychological payoff known as a racket feeling (Woolams and Brown, 1979). Continuing to collect bad feeling payoffs in the present also leads to a buildup of emotional energy in the body. As basic hungers are not met (touching, intimacy, drama) nor closure achieved about expressing feelings, the person may feel like exploding or appear so bound up that some important function such as walking, talking or thinking is impaired.

The dilemma for the therapist is how to facilitate a physical release of those feelings, in order to allow the person freer psychological and physical function-ing. To provide the actual release of long-repressed emotions, as well as more recent and here-and-now feelings, a therapeutic strategy is devised where the child cathects his or her energy into the defended feelings. For example, a child who is angry with his or her mother, may choose to come into group and use a cloth covered bat (bitacca) and pound on the floor while telling his or her mother all the stamps that (s)he has saved for six months.

In some cases the child may come to group very shut down, flushed and withdrawn, signaling that internally (s)he is very escalated, but externally show-ing no reaction. Having the child push on the therapist's hands or wrestle may allow the child to release the bound-up energy. The child will not only feel less tense and rigid, but will have experienced a situation where it is OK to feel feel-ings, and no one died or got hurt.

Anger is the primary feeling expressed in energy work and release may be achieved in many forms. Hitting and pushing objects, wrestling, biting towels and hard rubber objects, or being totally restrained while moving into an angry rage are all vehicles for the child or adolescent to achieve some catharsis of feel-ings. It is not unusual for the angry feelings to cover a layer of fear and sadness, and after reaching the top level of anger, the child may flow naturally into feel-ings of sadness, loneliness and despair.

John, a 16 year old adolescent, came to group one night with a flushed red face while refusing almost all eye contact. Several queries of what was going on produced evidence of him being extremely angry with his parents. Using the bitacca, he was able to release, by yelling and pounding, the anger pent up around his parents not trusting him and not appreciating his efforts in keeping the house clean. Similarly, Rich was restrained by six to eight members of the group and several old memories surfaced—the memories of having his ear drums punctured at the doctors, and his resentment of being ostracized and teased for not being able to hear. The repressed anger emerged in a rage capable of hurting and killing, followed by the sobs of a boy who felt alone, and closed out from his peers.

Whether the situation is current or archaic, energy work allows the move-ment of organs and muscles which flinched or constricted at the time the need and feeling was repressed (Erskine, 1980). This flow of feeling energy coincides with the emergence of script beliefs formulated during the event or situation. As such, energy work involves all levels of change—affective, cognitive, behavioral and neuromuscular.

Energy work, though an important therapeutic strategy, needs to be used by therapists comfortable with physical contact with children and adolescents, especially contact requiring the expression of intense emotions. A child who needs to express feelings at an intense level demands a potent therapist who is not afraid of the child's emotions and who can provide safety and assurance for himself or herself and others.

Ego State Dialogues

A particularly useful process in working with preadolescent and adolescent age children is structuring a dialogue between two or more of the child's ego states. This process externalizes the conflicts which is already occurring internally and brings into Adult awareness the positions of competing and conflicting ego states. The therapist facilitates the child in identifying the parts of the personality that are in disharmony and invites him or her to talk to that person or entity as if it were present. The use of pillows, an empty chair, or a doll may help differentiate the two parts and permit the child to have something concrete at which to aim his or her attention. For example, Jason, age 17, was experiencing a tremendous conflict between his maternal introject (mother part of Parent ego state) and his Child ego state as to whether he would continue to live with his father or move back home and live with his mother. In this particular situation, Jason was the confidant and emotional support for the mother, who was experiencing problems in emotional instability and lack of an external support system. The approach-avoidance conflict resulted in Jason being depressed, tense and undecided. A dialogue which began from his mother part focused her concern about losing him, her fear of rejection, and her going crazy. His Child ego state responded with anger about not being able to separate and join his peers, anger at her for not being able to take care of herself, and his wish to grow in a relationship with another woman his own age. The therapeutic gain for Jason was the expression of repressed feelings, closure of several unfinished scenes from the past, and the focusing of his own need for individuation.

The variety of ego state dialogues can be many and varied. Susan's conversation with her nasty counselor at camp, Jim's conflict between the rebellious and adapted parts of him with regard to grades, and Marcie's chat with the part of her that stays sick are all examples of how the therapist may utilize the dialogue technique to increase awareness and solve problems.

A similar therapeutic process allows the therapist to do therapy with the parental introject and thus provide a sense of internal relief for the child who must continually deal with demands of the parents inside his head. Because the introject is an incorporation of thoughts, feelings, and behaviors of the parent (or some other significant figure), a dialogue with the parent will reveal much about his or her personal issues and how he grew and made decisions about his own life. Interventions aimed at meeting some of the needs of the parental introject will relieve the child of the abuse or taking care (rescuing) of that parent. An example of this was Jenny's father who was rejected and excluded by his mother, and told that he was bad and would never succeed. The anger he held for his mother was passed on to Jenny and she incorporated the same sense of badness and failure. An interview with the father part of her was devised which facilitated her dad expressing his angry and sad feelings toward his mother. The therapeutic work with her dad resulted in Jenny not having to fight the internal crazy voices that would call her bad, and allowed her the freedom to relax and succeed.

The ultimate outcome or result of ego state dialogues is the child's shedding of the pathology of the past and a new decision to move forward and experience the present in an exciting and unencumbered manner. This process of making new decisions is known as a "redecision." "In redecision therapy the client experiences the Child part of himself, enjoys his childlike qualities, and creates fantasy scenes in which he can safety give up constricting decisions he made in childhood" (Goulding and Goulding, 1979, p. 9).

The following transcript is an example of an ego state dialogue which ends in a redecision. The dialogue begins when Ann imagines talking with her fatness, and attempts to resolve a continuing conflict in her life by living it in the present and creating a new ending.

Ann: I'm tired of being fat and ugly.
Therapist: Are you willing to try an experiment?
Ann: Maybe. OK.
Therapist: Be your fatness and describe yourself.
Ann: I am soft flab and I bulge everywhere.
Therapist: Tell Ann your importance in her life.
Ann: I am with you all the time just to remind you that nobody wants you.
Therapist: Be you (switch).
Ann: Just go away, I'm tired of being so fat.
Therapist: Be your fatness (switch).
Ann: I won't go away.
Therapist: Fatness, you said you must remind Ann of her not being lovable. Say more about that.
Ann: That's right, she's a blimp! No boy will even look at her! She will never get a date.
Therapist: And the reason you have made up that Ann should not have a date?

Ann: Then she won't be tempted to do bad things.
Therapist: You mean have sexual feelings and act on those feelings. (switch)
Ann: I just though of something. I remember my mom talking about not letting boys do anything to me, and if I did, how bad I would be.
Therapist: And how is that related to your fatness?
Ann: It's like I stay fat so I won't feel sexy feelings. Oh gosh! I don't have to be fat in order not to get pregnant. I can be slim and trim like other girls.
Therapist: That's right, you can.

In this case, Ann was able to bring an archaic conflict into her awareness, and redecide the essential OKness of feeling her sexual feelings and changing her shape.

It is obvious from the description of the ego state dialogues and redecision work that a certain level of cognitive development is necessary. Because the child must have a sense of several ideas simultaneously, this technique is more rapidly applicable for children who have or are near the development of formal operational thinking. Thus, the formal use of dialogues is most promising with adolescent age children who have the capacity for abstract thinking. However, derivatives of this technique with younger children using art work and puppets allows the child to project onto the object the conflicted parts of himself or herself and primitive incorporation of parental figures (Oaklander, 1978). In this case, the more concrete the medium, the easier the child will be able to externalize his or her internal feelings, ideas, and fantasies.

SUMMARY

Recent estimates of emotional problems in children and adolescents suggest that there is a continuing need for text sources which offer a workable and a realistic set of intervention strategies for working with this population. Transactional Analysis is a theory of personality and system of psychotherapy techniques designed to help people understand and change their feelings and behaviors.

TA is an interpersonal theory that focuses upon relationships between people. The theory outlines the importance of how we transact with others, the beliefs we develop about ourselves and others, and the defensive maneuvers we employ to maintain our belief systems.

Intevention strategies from a TA perspective are aimed at analyzing troubled and broken transactions, discovering hidden decisions about self and others, investigating script themes in a child's life, and helping the child make healthy decisions about how to live differently in the present and the future.

REFERENCES

Anthony, E. J. Psychoneurotic disorders of Childhood. In A. M. Freedman and H. Kaplan (Eds.), *Comprehensive textbook of psychiatry*. Baltimore, Maryland: Williams & Hopkins, 1967.

Axline, V. M. *Play therapy*. New York, New York: Ballantine Books, 1947.

Babcock, D. E. and Keepers, T. D. *Raising kids OK*. New York, New York: Grove Press, 1976.

Becker, W. C. *Parents are teachers*. Champaign, Illinois: Research Press, 1971.

Bendell, D. and Fine, M. Increasing personal responsibility in acting-out boys. *Transactional Analysis Journal*, 1979, *9*, 85–87.

Bloomfield, B. and Goodman, C. A TA approach to children's feelings. *Transactional Analysis Journal*, 1976, *6*, 323–325.

Berne, E. *Games people play*. New York, New York: Grove Press, 1964.

Chapman, A. A. *The games children play*. New York, New York: Berkley Publishing Corp., 1971.

Crossman, P. Permission and protection. *Transactional Analysis Bulletin*, 1966, *19*, 152.

Dreikurs, R. and Grey, L. A. *A new approach to discipline: Logical consequence*. New York, New York: W. Clement Stone, 1968.

Dusay, J. Response. *Transactional Analysis Bulletin*, 1966, *5*. 136–137.

Edwards, S. A. Hyperactivity as passive behavior. *Transactional Analysis Journal*, 1979, *9*, No. 1, 60–62.

Erskine, R. G. Script cure: Behavioral, intrapsychic and psysiological. *Transactional Analysis Journal*, 1980, *10*, (2) 102–106.

Goulding, M. M. and Goulding, R. L. *Changing lives through redecision therapy*. New York, New York: Brunner/Mazel, 1979.

Hansen, M. Dealing with the rebellious teenager. *Transactional Analysis Journal*, 1978, *8*, 222–226.

Harris, T. A. *I'm OK—You're OK*. New York, New York: Harper & Row, 1969.

Henry, H. Disciplining in an inner city high school. *Transactional Analysis Journal*, 1979, *9*, 143.

James, M. *Transactional analysis for moms and dads*. Reading, Massachusetts: Addison-Wesley, 1974.

Joint Commission on the Mental Health of Children. *Crisis in child mental health: Challenge for the 1970's*. New York, New York: Harper & Row, 1969.

Karpman, S. Script drama analysis. *Transactional Analysis Bulletin*, 1968, *7*, 39–43.

Klein, M. *Lives people live*. New York, New York: John Wiley & Sons, 1980.

Moustakas, C. E. *Psychotherapy with children*. New York, New York: Ballantine Books, 1959.

Mussen, P. H., Conger, J. J., and Kagan, J. *Child development and personality*. New York, New York: Harper & Row, 1974.

Newbrough, J. R. Concepts of behavior disorder. In S. E. Golann and C. Eisdorfer (Eds.), *Handbook of community mental health*. New York, New York: Appleton-Century-Crofts, 1972.

Oaklander, V. *Windows to our children*. Moab, Utah: Real People Press, 1978.

Steiner, C. M. *Scripts people live*. New York, New York: Bantam Books, 1974.

Woolams, S. and Brown, J. *The total handbook of transanctional analysis*. Englewood-Cliffs, New Jersey: Prentice-Hall, 1979.

PART III

Additional Considerations

10

A Holistic Approach to the Assessment of Emotionally Disturbed Children

ROBERT G. HARRINGTON

Mark was a husky eight-year-old boy who attended elementary school in a small town in the midwest. His teacher had been concerned for some time because Mark seemed quite sullen, withdrawn and lethargic. He would get into frequent fights on the playground and his school work was getting progressively worse. Mark seemed to have no friends and other students made fun of him in class. Mark's parents reported that he had been obstinate at home lately and constantly teased and fought with his younger brother. Mark refused to talk with his parents about the problem. With permission of his parent's, Mark's third grade teacher referred him for psychological assessment to see if some emotional disturbance was at the root of the problem.

A referral such as this one raises a number of important questions for the psychologist. How should the assessment proceed? Should the problem be diagnosed, classified and labeled? What assessment instruments should be used? Are the assessment results valid and reliable? What other information should the assessment provide besides a description of problem behavior? How can assessment information be used to determine the presence of emotional disturbance? What direction can assessment give to subsequent interventions?

HOLISTIC ASSESSMENT

It is my purpose in this chapter to present to you what I consider to be a holistic approach to behavior and personality assessment of children, like Mark, suspected of emotional disturbance. By employing this multifaceted approach, a clinician should be in a better position to respond to the above questions and develop an appropriate treatment plan to deal with the referral problem.

How should the assessment proceed? Previous approaches to the assessment of emotionally disturbed children have sometimes emphasized one theoretical approach to the exclusion of others. For example, psychodynamic assessment procedures have historically focused on the identification of intrapsychic conflicts and anxiety occurring during one of the psychosexual stages of development (Erickson, 1982). Behavioral psychologists, on the other hand, have generally discounted such mentalistic approaches. They have sought rather to describe the "controlling" environmental variables that may have shaped the maladaptive behavior exhibited by the child (Nelson and Hayes, 1979). Other theorists have attempted to assess the dynamic organization of an individual's personality traits (Cattell and Dreger, 1977). Phenomenologists have preferred to assess the child's own unique perceptions of his or her maladaptive behavior (Reinert, 1980). The problem with any one of these approaches is that behavior is complex and no one ideology has been able to satisfactorily explain every facet of human behavior (Lanyon and Goodstein, 1982).

A holistic approach does not recognize a single psychoanalytic or behavioral explanation for every emotional problem in childhood. A holistic approach attempts to assess the whole child. Some of the hallmarks of a holistic approach are the following. First, a holistic approach assesses the whole child by employing multiple assessment instruments and procedures and not just one partisan approach. Each of the approaches may provide information about different facets of the problem. Single assessment approaches may be limited due to methodological shortcomings in the assessment device, especially regarding reliability and validity (Cascio and Silbey, 1979). Multiple assessment may increase the reliability of the final assessment results by employing multiple criteria measures (Nay, 1979). A second distinguishing feature of the proposed holistic approach is that the child's behavior is evaluated in more than one setting, such as in the classroom, at home, or on the playground. It is important to know if the behavior problems are situation specific or generalized. If an individual child cannot meet the behavioral requirements of a particular setting this may help to clarify the extent of the problem and to detail problem situations (Alessi, 1980). Third, the holistic approach requires that assessment be considered an ongoing process. This permits the clinician to reformulate and modify initial impressions as circumstances change or as the child under study develops or otherwise improves his or her behavior (Phillips, Draguns, and

Bartlett, 1975). Ongoing assessment also allows the clinician to follow and evaluate improvement due to treatment (Ysseldyke, 1979). Finally, a holistic approach requires that multiple participants contribute to the assessment process. These significant others might include not only teachers, but also parents, school counselors, peers, siblings as well as the child. It is only by comparing the agreement of each individual's impressions that the most reliable description of multiple facets of the problem can be obtained (Schwartz and Johnson, 1981). At this point, the clinician needs to answer the question, "Should the problem be diagnosed, classified and labeled?"

CLINICAL DIAGNOSIS vs. PROBLEM FORMULATION

With this information a *formulation*, rather than a *final diagnosis*, of the current problem is developed (American Psychiatric Association, 1980). The difference between these two terms is that a formulation recognizes the flexibility of children's adaptive abilities (Phillips, Draguns and Bartlett, 1975) and may permit the examiner to rethink his or her original formulation of the problem and modify original impressions. A final diagnosis, on the other hand, may permit individuals to draw false inferences about a particular child. Furthermore, a diagnosis usually says more about problem areas for a child than where (s)he is coping well. In contrast to diagnosis, a formulation has far more descriptive and explanatory potential (Achenbach, 1982). Certainly, there will be those situations when a diagnostic label must be applied for eligibility and funding for a special placement such as a class for emotionally disturbed children or for third-party payments (Hobbs, 1975; Ulman and Krasner, 1975). This requirement, however, should not preclude the skilled clinician from reformulating the case to adjust the intervention program to the current needs of the child.

ASSESSMENT PROCEDURES

Faced with a referral like Mark's, the clinician might ask, What behavior and personality assessment instruments should be used?" The answer to this question is, of course, that not every facet of the behavior problem can be assessed. This would not be efficient and some of the information would not be useful. What I am about to present to you are five methods of data collection important in the identification and description of emotionally disturbed children. These five sources of personality information include: 1) referral consultation, 2) interview techniques, 3) objective personality measures, 4) projective tests, and 5) behavioral assessment. Each of these methods can supply different types of information and may be more or less critical to the formulation of the case depending on the circumstances of the emotional problem behavior. Consequently, in a particular case one or another assessment procedure might be stressed above the others but the potential contribution of each procedure would always be considered in beginning to formulate the case. Furthermore, information will accompany the discussion of each assessment approach which should be helpful in answering the question, "Are the assessment results valid and reliable?"

REFERRAL CONSULTATION

Even before the child is seen by the psychologist the assessment process is begun by reviewing the reason for referral. Sometimes referral reasons may be vague and imprecise, such as "Mark seems upset," or "Mark is having problems." For the most part, teachers and parents have not been given any direction concerning what should be considered deviant behavior (Algozzine, Schmid, Mercer, 1981). When left to their own resources, teachers have reported over 40% of their students when asked to identify those with behavior problems (Rubin and Balow, 1971, 1978). Moreover, it is not uncommon for this initial referral information to become the basis for all subsequent decisions about the child regardless of any new data provided by the assessment (Goldstein, Arkell, Ashcroft, Hurley and Lilly, 1976). Therefore, the psychologist's initial task should be to identify and redefine the referral problem(s). Not only should the view of the parents, teachers and others knowledgeable of the problem be considered, but also the concerns of the referred child.

One approach is to first consult with the person who made the referral. After discussing the problem and identifying the behaviors of concern, work together to develop an agreed upon definition of those behaviors. Check this definition with others who may have observed the problem behavior and also with the child. The psychologist should look for areas of agreement and disagreement among these individuals. Definitions should be restricted to problems that are observable. Most referral problems will fall into one of three broad categories—those behaviors the referral agent would like to see decreased, increased, or completely eliminated (Alessi, 1980). The first category may include discipline problems, the second academic preparation or performance problems and the third highly unusual or bizarre habits or agressive behaviors. At the referral stage of the assessment process inferences should be avoided. Factual observations need to be the foundation for later, more helpful and credible inferences. Throughout the referral process the clinician should be prepared to deal with possible resistance on the part of the parent and child, especially if neither one had a part in the initial referral nor were aware of the problem (Knopf, 1979). The parents may prefer to think the child will "grow out of it" and the child may feel defensive and angry about being "blamed" with the problem.

INTERVIEW TECHNIQUES

Teacher Interview

The next logical step in the assessment process is the interview. When the behavior of concern occurs primarily in the school setting, the child's classroom teacher is probably the person who can provide the most relevant information about the problem. In that case, the teacher should probably be interviewed first. In order to structure and focus this first interview, the teacher might be asked to keep some daily log or running record of the child's inappropriate behavior prior to this meeting (Irwin and Bushnell, 1980). This type of informal observation may help the teacher clarify the problem definition and severity, and more efficiently specify when the problem occurs most frequently. Sometimes a teacher may be somewhat unsure of all the ways in which a particular child's behavior problem has manifested itself in the class. An informal behavior problem rating scale or checklist could be completed by the teacher to provide a profile of several problem domains. Kiraly's (1977) Checklist of Student Problem Behaviors is one example of such an informal rating scale. The domains covered by this checklist include behavior problems such as temper tantrums, communications problems such as excessive talking, socialization problems including stealing and academic problems such as reading problems. The interviewer should attempt to elicit from the teacher how long this behavior has been a problem; during which class period and time of day the problem is most prevalent; what (s)he has done to deal with the problem; what is the reaction of the rest of the class when the behavior problem occurs; and whether the problem occurs in other classrooms. The teacher might also be asked whether (s)he thinks there is a relationship between the child's maladaptive behavior and present level of academic performance (Hallahan and Kauffman, 1977). The interviewer should also work with the teacher to evaluate the appropriateness of the intervention goals they choose (Walker and Hopps, 1976). Access to the child's educational folder or case file can provide valuable insights into the history of the maladaptive behavior such as previous emotional problems, interventions, placements and school performance.

Besides interviewing the teacher, parents may also be interviewed about such issues as the child's early development and his or her relationship to family members. Of course, how the interview is actually conducted and the meaning one assigns to the interview results will vary depending on the orientation and training of the interviewer. For example, the psychodynamically oriented interviewer may inquire about the relationship of a child's early childhood experiences with his or her psychosexual development (Sundberg, 1977). A behavioral interviewer would emphasize current behavior problems and the operant, respondent or cognitive variables that maintain them (Linehan, Goldried, and Goldfried, 1977). A trait theorist might look for consistent personality characteristics underlying the child's behavior problem. These three distinct approaches need not be mutually exclusive. For example, research suggests that it is not uncommon for some behavior therapists to combine all three of these approaches when evaluating a case (Wilson, 1980).

Parent Interview

Parents may provide a unique alternative perspective to the teacher interview. The parent interview procedures to be presented here could be applied by clinicians from any one of the three orientations represented above. It has been suggested that the parent interview serve the multiple purpose of establishing rapport, eliciting information about the child's problems, observing how parents relate to each other and obtaining historical data on the family and child (Knopf, 1979). More specifically, the examiner might investigate some or all of the following areas depending on the nature of the case (O'Leary and Johnson, 1979). Do the parents agree on what is the problem behavior? Is there something in the child's physical or psychological developmental history which may be influencing the problem? What is the emotional tone of the parents toward their child? When do they see the problem occurring most often? What disciplining methods have they used to control the behavior in the past? Do the parents agree on how the child should be disciplined? What do the parents want done about the problem? How do the parents react to the problem—guilty, embarrassed, angry? Are the parents motivated to change their own behavior? Do the parents believe an intervention can be successful? Have there been any dramatic life changes in the child's environment recently such as a death in the family, a divorce, the birth of a new sibling, a move to a new residence? What are the child's greatest strengths and adaptive skills? Are the parents seeking treatment themselves independent of or in concert with the problems of the child?

Research indicates that the parents' answers to questions about the child's early developmental history will most likely be unreliable and will be biased in either a positive or negative direction depending on whether they perceive a problem or not (Spitzer, Endicott, and Robins, 1978). Nevertheless, the parents' long-term perceptions of the child provide valuable information about their attitude toward the problem. Fortunately, parental reports about their child's most current child-rearing practices do concur with other independent reports (Rutter and Graham, 1968). The reliability of these reports can be increased even further when parents are asked very concrete questions (e.g., Does your child have any nervous tics?) and decreases rapidly when they have to make interpretations (e.g., When is your child anxious?).

Some clinicians may choose to interview the entire family together including the problem child. In this way family dynamics may be observed. Most children are members of a family. They are influenced by that family's conflicts and their lives are shaped by the rewarding and punishing aspects of relationships with parents and siblings. If one accepts this viewpoint, then children's problems can only be understood as an integral part of the family system. When both parents are available, a special effort might be made to ensure that they both participate in the interview. By attending the interview, they affirm their commitment and cooperation in solving this problem. Their impressions of the etiology can be compared for accuracy and bias. By far the most compelling reason, however, for including both parents in the entire assessment program is because involvement of both parents has been positively correlated with reports of successful interventions (Kahn, 1981).

Child Interview

While research has not supported the reliability of most structured child interviews (Fear, 1978), still, some information crucial to the formulation of the case may be gained from such a meeting with the child. In the past, clinicians have relied on some rather indirect methods such as play examinations (Murphy and Krall, 1960), puppetry (Woltmann, 1960), drawings (Swensen, 1968), and indirect questioning (Zubin, 1965), to get the child to provide information which might not have been available by more direct methods. The child's responses to the stimuli have been interpreted depending on the theoretical orientation of the examiner. Research has provided some structured child interview methods which may prove to be more diagnostically useful (Rutter and Graham, 1968; Wiens, 1976).

One such structured interview in particular was developed by Herjanic, Herjanic, Brown and Wheatt (1975). As much as possible the interview permits "yes" or "no" answers and follows the usual content of the psychiatric examination of the child. By using this instrument, clinicians have been successful in distinguishing between disturbed and nondisturbed children (Herjanic and Campbell, 1977; Herjanic, Herjanic, Brown and Wheatt, 1975; Rutter and Graham, 1968). As Rutter, Tizard and Whitmore (1970) pointed out previously, this interview confirms that the more problems a child has in relating to others and functioning in school the more likely (s)he is to need psychological care. Furthermore, when children's (ages six to sixteen) responses on this structured interview are compared with those of their mothers' there is an overall 80% level of agreement. This structured interview format appears to be highly reliable.

As an alternative to conducting a structured interview with the child, the examiner might investigate some other areas using less formal and less structured interview techniques (Greenspan, 1981). One approach is to choose relevant items from some child interview format (Harrington, 1982) or the interviewer may conduct the interview around specific issues or themes related to the referral problem. Some areas which might be investigated include the following:

Does the child's initial perception of the problem match that of significant others? Would the child like to modify his or her behavior? What are the child's feelings toward people wanting him or her to change? What does the child think others would like to see done about the problem? What may limit or enhance the child's ability to meet these goals?

During the interview phase of the assessment process a broad description of the problem from the perspectives of the teacher, parent and child has been the primary goal. The purpose of the next stage of assessment is to more precisely define and specify the parameters of the problem.

OBJECTIVE PERSONALITY MEASURES

By employing standardized, norm-referenced instruments during this phase of the assessment process the examiner can compare the number and types of problem behaviors a child is exhibiting with some standard or reference group. Without these instruments the examiner might be forced to make value judgments about what constitutes disturbed behavior based solely on data from the interview. Objectively scored measures of personality include true-false, multiple choice, and other predetermined response categories. Some are meant to be completed by a parent or teacher, and others require the child to self-report. The rater is required to indicate the degree with which (s)he agrees with specific statements made in the scale. This rating should be based on numerous observations of the child's behavior and should represent current behavior usually within the previous month. The advantages of objective rating scales are that they are efficient, and provide information that is representative of the child's current functioning.

Since there are hundreds of objectively scored instruments for the measurement of child personality development a comprehensive review of these scales is beyond the scope of this chapter (For extensive reviews see Cone and Hawing, 1977; Shea, 1978). Instead, four dimensional rating scales will be presented as representative of the state of the art.

Behavior Problem Checklist (BPC)

The Behavior Problem Checklist (BPC) (Quay, 1977; Quay and Peterson, 1975) is a factor analytically-derived dimensional rating scale. Each of the 55 items represents a problem area which is rated on a three-point scale in regard to its severity. The checklist measures four primary dimensions: Conduct Problems, Personality Problems, Inadequacy-Immaturity, and Socialized Delinquency. Interrater and test-retest reliabilities of the BPC have been high. Ratings by husbands and wives have correlated at approximately .70. In contrast, as would be expected, correlations of parent and teacher ratings were only .23 to .41 (Quay, Sprague, Shulman, and Miller, 1966). Test-retest reliabilities of teacher ratings of fourth-grade children across a two-week interval have been very satisfactory at .82 to .98 (Evans, 1975).

Numerous validation studies have been performed using the BPC. The BPC has successfully distinguished clinic children from their siblings as well as from a nonclinic control group (Speer, 1971). It has also been used to distinguish various groups of problem children such as residents of facilities for emotionally disturbed from normal matched or randomly selected controls (Campbell, 1974; Paraskevopoulos and McCarthy, 1970; Sultana, 1974). Because of extensive normative data accumulated about the BPC (Speer, 1971; Touliatos and Lindholm, 1976; Victor and Halverson, 1976), the BPC is an excellent instrument for determining how similar a child is to a normal or some "disturbed" group. Since items for the BPC were selected from a pool of the most frequently occurring behaviors of children referred to a psychiatric clinic, the scale may be somewhat limited when applied to children in other settings.

Devereaux Elementary School Behavior Rating Scale (DESB)

Spivack and Swift (1967) developed the DESB to evaluate child behavior problems specifically related to classroom performance. The scale contains 47 items defining 11 behavioral factors. The rater is directed to compare the child to the "average child in the normal classroom" and indicate how often (s)he engages in the behaviors listed. The 11 factors include: classroom disturbance, impatience, disrespect-defiance, external blame, achievement anxiety, external reliance, comprehension, inattention and withdrawal, irrelevant responsiveness, creative initiative, and closeness to the teacher.

Test-retest reliabilities for the 11 scales on the DESB have ranged from .49 to .86 with medians in the low .70's (Schaefer et al., 1975; Wallbrown, Wallbrown and Blaha, 1976). Teacher and teacher-aide interrater reliabilities on the DESB have ranged from .67 to .87 with a mean of .80.

Regarding validity of the DESB, when IQ is partialed out, each of the eleven factors has shown low but significant negative correlations with achievement measures (Spivack and Swift, 1966). As grades have gone down, the number of deviant factor scores has gone up. For example, Swift and Spivack (1969) have reported that eighty percent of children sampled with report card grades of A and B had only one or no deviant factor scores. On the other hand, 85% of children receiving grades of D or F had two or more deviant scores and 65% had four or more. This is an important finding since the items selected for the DESB were behaviors thought by teachers to interfere with academic achievement. Likewise, factor scores of emotionally disturbed children have been found to be significantly different from those of normal classroom populations (Spivack and Swift, 1966). In summary, the DESB is probably best used as a screening instrument in situations where the child's emotional problem is school-based and is related to an inability to achieve in school.

Personality Inventory for Children (PIC)

The PIC has 16 separate scales for males and females and 17 supplemental scales. The supplemental scales were assigned to identify more specific areas of parental concern. Each profile sheet contains three validity scales, one screening scale for general maladjustment and 12 clinical scales. The clinical scales are: Achievement, Intellectual Screening, Development, Somatic Concern, Depression, Family Relations, Delinquency, Withdrawal, Anxiety, Psychosis, Hyperactivity, and Social Skills.

The test manual (Wirt, Lachar, Klinedinst, and Seat, 1977) provides a considerable amount of information about test development and profile analysis including empirical validity data for most but not all of the scales. A major validity study has been conducted by Lachar and Gdowski (1979) involving an actuarial interpretation system for the PIC. Over a 16 month period 200 children (mostly ages six through twelve) and 231 adolescents (ages 13–17) were evaluated at an urban university-affiliated clinic. Hundreds of items of criterion information were collected on these children including a preappointment questionnaire, teacher ratings, school information and diagnostic interview results. Those criterion items that correlated significantly with high or low scores on each of the scales were separated by sex and age and also in combination. The range of scores on each of the scales where the relationship with a criterion variable was the strongest was also reported. The results of this study were used as the basis for a computerized scoring and interpretation system.

The PIC is a relatively new objective personality measure but its use at child guidance clinics has increased because it provides more comprehensive and clinically relevant personality descriptions than more subjective measures. Furthermore, the PIC format fits well with the typical parent interview of their child's problem behaviors which most clinicians perform. The historical perspective which the PIC elicits regarding family life style, school performance, social relationships and other environmental factors may also be helpful in formulating the case and developing treatment plans. Differences in profiles from each parent may highlight alternative ways of formulating and understanding the case. The computerized scoring and automated interpretation should make this portion of the assessment process more efficient. Because of its careful development relying mostly on empirically-derived data, the PIC promises to be a clinically useful tool for differentiating emotionally disturbed from normal children.

Child Behavior Check List (CBCL)

Another relatively new and promising objective measure of emotional disturbance is the Child Behavior Check List (CBCL) and its accompanying Child Behavior Profile (CBP) (Achenbach, 1978; Achenbach and Edelbrock, 1979). Unlike other checklists which have yielded either a small number of broad-band behavior problem factors (Quay and Peterson, 1767) or a large number of narrow-band factors (Baker and Dreger, 1973) the CBCL yields both narrow- and broad-band factors. This fact is important because while broad-band factors may represent general behavior patterns, only the narrow-band factors can uncover syndromes that vary with such characteristics as sex and developmental level. Another innovation of the CBCL is that it includes measures of children's adaptive competencies as well as behavior problems.

The CBCL consists of 188 behavior problem items to be rated 0, 1, 2 plus seven multidimensional items related to social competencies. The pool of items for the scale was developed based on existing literature on the assessment of children's problems plus 1000 psychiatric case histories. Parents can complete the checklist in about 18 minutes. There are six separate forms of the scale – by sex and by three different age groupings: four and five, six through eleven, and 12 through 16. Factor analysis of the items on each form of the CBCL has consistently revealed eight or nine narrow-band categories depending on the age or sex of the child. Scales describing narrow-band factors which occur on at least four of the six scales include the following: Somatic Complaints, Aggressive, and Hyperactive. Each of the eight or nine narrow-band factors on each scale loads on one of two second-order broad-band factors entitled Internalizing and Externalizing. The three social competence scales which tap participation in various activities, social relationships and school success are the same for all six forms.

Some of the scales of the CBCL have reported reliability data, but some of these same scales have so few items that their reliability remains in question. There is not much research evidence available for the external validity of the CBCL either (Lanyon and Goodstein, 1982). The CBCL, however, is quite new, and the precision with which the scale was developed promises the potential for satisfactory validity.

The benefits of utilizing a scale like the CBCL in the assessment of an emotionally disturbed child are three-fold. First, the computer scored Child Behavior Profile derived from a parent's response to the CBCL permits the clinician to scan how a child's problems and competencies cluster and how the child compares with normal children of similar age and sex. Second, the Child Behavior Profile provides more idiosyncratic information about an individual child based on the scale profiles than does classification into mutually exclusive categories according to individual syndromes. Third, the scale is potentially sensitive to quantitative assessment of change in an emotionally disturbed child's behavior (Achenbach, 1978; Achenbach and Edelbrock, 1979; 1982).

PROJECTIVE TECHNIQUES

In contrast to the nomethic or group comparison approach to assessment embodied in the checklists and rating scales presented in the previous section, projective techniques represent idiographic assessment methods. That is, one of the primary purposes of projective assessment of the child is to reveal the specific unconscious motives and conflicts influencing a particular child's ego development. The rationale behind the projective technique is that the most significant aspects of personality are not open to direct observation or self-report. The child may employ a variety of defense mechanisms to protect the ego from intrusive anxiety-arousing thoughts. Projective techniques permit the child to respond in some form, usually either verbally or through drawings to an ambiguous or neutral stimulus. These projective techniques are based on the premise that children will unconsciously reject their own emotionally unacceptable impulses and will attribute them to these stimuli. Even more than the other assessment methods discussed in this chapter projective techniques require extensive training, supervision and clinical sensitivity before they can be successfully employed in the assessment of emotionally disturbed children. The selection of one projective technique over another will depend upon not only the theoretical orientation and skill of the examiner but also on the age, mental ability and problems of the child being assessed. Two representative projective techniques will be presented in the next section including the Thematic Apperception Test (TAT) and the Sentence Completion Method. Of course, there are many other projective techniques available including the Rorschach Psychodiagnostic Technique (Buros, 1978; Peterson, 1978a; Weiner, 1977; Dana, 1978; Klopfer and Taulbee, 1976), the Holtzman Inkblot Technique (Hill, 1972; Klopfer and Taulbee, 1976; Peterson, 1978b), and picture drawing techniques (Brown and McGuire, 1976; Piatrowski and Keller, 1978). The TAT and Sentence Completion Method are included only as examples of how projective instruments might be integrated into the total assessment process.

Thematic Apperception Test (TAT)

The Thematic Apperception Test (TAT) (Murray, 1943) is a rational-theoretical assessment technique. It consists of 31 cards, 30 depicting various people and situations, and one blank card. Typically, a child is administered only ten or eleven cards chosen according to sex, age, and problem nature and asked to tell as dramatic a story as possible to each card. The youngster is asked to describe what is happening in the picture, what led up to the action shown, how the story will end, and how the figures feel. The assumption is that the stories will reveal aspects of the youngster's own personality by attributing his or her fantasies, motivations, conflicts, needs, values, and attitudes to the hero in each picture. The more intense an attitude or need is, the more often the theme will occur in the stories and less ambiguous pictures tend to produce longer and more reliable stories than more ambiguous pictures.

The Children's Apperception Test (CAT) (Bellak and Bellak, 1974) is an adaptation of the TAT for children up through age ten. Anthropomorphic animals in a variety of situations replace human figures in the drawings. The situations are meant to elicit children's unconscious attitudes toward parents, peers, aggression, fear, loneliness and other personality characteristics.

The TAT and its companion, the CAT, currently represent two of the most widely used methods for the clinical assessment of the inner personality structure of emotionally disturbed children. Despite this fact, the instruments lack formal normative data, and have low reported reliability and validity (Holt, 1978; Swartz, 1978). The response to this criticism of the TAT, as with most other projective tests, is that the clinical validity of the TAT needs to be established for each investigator because the "measuring instrument is not the test, but the test plus interpreter" (Rabin, 1981, p. 94). It is further argued that the TAT is not generally used in isolation and its validity is increased when used with other methods.

The clinical value of the TAT and CAT seems to be that the examiner can directly observe some of the feelings a child may have regarding the referral problem. In fact, the more undeveloped egos of children may permit less awareness and/or concern about direct projection of needs onto the projective protocol (Swartz, 1978). For a child who is shy or reluctant to be interviewed or who has repressed some of his feelings about the problem, the TAT could be an excellent method for uncovering pertinent material unavailable through more direct methods (Koppitz, 1982).

Sentence Completion Method

Another projective technique widely used by clinicians is the sentence completion method. The procedure consists of a set of incomplete sentences that the child is asked to finish, as "My mother and I _____" or "In the future there are going to be _____". Depending on the test, a child may be asked to complete between 40 to 100 stems. The Rotter Incomplete Sentences Blank (ISB) (Rotter and Rafferty, 1950) enjoys the widest use. The rationale is that the trained clinician can infer how the child feels about the problem in question by the consistency of themes found in the completed sentences. Some examiners may prefer to use the rationally derived scoring system accompanying the ISB. It yields a single index of adjustment–maladjustment. Each response can be scored on a seven-point scale as to whether the response is a Conflicted, Neutral, or Positive reaction. Relatively high reliability and validity have been reported in the ISB manual for this maladjustment index and have been substantiated in later studies (Goldberg, 1965).

The incomplete sentence method can be a useful clinical instrument for several reasons. It is quickly and easily administered either to individuals or groups of children. Sentence stems can be read aloud to nonreaders and responses can be dictated to the examiner when a child cannot write well. The method is flexible. There is a wide variety of sentence completion blanks available aimed at addressing such areas as peer relationships, school work, family attitudes, and anxiety. It is also possible for a clinician to adapt an existing scale or to add some stems specifically related to the referral problem. (Reinert, 1980). One of the drawbacks of the sentence completion method is that it elicits little unconscious or involuntary information. Explicit stems make it fairly clear what psychological issue is being raised. Consequently, precocious children may choose to reveal little about their inner conflicts and concerns by giving a humorous or evasive response. Less intelligent children may give stereotypes or one-word answers. Incomplete sentences are most helpful when the child is motivated and capable of sharing his feelings with the examiner. Murstein (1965) has called this method "probably the most valid of all projective techniques" because of its use in predicting selected criteria consistent with the response mode of the test, i.e., verbal and consciously controllable material. Probably the best use of this method with emotionally disturbed children is to delineate several problem-related themes and to clinically assess affective reactions toward those themes. This data should provide some good insights into which environments, relationships or situations will require further investigation in the next phase of the assessment process.

BEHAVIORAL ASSESSMENT

The purpose of the previously discussed assessment approaches have been to answer the following questions: What is the operational (i.e., public and observable) definition of the problem behavior? When and where does this behavior occur most frequently? Is this behavior normal or abnormal for this child's age? What role have significant others played in the development of this behavior? What has been the reaction of the child and others to this problem behavior? What is the motivation to change behavior on the part of the child and others involved with this problem behavior? Having answered these questions, one more question must be asked before any conclusions can be arrived at how to formulate the case. "How is this child's problem behavior maintained or controlled?" That is, are there factors in this child's daily life that precipitate these behavior recurrences? The method proposed to answer this question is behavioral assessment.

The goal of clinical behavioral assessment is to target certain maladaptive behaviors, carefully define them and systematically observe and record them, usually as they occur in the child's natural environment. Sometimes the behaviors of significant others will simultaneously be observed and recorded in order to assess their influence on the target behaviors. These records are then used to identify who or what in the environment is eliciting or cueing the child's maladaptive behavior and how this behavior is being reinforced or maintained. These controlling variables are called antecedents and consequences (O'Leary, 1979).

Contrary to what might be expected, clinical behavior assessment techniques and traditional trait and psychodynamic measures are not necessarily incompatible (Wade, Baker, and Hartmann, 1979). Clinical behavior assessment recognizes that the cause of behavior is a product of both organismic variables and environmental variables (Nelson and Hayes, 1979). Clinical behavioral assessment also recognizes that problem behaviors in children do not only take the form of overt motor events but may also include covert thoughts or feelings.

The first task in conducting a behavioral assessment is to operationally define the problem behavior in concrete and observable terms and to specify the environmental stimuli controlling the behavior (Myerson and Hayes, 1978). One common procedure helpful in completing this task is to have the child, if possible, or a parent or teacher, keep anecdotal records about when each instance of the problem behavior occurs, where it occurs and what else is happening immediately preceding and just after the problem behavior occurs.

The next step is to designate the sampling procedure to be used in the subsequent observation. One of the most widely used sampling procedures is the time sample. Time sampling requires that behavior be observed at predetermined intervals for specified periods of time. For example, observations could take place for one minute during each five minutes of a one-hour session. The advantage of the time sample is that it heightens the representativeness of the sampled behavior.

The clinician must next choose a method of observation (Kratochwill, Alper and Cancelli, 1980). The choices include uncontrolled, or naturalistic observation; controlled, or structured observation; self-observation; and written self-reports. Usually, childhood behavior problems will be observed and recorded by an independent observer as they occur in the natural environment. The advantage of this approach over a laboratory observation is that real-life antecedent stimuli and consequences of the behavior can be observed directly. One disadvantage of the naturalistic observation approach is the cost in time and energy. A second problem is reactivity; sometimes behavior will change due to the observational process itself. A third difficulty of direct observation involves invasion of privacy. This is especially problematic in personality assessment where the behaviors to be observed include such constructs as phobias, aggression or sexual identification. One suggestion which may resolve all three problems is to employ a participant observer (Haynes, 1978). By having observers already present in the setting recording the behaviors, the clinician can be saved the time involved in directly observing the behaviors, reactivity to an outside observer is avoided, and the privacy of the situation can be maintained.

The final step in the process of behavioral assessment is to interpret the data. There are no standard procedures or absolute criteria. It is generally agreed, however, that observational data should answer at least these three questions (Alessi, 1980): (1) On the average, how frequently does the problem-behavior occur? (2) Is the frequency of occurrence severely discrepant from what one would expect for a child at this age? (3) What are the antecedent environmental situations and what are the consequences of the problem behavior occurring?

Like all other assessment approaches, behavioral assessment must be evaluated for its psychometric qualities. Because of its individualized approach, however, clinical behavioral assessment has avoided, until recently, complying with the psychometric standards of validity and reliability (Curran, 1979; Goldfried, 1979). One threat to the reliability of these methods involves inadequate sampling over time, situations, and subjects during behavior observation (Kazdin, 1979). Another is the reactive effect of the observation process on the observed behavior itself. Unreliability can also be introduced due to observers' own biased expectations (Lipinki and Nelson, 1974). On the other hand, the external validity of a behavioral assessment procedure may be reduced when contrived laboratory observations are substituted for naturalistic observations. Lack of standardized observation procedures and norms can also bring the validity of this technique into question. Finally, when behavioral assessments always involve only motor behaviors and never cognitive or affective behaviors, content validity may be called into question (Lazarus, 1976; Lobitz and Johnson, 1975; Patterson, 1974; Linehan, 1980). These are problems which are not insurmountable but which must be controlled if accurate interpretations of observations are to be made.

What has been presented in this final assessment approach has been a rather brief and simplified introduction to the practice of clinical behavioral assessment. Expertise in this area of assessment requires intensive training and supervision. The intent has been merely to place behavioral assessment in the context of a holistic assessment and to discuss its benefits.

FORMULATING A CASE
USING THE HOLISTIC APPROACH

Most probably all of us have seen children whom we have suspected of being "emotionally disturbed." These children may be characterized as showing one or more of the following characteristics (Gearheart, 1980): avoids contact with others, avoids eye contact, displays temper tantrums, disturbances of sleep or eating habits, chronically disobedient, emotional isolation, covert or overt hostility, exaggerated or bizarre mannerisms, disorganized in routine tasks, few or no friends, displays ritualistic tasks, frequent verbalizations about suicide, frequent illnesses, physical withdrawal from touch, frequent unexplained crying, physically aggressive, frustration level is low, rapid and severe mood changes, hyperactivity, refuses responsibility of actions, inability to complete tasks, requires constant reassurance, inappropriate verbalizations and noise, repetitive behavior, inattentiveness, seeks attention excessively, inconsistent academic performance, self-mutilation, inconsistent friendships, self-stimulating, lethargic, severe reactions to schedule changes, out of touch with reality, and sexual deviations. As a matter of fact, most children at one time or another will show one or more of these characteristics (Lapouse and Monk, 1964). If this is the case, then how can the clinician differentiate the emotionally disturbed child from the normal child? One determining factor relates to the differing expectations of others. A behavior acted out in one social or cultural context may be considered maladaptive while in another it would not be. This is one way the values and mores of subgroups of society help define deviance. Another way in which emotional disturbance can be discerned is by its intensity, duration and/or frequency. Maladaptive behaviors which are not severe, which are brief and which happen infrequently are not likely to be classified as disturbed. These determinations of intensity, severity and duration of behavior problems are made in comparison with the child's own sex and age group. For instance, what is appropriate behavior at age five may not be appropriate at age seven. Lastly, decisions about emotional disturbance may also be influenced by the specific situation in which the behavior is displayed. What is acceptable and expected in one situation may be seen as bizarre or disruptive in another.

A logical question at this point might be to ask "How can the five assessment approaches in this chapter be combined to assist in the determination and description of an emotionally disturbed child?" Mark's case, which was introduced earlier, will be used as an example. The clinician might begin by consulting with the referral agent to clearly define the problem behavior. In the case of Mark, the clinician might work to operationally define what the referral agent meant by describing Mark as "sullen and withdrawn." The clinician might cross-check these impressions with significant others such as the parents and try to define what their own concerns might be.

Having operationally redefined the problem, the clinician might continue the assessment process by interviewing Mark's teacher, his parents and Mark himself about the frequency, intensity, duration and chronicity of the problem behavior. By interviewing these people, it could be discovered, for example, that Mark's parents are in the midst of divorce proceedings and his response may not be so unexpected given the circumstances. During these interviews, tentative hypotheses should be developed regarding the causes of the problem behavior. One reason why hypotheses gained through interview techniques are usually only tentative is because the clinician cannot always feel confident that the distressing behavior described by the referral agent(s) is really any deviation from the norm. Standardized rating scales and checklists like the Personality Inventory for Children, the Child Behavior Checklist, the Behavior Problem Checklist or the Devereaux Elementary School Behavior Rating Scale can help the clinician make the necessary norm-based comparisons between Mark's behavior and that of other children of his same age, grade and sex. In this way the clinician may determine to what degree Mark's behavior is atypical.

While the information gained through the assessment process so far may be helpful in *describing* Mark's behavior problem it is not very helpful in telling the clinician *why* Mark behaves the way he does. The medium of fantasy projection in projective tests is a natural way for a young child like Mark to communicate to the clinician the circumstances of his anxieties and aspirations. Projective tests like the CAT or Incomplete Sentences Blank could provide insight into what it is about himself, others or his environment that has made Mark so depressed, fight with others, and fail in his school work. Furthermore, the tests may reveal how Mark feels about his future and his motivation to change.

Another approach which may tell the clinician more about the causes of Mark's behavior and some clues as to how it might be controlled is behavioral assessment. A systematic behavioral observation could help determine how the environmental context may be reinforcing his fights with his brother or his refusal to talk with his parents. A behavioral assessment could also provide data regarding how environmental stimuli could be controlled or how naturally occurring rewards and punishments could be used to modify Mark's behavior.

Mark's case illustrates how complex the assessment of emotional disturbance can be and that no single assessment approach alone can be used to adequately formulate a referral problem. Each approach has its advantages and disadvantages and the limited reliability and validity of decisions based on a single approach may be increased when multiple methods are combined (Nay, 1979). Each approach contributes some unique bit of information to the holistic assessment of the child.

LINKING ASSESSMENT AND INTERVENTION

Multifactored assessment and a holistic formulation of the case can be the key to appropriate interventions with emotionally disturbed children. The problem is that psychologists may not make the link between their assessment results and their interventions. Their assessments may not answer the ultimate question, "What direction can this assessment provide for subsequent interventions?" This becomes even more of a problem in cases where the psychologist is not providing the treatment directly. When parents, teachers, counselors or other psychologists are treating the child they vitally need "linkages" between assessment and treatment made for them by the clinician (Bagnato, 1980). Three reasons why psychologists may not make the appropriate assessment-intervention linkages include: failure to identify the original purpose(s) of the assessment; vague, imprecise presentation of functional information in psychological reports; and failure to link the child's needs to specific intervention goals and targets (Bagnato and Neisworth, 1981).

When the original purpose of conducting the assessment is not identified, the meaningfulness of the subsequent report will be decreased. Some psychologists may assume that the primary purpose of assessment is to predict future behavior. Such predictive statements may be only of limited use to those individuals trying to intervene with an emotionally disturbed child. Three fundamental purposes underlie most psychological assessments. They include redefining the referral problem, detecting whether the problem requires intervention and deciding what factors are maintaining the problem. It is important to have clear assessment questions in mind at the outset in order to link the purposes of the assessment with subsequent interventions.

One of the primary vehicles by which psychologists can make linkages between the purpose(s) for the assessment and later interventions is through the psychological report. Traditional reports often focus on scores on tests. Consequently, they may be filled with jargon that sounds authoritarian, confusing and ambiguous to the reader (Bersoff, 1973). In order to see the link between assessment results and intervention strategies, the reader of a psychological report needs to know the following: How would I as a clinician operationally define the problem behavior? Who is involved in the problem besides the child? When and where does the problem occur most frequently? What do I think is causing the problem behavior to persist? What are the base rates (i.e., how common is this problem among other children of similar age) (Lanyan and Goodstein, 1982)? What are the child's adaptive strengths and weaknesses? How can this test data be used to answer the original referral question?

Beyond linking the purpose(s) of the assessment with the content of the psychological report, a final link needs to be made. That link is between the child's own particular needs and specific intervention goals. Useful assessment intervention linkages answer these questions. What mode of treatment will be most likely to effect behavior change? Should the intervention involve individual counseling, behavior therapy, family therapy, or some other form of treatment? Assessment information should also provide direction regarding who should be involved in the treatment, the likelihood of success in treating the problem, how the adaptive strengths of those involved can be employed to resolve the problem, the environmental variables that seem to maintain the problem situation, and the present baseline level of the behavior problem for use in measuring and comparing future behavior change maintenance, and generalization (Haynes, 1978).

By integrating assessment information in this way, the appropriate links between the *purpose*(s) of the assessment, specific *target* behaviors and matching *interventions* can be made to complete the holistic assessment of the emotionally disturbed child.

REFERENCES

Achenbach, T. M. The Child Behavior Profile: I. Boys aged 6-11. *Journal of Consulting and Clinical Psychology*, 1978, *46*, 478–488.

Achenbach, T. M. *Developmental psychopathology*, (2nd edition) New York, New York: John Wiley and Sons, Inc., 1982.

Achenbach, T. M. and Edelbrock, C. S. The Child Behavior Profile: II. Boys aged 12-16 and girls aged 6-11 and 12-16. *Journal of Counseling and Clinical Psychology*, 1979, *47*, 223-233.

Alessi, G. Behavioral observation for the school psychologist: Responsive discrepancy model. *School Psychology Review*, 1980, *9*, 31–45.

Algozzine, R., Schmid, R. and Mercer, C. D. *Childhood behavior disorders*. Rockville, Maryland: An Aspen publication, 1981.

American Psychiatric Association. *Diagnostic, and Statistical Manual of Mental Disorders*, (3rd edition) Washington, D.C.: American Psychiatric Association, 1980.

Bagnato, S. J. The efficacy of diagnostic reports as individualized guides to prescriptive goal-planning. *Exceptional Children*, 1980, *48* 554-557.

Bagnato, Stephen J and Neisworth, John T. *Linking Developmental Assessment and Curricula*. Rockville, Maryland: Aspen Publication, 1981.

Baker, R. P. and Dreger, R. M. The preschool behavioral classification project: An initial Report. *Journal of Abnormal Child Psychology*, 1973, *1*, 88–120.

Bellak, L. and Bellak, S. S. *Children's Apperception Test* (6th and revised edition). Larchmont, New York: C.P.S., Inc., 1974.

Bersoff, D. N. The psychological evaluation of children: A manual of report writing for psychologists who work with children in an evaluation setting. Unpublished manuscript, 1973.

Brown, W. R. and McGuire, J. M. Current psychological assessment practices. *Professional psychology*, 1976, *7*, 475–484.

Buros, O. K. *Eighth mental measurements yearbook*. Highland Park, New Jersey: Gryphon, 1978.

Campbell, S. B. Cognitive styles and behavior problems of clinic boys: A comparison of epileptic, hyperactive, learning disabled, and normal groups. *Journal of Abnormal Child Psychology*, 1974, *2*, 307–312.

Cascio, W. F. and Silbey, V. Utility of the assessment center as a selection device. *Journal of Applied Psychology*, 1979, *64*, 107–118.

Cattell, R. B. and Dreger, R. M. (Eds.). *Handbook of modern personality theory.* Washington, District of Columbia: Hemisphere, 1977.

Cone, J. D. and Hawking, R. P. (Eds.). *Behavioral assessment: New directions in clinical psychology.* New York, New York: Bruner/Magel, 1977.

Curran, J. P. Pandora's box reopened? The Assessment of social skills. *Journal of Behavioral Assessment*, 1979, *1*, 55–72.

Dana, R. H. Review of the Rorschach. In A. K. Buros (Ed.) *Eighth mental measurements yearbook.* Highland Park, New Jersey: Gryphon, 1978.

Erickson, M. T. *Child psychopathology* (2nd edition). Englewood Cliffs, New Jersey: Prentice-Hall, Inc., 1982.

Evans, W. R. The Behavior Problem Checklist: Data from an inner-city population. *Psychology in the Schools,* 1975, *12*, 301–303.

Fear, R. A. The evaluation interview, (2nd revision and edition) New York, New York: McGraw Hill, 1978.

Gearheart, B. R., *Special education from the 80's.* St. Louis: C. V. Mosby, 1980.

Goldberg, P. A. A review of sentence completion methods in personality assessment. *Journal of Projective Techniques and Personality Assessment,* 1965, *29*, 12–45.

Goldfried, M. R. Behavioral assessment: Where do we go from here? *Behavioral Assessment,* 1979, *1*, 19–22.

Goldstein, H., Arkill, C., Ashcroft, S. C., Hurley, O. L., and Lilly, M. S. Schools. In N. Hobbs (Ed.) *Issues in the classification of children* (Vol. II). San Franscico, California: Jossey-Bass, Inc., 1976.

Greenspan, S. I. *The clinical interview of the child.* New York, New York: McGraw-Hill, 1981.

Hallahan, D. P. and Kauffman, J. M. Labels, categories, behaviors: Ed, Ld, and EMR reconsidered. *Journal of Special Education,* 1977, *11*, 139–149.

Harrington, R. G. *A proposed child interview format.* Manuscript submitted for publication, 1982.

Haynes, S. N. *Principles of behavioral assessment.* New York: Gardner Press, 1978.

Herjanic, B. and Campbell, W. Differentiating psychiatrically disturbed children on the basis of a structured interview: *Journal of Abnormal Child Psychology,* 1977, *5*, 127–134.

Herjanic, B., Herjanic, M., Brown, F., and Wheatt, T. Are children reliable reporters? *Journal of Abnormal Child Psychology,* 1975, *3*, 41–48.

Hill, E. F. *The Holtzman inkblot technique.* San Francisco, California: Jossey-Bass, Inc., 1972.

Hobbs, N. *Issues in classification of children.* Vol. 1. San Francisco, California: Jossey-Bass, Inc., 1975.

Holt, R. B. *Methods in clinical Psychology, Vol. I: Projective assessment.* New York, New York: Plenum Press, 1978.

Irwin, D. M., and Bushwell, M. M. *Observational strategies for child study.* New York, New York: Holt, Rinehart and Winston, 1980.

Kahn, Marvin W. Mental health practitioners. Cambridge, Massachusetts: Winthrop Publishers, Inc., 1981.

Kazdin, A. E. Situation specificity: The two-edged sword of behavioral assessment. *Behavioral Assessment,* 1979, *1*, 57–75.

Kiraly, J. *Checklist of student problem behaviors.* Unpublished manuscript, University of Iowa, 1977.

Klopfer, W. G. and Tulbee, E. S. Projective tests. *Annual Review of Psychology*, 1976, *27*, 543–567.

Knopf, I. J. *Childhood psychopathology*. Englewood Cliffs, New Jersey: Prentice-Hall, 1979.

Koppitz, E. M. Personality assessment in the schools. In C. R. Reynolds and T. B. Gutkin (Eds.). *The handbook of school psychology*. New York, New York: John Wiley and Sons, 1982.

Kratochwill, T. R., Alper, S., and Cancelli, A. A nondiscriminatory assessment in psychology and education. In L. Mann and D. A. Sabatino (Eds.), *Fourth review of special education*. New York, New York: Grune & Stratton, 1980.

Lachar, D. and Gdowski, C. L. *Actuarial assessment of child and adolescent personality: An interpretive guide for the Personality Inventory for Children Profile*. Los Angeles, California: Western Psychological Services, 1979.

Lanyon, R. I. and Goodstein, L. D. *Personality assessment*, (2nd edition). New York, New York: John Wiley and Sons, Inc., 1982.

Lapouse, R. and Monk, M. A. Behavior deviations in a representative sample of children: Variation by sex, age, race, social class and family size. *American Journal of Orthopsychiatry*, 1964, *34*, 436–446.

Lazarus, A. A. *Multimodal behavior therapy*. New York, New York: Sprenger, 1976.

Linehan, M. M. Content validity: Its relevance to behavioral assessment. *Behavioral Assessment*, 1980, *2*, 147-159.

Linehan, M. M., Goldried, M. R., and Goldfried, A. P. Assertion therapy: Skill training or cognitive restructuring. *Behavior Therapy*, 1979, *10*, 372–388.

Lipinski, D. and Nelson, R. O. Problems in the use of naturalistic observation as a means of behavioral assessment. *Behavior Therapy*, 1974, *5*, 341–351.

Lobitz, G. K. and Johnson, S. M. Normal versus deviant children: A multimethod comparison. *Journal of Abnormal Child Psychology*, 1975, *3*, 353–373.

Murphy, L. B. and Krall, U. Free play as a projective tool. In A. I. Rabin & M. R. Haworth (Eds.), *Projective techniques with children*. New York, New York: Grune & Stratton, 1960.

Murray, H. A. *Thermatic Apperception Test Manual*. Cambridge, Massachusetts: Harvard University Press, 1943.

Murstein, B. I. (Ed.) *Handbook of projective techniques*. New York, New York: Basic Books, 1965.

Myerson, W. A. and Hayes, S. C. Controlling the clinician for the client's benefit. In J. E. Krapfe and E. A. Vargas (Eds.), *Behaviorism and ethics*. Kalamazoo, Michigan: Behaviordelia, 1978.

Myerson, W. A., Tizard, J., and Whitmore, K. (Eds.) *Education, health, and behavior*. London: Longman, 1970.

Nay, R. W. *Multimethod clinical assessment*. New York, New York: Gardner Press, Inc., 1979.

Nelson, R. O. and Hayes, S. C. Some current dimensions of behavior assessment. *Behavioral Assessment*, 1979, *1*, 1–16.

O'Leary, K. D. Behavioral assessment. *Behavioral Assessment*, 1979, *1*, 31–36.

O'Leary, K. D. and Johnson, S. Psychological assessment. In Herbert C. Quay and John S. Werry (Eds.) (2nd edition). *Childhood psychopathology*. New York, New York: John Wiley and Sons, 1979.

Paraskevopoulos, J. and McCarthy, J. M. Behavior patterns of children with special learning disabilities. *Psychology in the Schools*, 1970, *7*, 42-46.

Peterson, R. A. Review of the Holtzman Inkblot Technique. In O. K. Buros (Ed.) *Eighth mental measurements yearbook*. Highland Park, New Jersey: Gryphon, 1978b.

Peterson, R. A. Review of the Rorchbach. In O. K. Buros (Ed.) *Eighth mental measurement yearbook*. Highland Park, New Jersey: Gryphon, 1978a.

Patterson, G. R. Interventions for boys with conduct problems: Multiple settings treatments and criteria. *Journal of Consulting* and *Clinical Psychology*, 1974, *42*, 471–481.

Phillips, L., Draguns, J. G., and Bartlett, D. P. Classification of behavior disorders. In N. Hobbs (Ed.) *Issues in the classification of children. Vol. I.* San Francisco, California: Jossey-Bass, Inc., 1975.

Piotrowski, C., and Keller, J. W. Psychological test usage in Southeastern outpatient mental health facilities in 1975. *Professional Psychology*, 1978, *9*, 63-67.

Quay, H. C. Measuring dimensions of deviant behavior: The Behavior Problem Checklist. *Journal of Abnormal Child Psychology*, 1977, *5*, 277–289.

Quay, H. C. and Peterson, D. R. *Behavior problem checklist and manual*. Champaign, Illinois: University of Illinois, 1967.

Quay, H. C. and Peterson, D. R. *Manual for the behavior problem checklist*. Unpublished, 1975.

Quay, H. C., Sprague, R. L., Shulman, H. C., and Miller, A. L. Some correlates of personality disorder and conduct disorder in a child guidance sample. *Psychology in the Schools*, 1966, *3*, 44–47.

Rabin, A. I. (Ed.). *Assessment with projective techniques: A concise introduction*. New York, New York: Springer Publishing Company, 1981.

Reinert, H. C. *Children in conflict* (2nd edition). St. Louis, Missouri: Mosby, 1980.

Rotter, J. and Rafferty, J. *Manual for the Rotter Incomplete Sentence Blank*. New York, New York: Psychological Corporation, 1950.

Rubin, R. A. and Balow, B. Learning and behavior disorders: A longitudinal study. *Exceptional Children*, 1971, *38*, 293–299.

Rubin, R. A. and Balow, B. Prevalence of teacher identified behavior problems: A longitudinal study. *Exceptional Children*, 1978, *44*, 102–111.

Rutter, M., Tizard, J. and Whitemore, K. *Education, health and behavior*. London: Longman, 1970.

Rutter, M. and Graham, P. The reliability and validity of the psychiatric assessment of the child. I. Interview with the child. *British Journal of Psychiatry*, 1968, *114*, 563–579.

Schaefer, C., Baker, E., and Zawel, D. A factor analytic and reliability study of the Devereaux Elementary School Behavior Rating Scale. *Psychology in the Schools*, 1975, *12*, 295–300.

Shea, T. M. *Teaching children and youth with behavior disorders*. St. Louis, Missouri: C. V. Mosby, 1978.

Schwartz, S. and Johnson, J. *Psychopathology of childhood: A clinical-experimental approach*. New York, New York: Pergamon Press, 1981.

Speer, D. C. The Behavior Problems Checklist (Peterson-Quay): Baseline data from parents of child guidance and nonclinic children. *Journal of Consulting and Clinical Psychology*, 1971, *36*, 221–228.

Spitzer, R. L., Endicott, J., and Robins, E. Research Diagnostic Criteria: Reliability and Validity. *Archies of General Psychiatry*, 1978, *35*, 773–782.

Spivack, G. and Swift, W. The Devereaux Elementary School Behavior Rating

Scales: A study of the nature and organization of achievement related disturbed classroom behavior. *Journal of Special Education,* 1966, *1,* 71–90.

Spivack, J. and Swift, M. Devereaux Elementary School Behavior Rating Scale manual. Devon: The Devereaux Foundation, 1967.

Sultana, Q. An analysis of the Peterson-Quay Behavior Problem Checklist as an instrument to screen emotionally disturbed children. Unpublished doctoral dissertation, University of Georgia, 1974.

Sundberg, N. D. *Assessment of persons.* Englewood Cliffs, New Jersey: Prentice-Hall, 1977.

Swartz, J. Review of the Thematic Apperception Test. In O. K. Buros (Ed.) *Eighth mental measurement yearbook.* Highland Park, New Jersey: Gryphon, 1978.

Swenson, C. H. Empirical evaluations of human figure drawings: 1957-1966. *Psychological Bulletin,* 1968, *70,* 20–44.

Swift, M. and Spivack, G. Clarifying the relationship between academic success and overt classroom behavior. *Exceptional Children,* 1969, *36,* 99–104.

Touliatos, J. and Lindholm, B. W. Relationships of children's grade in school, sex, and social class to teachers' ratings on the Behavior Problem Checklist. *Journal of Abnormal Child Psychology,* 1975, *3,* 115–126.

Ulmann, L. P. and Krasner, L. *A psychological approach to abnormal behavior.* (2nd edition) Englewood Cliffs, New Jersey, Prentice-Hall, 1975.

Victor, J. B. and Halverson, C. F., Jr. Behavior problems in elementary school children: A follow-up study. *Journal of Abnormal Child Psychology,* 1976, *4,* 17–29.

Wade, T. C., Baker, T. B., and Hartmann, D. P. Behavior therapists self-reported views and practices. *The Behavior Therapist,* 1979, *2,* 3–6.

Walker, H. M. and Hopps, H. Use of normative peer data as a standard for evaluating classroom treatment effects. *Journal of Applied Behavior Analysis,* 1976, *9,* 159–168.

Wallbrown, J., Wallbrown, F., and Blaha, J. The stability of teacher ratings on the Devereaux Elementary School Behavior Rating Scale. *Journal of Experimental Education,* 1976, *44,* 20–22.

Weiner, I. B. Approaches to Rorschach validation. In M. A. Rickers-Ousiankina (Eds.) *Rorschach psychology,* (2nd edition) Huntington, New Jersey: Krieger, 1977.

Wiens, A. N. The assessment interview. In I. B. Weiner (Ed.) *Clinical method in psychology.* New York, New York: John Wiley and Sons, 1976.

Wilson, C. Chrisman. Behavioral assessment: Questionnaires. *School Psychology Review,* 1980, *9,* 58–66.

Wirt, R. D., Lachar, D., Klinedinst, J. K., and Seat, P. D. *Multidimensional description of personality.* Los Angeles, California: Western Psychological Services, 1977.

Woltmann, A. G. Spontaneous puppetry by children as a projective method. In A. I. Rabin and M. R. Haworth (Eds.) *Projective techniques with children.* New York, New York: Grune & Stratton, 1960.

Ysseldyke, J. E. Issues in psychoeducational assessment. In D. Reschly and G. Phye (Eds.) *School Psychology: Methods and Roles.* New York, New York: Academic Press, 1979.

Zubin, J., Eron, L. D., and Schumer, F. *An experimental approach to projective techniques.* New York, New York: John Wiley and Sons, 1965.

11

The Parent–School–Therapist Alliance in the Treatment of Emotionally Disturbed Children

NATALIE HILL

An historical review reveals a number of shifts and changes in the philosophical underpinnings of the treatment of emotionally disturbed children. Early in the century the child guidance movement addressed the impact of sociocultural and familial forces acting on the child and treatment efforts were essentially attempts to remodel and reconstruct the elements comprising the child's environment. Later, as the influence of psychoanalytic theory spread throughout the country, attention was turned from external to internal variables and personality development was viewed from the perspective of powerful instinctual driver exerting influence on a three-dimensional personality structure. Within this context, external determinants were cast in a secondary role. As ego psychology gained favor, attention was shifted from the drives to the ego, which was freed from its inherited dependence on instinctual drive energy by Hartman's proposition that it contained an autonomous sphere with energies and functions of its own (Hartman, 1964). With this new status granted the ego, its adaptive functions and concomitant negotiations with the external as well as internal world were given a prominent place in the scheme of personality organization. This in turn renewed interest in environmental factors, particularly interactions with significant others in the child's daily life, and treatment methodologies were designed to include these. In response to this need for a systematic therapeutic approach to the child's interactions with family members, family therapy techniques were developed, refined and gained a secure place in the treatment armamentarium for children.

Parallel to these changes occurring in the theoretical and practical field, the late 1960s and 70s spawned a social revolution that altered the very core of family structure. The rising divorce rate, the women's movement, and increasing social tolerance of sexual freedom and alternative life styles caused family constellations to emerge that no longer resembled the established blueprint of traditional family life, either in composition or function. The customs and traditions designed for the two-parent family model that had long served as guidelines for raising children were no longer applicable across the board and required revision to meet the needs of the rapidly growing ranks of new and different family structures.

An equally powerful force in altering our approach to the treatment of emotionally disturbed children was the community mental health movement which reduced the stigma of mental illness by advocating that mental health services be available to all members of society within the confines of the local community. This generated more referrals from schools, physicians, judicial systems and local social and rehabilitation workers, and many of these were clientele experiencing severe difficulties in their broader social adaptation with only minimal internal discomfort, resulting in low motivation for treatment. This segment of the clinic population has probably presented the greatest challenge of all to mental health clinicians, not only because of the motivational problem but the fact that they do not often have the typical personality organization nor supportive resources within their own environment to make them "good" candidates for our time honored repertoire of treatment modalities.

The historical overview presented above is testimony to the fact that mental health professionals have traditionally retained the necessary flexibility to expand boundaries of their practice skills and create new strategies and models to meet contemporary problems. Such flexibility is particularly vital when the parents of the emotionally disturbed child referred for treatment are unmotivated or have certain ego deficits that prevent them from effectively utilizing our standard methods. No child should be denied treatment or professional attention because of parental limitations and it is the purpose of this paper to demonstrate that when such conditions prevail, collateral resources can be mobilized to aid the therapist in his efforts to treat the child.

The enlistment of others close to the child as members of the treatment team has been proposed by others and some years ago Josselyn devoted an entire paper to the notion that "the treatment team be extended to include those people who have significant roles in the child's daily life" (Josselyn, 1964, p. 734). In many cases where parents are incapable of providing the child with the necessary milieu to promote emotional growth or are unwilling to invest themselves in a therapeutic process, school personnel such as teachers, counselors, etc., can be drawn into the treatment program, not only to facilitate a better understanding of the total picture, but to actually supplement the role played by parents.

RATIONALE

The home and the school constitute the two most important environments in the child's daily life, and the problems of the emotionally disturbed child, regardless of the nature and form they may take, are usually manifested in one or both of these settings.

The significance of the family relationship factor in the evolution and development of the child's psychopathology and thus, the importance of the parents' involvement in the treatment program enjoys wide endorsement by mental health practitioners. On the other hand, involvement of school personnel is thought to be a wise but not essential practice and is usually employed for specific purposes such as gaining additional insights into the youngster's problem via information about classroom behavior or perhaps imparting suggestions and advice to teachers on the control of selected behavior problems presented at school. The classic paradigm for therapist-teacher relationships is that of the therapist assuming the role of consultant while the teacher poses as a somewhat passive recipient of advice and suggestions transmitted to her through the greater wisdom of the consultant. This paper suggests that we expand our boundaries in working with school personnel and enlist them, along with the family, as members of the therapy team in ways similar that therapist, teacher, and houseparents join together in providing the therapeutic milieu for a child in residential treatment.

IMPORTANCE OF THE SCHOOL IN THE LIFE OF THE CHILD

Starting school usually represents the first solid separation of the child from his family in the sense that it is a daily separation for the major portion of the day and is mandatory. Whereas day care or babysitting arrangements for the preschooler are voluntary on the part of the parents and well within their control, formal education is not and parents and child both must comply with the letter of the law.

School provides the child with his first exposure to the larger social world where he is required to participate as a member, perform certain functions and become receptive to some form of systematic instruction (hersor, 1977; Erickson, 1968). By the time the child reaches first grade, the number of hours spent in school usually equal and at times exceed the number spent at home, and the relationships he forms within that setting and the experiences he has there can play a major role in his ongoing emotional and social development (Erickson, 1968). Thus, when the child begins school, the central importance of home and family is suddenly rivalled by that of school and teacher. The teacher becomes not only an authoritative figure and transmitter of knowledge but an object of identification as well (Freud, 1965); as the school competes in importance with home as a conveyor of knowledge and social values, so the teacher occupies a part of the child's internal object-attachment world, heretofore reserved only for parents.

A wise educator realizes (s)he is responsible for more than just the cognitive growth of the child and acts accordingly. (S)he passes judgement on many of the child's functions lying outside the realm of academic performance. (S)he must monitor the child's behavior for about one third of the day and intervene and control both the overt and the more subtle vicissitudes of the child's emotional and behavioral life. This places the teacher in a powerful position to influence the child's emotional as well as intellectual growth, and by the same standard (s)he can play a role in the child's pathology.

If the parents and teachers share similar goals and values concerning child development, the child benefits from these combined resources brought to bear on his behalf. In some cases, however, the home and school represent diametrically opposed systems of influence upon the child in terms of development of personal values and social responsibility. In most cases, we can count on the school to embrace a philosophy consistent with a sound code of ethics and training for children, though sometimes certain individuals within that system may fall short of incorporating these principles. We cannot always be so certain that this holds true in the child's home environment and if not, the child is faced with a critical conflict in loyalties and left with intense guilt if one set of values are incorporated at the expense of the other.

An overly conforming youngster might attempt to resolve this dilemma by relating to both settings in accordance with the demands of each, only to wind up with a sense of internal dissonance about acceptable behavior and relationships with others, rather than an integrated and cohesive sense of self and object relatedness. Another type of child might attempt rebellion in one or both arenas which would surely bring him into sharp conflict with those in charge, and create then a struggle between external and internal forces in contrast to the intersystemic one described above (Gordon, 1968). A third solution, and by far the more serious of the possible options is for the child to sense he is in a "no win" situation and to withdraw from meaningful interaction with both sets of conflicting forces. Rarely is a child so emotionally mature and intellectually well-endowed that he can weather such a conflict, select the best of both worlds and discard the unhealthy aspects of each. In the case of a youngster already showing signs of emotional disturbance, it could propel him further down the road to a borderline personality organization. A mental health clinician involved in the treatment of children must recognize not only the value of bringing the parents and school personnel into a working alliance but also the possible dangers of not doing so.

THE PARENT-THERAPIST ALLIANCE

Since I have elected to highlight the value of a collaborative network between parent, teachers and therapist, the omission of extensive discussion of the child-therapist alliance is deliberate and not meant to discount the validity or value of it in any respect.

Children come to the attention of the mental health clinician from a variety of sources. Ideally, the parents themselves are the first to note a cluster of characteristics that signal the child's distress, and initiate the evaluation without undue pressure from outside sources and show willingness to cooperate in the ongoing program prescribed by the therapist. With this type of family, our more traditional treatment approaches are usually effective, and the clinician has the luxury of choosing which modality is most appropriate. (Usually the choices include individual treatment of the child and parents, family therapy, or a combination.) There are even some instances when the therapist and parents can meet together and work out techniques to resolve the problem without the child's direct participation in the process. This is, of course, indicated only when the problematic behavior has been thoroughly evaluated and found to still lie between the child and the environment, and has not become internalized and integrated into his personality organization. It requires a set of parents who are able to examine their own interactions with the child and have sufficient ego strength and flexibility to make the required shifts in their reactions to the child without upsetting their own emotional equilibrium or that of other family members.

The above set of conditions do not often exist with respect to families who come to the attention of community mental health clinics. The contact may have been initiated by the parents themselves, but just as likely they may come by way of the judicial system, the local Social and Rehabilitation Service or quite possibly as the result of pressure from the school. The presenting problem may not be a specific complaint about the child's behavior or symptomatology but that of the parent or parents, as in the case of various forms of child abuse or deprivation and neglect. The family may consist of one parent only or the persons playing the parental role may be relatives or foster parents. Time and money are also more crucial variables than ever before, and both partners of a two-parent family system may quite likely be employed outside the home and not easily accessible for treatment purposes. The rising cost of treatment may preclude the possibility of working with the parents and child separately or as mentioned above, the parents may not possess the optimal internal resources to complement the child's emotional growth requirements. When the referral is initiated and strongly encouraged by an outside source such as schools, judicial system, etc., it is not uncommon for the parents to resent it and use whatever defensive measures available to sabotage the process. They may be angry at the child whose behavior has precipitated the referral and be willing to present him to the clinic so long as they can view it as a punishment tactic, or they may perceive the referral source as well as the clinic as a threat to the integrity of the family unit, and mobilize strong resistences designed to protect them and the child from meaningful exposure to the intervention.

Both external and internal factors can intervene and require us to settle for expedient methodologies rather than ideal ones. When such uneasy alliances are established between parents and therapist, the child can become the victim or pawn and it is important that we give top priority to his well-being at the same time we attempt to establish some kind of benign collaborative effort with the parents.

Working with these families can be a challenge, but at the same time can be a very frustrating experience for the therapist since their attitude and the paucity of personal resources prevent us from practicing our special skills and expertise. Insight-oriented techniques are not applicable, and often erratic work schedules and fluid family structures interfere with a family treatment approach. Even the more flexible strategies of the crisis intervention model are not entirely appropriate since these families usually do not perceive themselves in a state of crisis, which is largely due to the fact that their life style presents a chronic crisis and this particular situation at present does not differ qualitatively from any other.

In these situations the therapist must attempt to engage the parents in the treatment process on whatever level they can participate effectively. This involves an appraisal of the parents' personal resources, both internal and external, which can be accomplished by a skillful practitioner during the course of obtaining history on the child. Quite often the parents will become willingly involved at this stage since they can regard themselves simply as informers and are relatively unthreatened in this capacity. In the author's experience, most resistent parents can be successfully sustained in the ongoing process if they can continue to think of themselves as an informant or collaborator and identified then as a member of the treatment team rather than as a patient and participant in treatment. It is well to realize that it is not really necessary, and at times unwise, to force this issue of treatment participation, as any contact with them can usually develop naturally into a therapeutic encounter when they begin to feel comfortable in the presence of a skillful therapist.

Sometimes, though rarely, the parents cannot be successfully engaged on any level in the treatment program for the child. This can create a power struggle between parents and therapist and while the latter strives to involve them, they are busily designing ways to remain isolated from the entire procedure. On some occasions the treatment of the child is terminated on the grounds that it cannot succeed without some level of parental participation.

It is the author's belief that there is considerable room for disagreement with this approach and that therapy with the child can be of value to him even though the parents refuse engagement. It is here that insights gleaned from ego psychology can be applied most effectively. "When the ego is viewed as having a variable but relative autonomy from both drives and reality, the view provides a very different theoretical base from which to consider factors capable of producing therapeutic leverage" (Finzer and Waite, 1964). A therapist, like a parent and teacher, serves as an identification figure for the child, and this provides him with an opportunity for a positive introject which adds a dimension to his ego, super ego and ego ideal, thus modifying inner structures. Furthermore, a properly designed therapeutic encounter enables the child to define and maintain boundaries and through sensitive and well-timed interventions, learn to tolerate frustration and delay gratification. To maintain that the child could not benefit from such an experience without parental involvement is to conclude that the child is merely an extension of his parents and has no potential for an emotional life of his own. Such claims are never made on his intellectual life, as we always sanction and support his attendance in school without requiring parental support or approval; indeed, on the contrary, if they interfere, legal steps are taken to insure the child his right to uninterrupted education. Why would we do less concerning his emotional growth? When parental involvement in treatment is reduced for any reason, it is more important than ever to coordinate our efforts with others who influence him and play a part in his daily life. One of the most important and accessible resources in this respect is the school.

THE THERAPIST-TEACHER ALLIANCE

Many children who come to the attention of the clinician have already been identified as a problem in school, and a number of these children come to us as direct referrals from the school system.

There has been considerable interest and investment in developing models for effective collaboration between teachers and mental health workers (Caplan, 1961, Berlin, 1962) yet a truly comfortable and smooth communication between the two systems has not yet emerged. A part of the problem is the difference in training of the clinician and the teacher, as the former is concerned with developmental issues and psychopathology, and the teacher has been instructed in pedagogy and the content of her subject matter (Millar, 1966).

Another point of departure occurs when the concerns of the child's teacher are not considered the most crucial avenue of interest to the therapist who may, in his diagnostic appraisal of the child, feel attention should be directed to a symptom or problem other than that identified by the teacher. For example, a teacher may be primarily interested in seeking a quick solution to the child's disruptive behavior in the classroom, which may be seriously interfering with her primary objective of transmitting knowledge to the greatest number of children possible. This is far removed from the therapist's primary objective which is the comfort and emotional growth of the child under his care and treatment.

It is helpful for these differences to be recognized at the outset and that this be done without implying that the therapist is in possession of knowledge and skills superior to those of the teacher. The differences can correctly be perceived as positive ones in the sense that each has a set of observations to bring to the task at hand. The therapist can help the teacher understand what is occurring inside the child emotionally, but the teacher is in a unique position to offer the therapist valuable diagnostic data concerning the quality of the child's object relationships and what types of experiences throughout the day trigger certain responses in the child.

It can be assumed that the therapist will probably never have the opportunity to observe the child engaged in the broad range of relationships and activities that by nature are built into his school experience. Since this information is so crucial to the diagnostic understanding of the child and by association to the treatment plan, it can provide a natural entry to approaching the teacher and other school personnel in a liaison fashion with a collaborative intent rather than in the more traditional consultant role which suggests that the teacher assume the passive receptive position of carrying out suggestions of the therapist. As a liaison in the total process, the teacher becomes an active contributor to the understanding and resolution of the problem and thus a member of the treatment team. Just as a physician might refer a patient to a specialist for a more refined analysis of a given condition, the therapist can enlist the observational skills of the teacher in acquiring more specific knowledge about the child's reactions and behavior patterns, and her daily interactions with him can serve therapeutic aims.

The Collaborative Network Between Parents-Teachers-Therapists

It would be ideal to establish a model for the effective involvement of parents and teachers in the treatment program of the disturbed child, and apply this with minor variations to each case. However, the wide range of problems encountered in a community mental health clinic militate against the use of a rigid methodology for working with families and schools, and the therapist must improvise, compromise, create and experiment with new approaches designed to fit the resources available.

By the time the child is brought to the clinic, the parent and teacher may have already compared notes and attempted some strategies to resolve the problem. Both may be in agreement that the problem warrants professional attention, and a collaborative effort between parent and teacher already established. If such a liaison exists, the therapist's entry can be relatively smooth since no remedial work must be done between parent and teacher. Often this is not the case, however, and the therapist's first task is to become the linking person in the interface between the network members.

The existing relationship between teacher and parents may be a neutral one or on occasion, the battle lines may have already been drawn, and they are locked in conflict over one or more issues pertaining to the child. Resolution of this conflict is desirable if therapeutic work on behalf of the child is to proceed smoothly. Resolution can be difficult to achieve, however, and it is here that operationalizing the philosophy of the team approach is most useful. Since it is inappropriate for the therapist to cast himself in a "therapist" role in relationship to the parent-teacher dyad, he can often circumvent the conflict by enlisting the aid of each in working with him on goals of benefit to the child; thus, asking both sides to become his ally. In so doing, the opposing sides are brought together as team members and energy is expended on pursuing common goals that bind them together in an alliance rather than issues that divide. If at all possible, the therapist should attempt to engage the parents and teacher in working together on a specific task designed to resolve a mutually defined problem related to the child, making them an active part of the therapeutic process via discrete operational techniques. This not only benefits the child by providing a positive intervention but also serves to drain energy from the parent-teacher conflict, and the child's life is further enhanced by the easing of tensions between these all-important figures.

At various points in the collaborative effort, the emphasis may shift from one set of alliances to another. This is dictated partially by the nature of the child's problem as well as the personal resources of those involved. For example, at one point in the treatment course, it may be appropriate for the parents and teacher to play a more active role than the therapist; while at another time a stronger investment is indicated for the therapist-teacher or perhaps the therapist-parent alliance. In the event the parents are unable to act consistently as a positive influence in the child's life, the therapist can often engage the teacher and other school personnel in playing a stronger role in the child's program for the purpose of compensating for the weaker role of the parents. This is not to suggest that teachers be encouraged to perform parental functions nor become surrogate parents to the child; on the contrary, the teacher's role can be expanded to include some therapeutic functions as opposed to parental. The collaborative effort between therapist and teacher in cases such as this would form the core of the treatment program. In the words of one author, "there is no

more felicitous setting for intervention than where children naturally aggregate"
(Levy, 1973, p. 24). At first glance it may seem that this is placing a burden on
the teacher or asking her to perform in a capacity beyond her ability. In reality,
however, the teacher is usually already quite involved with the problematic
child, and is expending considerable time and energy in what may be futile attempts to facilitate his or her classroom adjustment. Designing a therapeutic
role for the teacher, with a more thorough understanding of his or her dynamics,
along with some specific interventions aimed at alleviating his or her distress,
will probably be a most welcome assignment, and should be within his or her
grasp, depending on the therapist's skill in translating theory into practice.

In this three-way collaborative network, none of the participants is required
to perform a role or function beyond his or her existing capabilities or those
limitations imposed by the setting in which (s)he operates. The "soft spot" in
the treatment created by the weakest link can be balanced out to some extent
by strengthening the impact of one or both of the other links in the system.
With pressure on the parents reduced, and anxiety alleviated, energies previously bound up in counter-productive defensive maneuvers can be released
and invested in more positive contributions. A smoothly operating alliance between parents, school and therapist acts as solid framework for the child, and a
secure frame itself has a therapeutic effect. The unity and cohesiveness in his
outer world, among such important persons in his or her life, with whom (s)he
is in constant contact, is validation of the reality of order and harmony, which
provides a strong sense of security and protection. Over time this experience
can aid in the development of unity and solidarity in the child's internal world.

The following case examples are presented to illustrate how the parent-
teacher-therapist collaborative network operates in practice, and how the various alliances can be shifted in function to meet the needs of the child while at
the same time compensate for a rather narrow range of parental participation.

CASE EXAMPLE A

Terry is a nine year old boy referred to the clinic by the school counselor
in early February, midway through third grade. He was an only child whose
parents divorced when he was an infant. Contact with the father was infrequent
and the mother had full charge of the parenting responsibility which, combined
with her borderline personality organization produced a quasi-symbiotic relationship between the two. She worked long hours in a fast-food chain and also
held a part-time job to supplement her income.

Terry was identified as a problem child by the school while in kindergarten,
and by the time he reached first grade the school authorities were urging the
mother to seek treatment for him. She avoided this, however, and when they

became insistent, she moved and enrolled him in another school. Problems soon surfaced in the new setting and finally the mother reluctantly presented the child for treatment.

The school reported multiple problems with Terry, which included academic difficulties in every area in spite of an intellectual potential falling solidly in the average range. Of most concern, however, was the youngster's uncontrolled aggression and defiance which at times took the form of violence directed toward anyone or anything he perceived as an obstruction. His peers were terrorized by him and in turn they excluded him from their activities. He usually sought the company of older boys after school, and was introduced to cigarettes, chewing tobacco, and at one point the mother expressed concern over drugs, although there was no hard evidence to substantiate this.

The mother spent most of the first session defending Terry's behavior, blaming the school for its inability to control him, and minimizing her own problems with him, although it soon became apparent she had little or no control over him herself, and attempted to manage him by bribery or threats. She had a borderline personality organization, was very threatened by the treatment process and made every effort to avoid involving herself except on a very superficial level.

While being strongly resistant at first, Terry was gradually able to develop an attachment to the therapist, and became comfortable and able to share during the hour. The situation at school was slower to change, however, and generally at some point during the day an episode would occur. It became apparent that the therapeutic measures to be taken toward helping this little boy would have to come from the combined resources of the therapist and the school, since the mother was clearly unable to play a sustained effective role. Thus, a strong alliance was developed between the therapist and the school personnel. The third grade teacher, the special education teacher and the therapist became the treatment team for Terry. Pressure was removed from the mother, and she was utilized in ways and on occasions she could be counted on to play a positive role and thus enjoy some success. As her anxiety about treatment diminished, she was at times able to initiate contact with the therapist to seek help in handling specific problems with Terry. By the end of the school year, the frequency of the classroom episodes had decreased, although the intensity of them remained the same.

The mother's remarriage has necessitated a move to another school district, but still within the operating range of the mental health clinic. The step-father is a welcome addition to the total picture, as he is open and warm, and is becoming a strong positive force in the boy's life, as well as in the treatment process. Thus, a therapist-father alliance is developing, and collaborative efforts between the therapist and the new school teachers have been instigated but are more difficult to sustain due to the distance involved. Goals at this point are to strengthen the father-teacher alliance and at the same time attempt to establish more frequent contacts with the parents as a couple.

Discussion

With regard to Terry, the school personnel and the therapist assumed the major responsibility for treatment and worked unusually closely in helping to reshape his emotional and behavioral responses. The mother was certainly a crucial factor in the total picture, particularly in light of the close, nearly symbiotic nature of her relationship with her son. It was apparent that loosening this tie and allowing others to play a significant role in the boy's life was a necessary step in the program. Permitting the mother freedom to remain somewhat distant from the treatment endeavors proved to be therapeutic for Terry, and enabled him to develop a bond with the therapist, further diluting the pathological attachment to his mother. With the therapist available, the school applied less pressure on the mother to provide controls for the child, became more comfortable in performing this function themselves, and involved the mother in Terry's school life in more positive ways. The school personnel worked out a rather creative system of their own in handling Terry since his behavior posed such problems that any one or even two persons would be strained beyond endurance after a period of time with him. The school counselor was pressed into service and would spend time with him for a portion of the day, thus, relieving the classroom and special education teachers. The advent of the stepfather has rounded out the picture, and provided the necessary stability and therapeutic component previously absent in the home environment. While the stepfather is an important link in the alliance network, it is vital that the mother's silent, but powerful influence not be minimized. Her personality dynamics must be taken into account and a role, compatible with these, provided for her or she could easily feel her relationship with her son so threatened and replaced by all these others, she could conceivably "fire us all," take her son and flee.

CASE EXAMPLE B

Sam was eight years old and in second grade at the time of the referral to the clinic, although he had shown severe psychopathology as a preschooler. The referral was made by the teacher toward the end of his second grade year and the parents were in full agreement, and promptly acted upon the recommendation. This little lad was at once recognized by the therapist as a severely disturbed youngster. He was poorly coordinated, had speech problems, quite slow academically and was beginning to demonstrate behavior in class and at home with a definite psychotic flavor to it. For example, he would frequently get down on all fours and imitate animal behavior and sounds, particulary when he felt under stress, and was showing an increasing inability to concentrate and attend to the tasks at hand. He was not a disobedient child, and could be brought under control fairly easily, but his bizarre behavior and inability to relate appropriately to others resulted in him being ostracized by classmates and elicited strong concern on the part of parents and teachers.

The parents were somewhat limited socially and intellectually, and although they had recognized the son's pathology for some time, there was gross denial concerning the severity of it, as they expected he might "outgrow" it. Both parents were quite passive-dependent in character structure and provided a very weak structure and control system within the home. In spite of their limitations, a basic caring and concern for Sam was evident. History revealed some peculiarities from birth and although a neurological work-up had been done as a toddler, no specific syndrome could be identified.

A number of conferences between school personnel, parents and therapist were held, and the school psychologist designed a program to meet Sam's academic needs. All agreed to share in the task of helping him develop more age appropriate social, emotional and behavioral patterns and thus a three-pronged alliance was developed. It became incumbent upon the therapist to caution both the school and parents against expecting any rapid changes in Sam, and it was emphasized that it might take two or three years before substantial improvement could be evident. In the meantime, however, it could certainly be expected that our combined efforts would result in checking the regression and keep Sam from moving further from reality. The therapist spent considerable time explaining and describing the nature of Sam's chaotic internal world, what happened to him at the times he exhibited the bizarre behavior and how he felt, as well as instructing both parents and teachers how and when to constructively intervene to interrupt the behavior pattern. This was done without casting any shadow of blame on these well-intentioned but relatively inadequate parents.

The therapist met with Sam in play therapy and sessions with Sam and his parents were held with some degree of regularity to observe and help them function more adequately in their parenting tasks. The special academic program at school was slow getting started due to some administrative obstacles, and when it finally became operable, Sam's use of it was minimal. After six months of treatment, the mother became discouraged with the total program since Sam's behavior at home was substantially the same, and began to entertain doubts about his ability to change at all. Although scholastically he had not shown improvement and his use of the play therapy hour continued to be erratic, his behavior at school was more appropriate and the therapist enlisted the help of the school personnel in communicating this to the mother. The physical education instructor was brought on the scene and each teacher described the changes observed in Sam's classroom and playground behavior. Knowing that a picture is worth a thousand words, a situation was set up where the mother could come to the school and observe the progress first-hand. The father worked rather long hours out of town and the financial situation would not permit a day off. A time was set up for the mother to observe Sam with his peers on the playground. As the mother observed some concrete changes in her son, this in turn enabled her to continue with enthusiasm her own part of the program.

By mid-fourth grade the youngster's therapy sessions were beginning to organize around some problem discussion as well as play activities, the latter of which had become goal-oriented. At this point in time Sam is in the middle of his fifth grade year with some improvement in academic work, but the major gains still lie within the psychosocial realm. The stuttering has all but vanished and he prefers now to sit in the therapist's office and converse rather than go to the playroom. The discussions have recently focussed on the very appropriate topic of the difficulties involved in adjusting to a new school, a circumstance brought about by the parents move to the country.

Discussion

This case material demonstrates how the school, parents and therapist played equally active roles in the treatment designed for this child. For Sam, the alliance between parents-teacher-therapist provided a secure frame to guard against further regression as well as firm boundaries to contain his impulses and test reality.

The school was a crucial resource in helping the mother understand and recognize her son's improvement which at that time was not in evidence at home nor in the therapy hour. Even if improvement had been noted in the therapy hour, there is no way this could have been so graphically illustrated to the mother as by the invitation to observe Sam on the playground in interaction with his peers. This demonstration gave her a sense of hope which sparked her motivation to continue with her assigned role in the treatment. Family therapy sessions were initially used for educational purposes, as the therapist worked with the parents around appropriately intervening when Sam displayed his bizarre behavior. As he improved, and could be counted on to participate more productively in the family sessions, conflict resolution became the focus. An unexpected and far-reaching benefit from the entire process was realized when the school counselor telephoned the therapist to propose a similar program for another child.

CASE EXAMPLE C

Jerry was referred to the clinic by the school psychologist toward the end of the first semester of his sophomore year in high school. Like so many children, behavioral and academic problems had surfaced during his early elementary years, and it was recommended then that the parents bring him to the clinic for evaluation. They evaded the issue, and each year the recommendation was repeated. By the time he was in senior high the problems pervaded most aspects of his life. He was placed in a Personal and Social Adjustment (PSA) class in high school where his behavior was grossly inappropriate and although he was not an actual physical threat to anyone, Jerry's verbal threats and frequent obscenities were intimidating to students and unbearable to the faculty. His emotional disturbance was manifested by very poor impulse control, low self-esteem and a compulsive eating pattern resulting in obesity.

By early November the PSA teacher who had him in class for a full five hours could no longer tolerate his behavior so he was again referred to the clinic, this time with the strong message that other action would be taken if the parent's did not comply.

The mother initiated the contact with the clinic and Jerry came in reluctantly. The therapist was able to establish some positive contact with him but he adamantly refused to discuss the events at school in terms of his own behavior, projecting all blame for his troubles onto another boy in class whom he disliked intensely. Although the parents made an effort to involve themselves, after five weeks work it was clear that outpatient therapy would not significantly alter the pervasive pathology in this youngster and his family, and would certainly not produce the changes necessary to keep him in the public school system. There was also serious concern about his potential for seriously acting-out in the community. The therapist met with the school personnel, shared her findings along with the recommendation that Sam undergo a 30 day evaluation program in the children's screening unit. The school authorities were at once in complete agreement, and had indeed reached the same conclusion prior to the clinic referral.

The next step was presenting this to the parents and Jerry. Knowing their strong opposition to even outpatient help for the son, the therapist elected to see the parents alone to introduce the idea, and was prepared for a total rejection of the proposal. Surprisingly, they accepted it and agreed to work with the therapist toward helping the son accept it.

Discussion

It seems plausible to speculate that Jerry's problems could have been treated more successfully on an outpatient basis had the parents acted on the school's referral years ago. On today's scene, with the increased collaboration between the school and mental health clinic, it is quite possible that the school officials would have enlisted the aid of the mental health clinician at the time they presented the recommendations to the parents, who might have been able to help them take a more realistic view of Jerry's maladaptive behavior patterns.

At an earlier age, the defense system, now crystallized and tightly organized around projective maneuvers, would have been less stable and more open to change. Also the school setting could have been used as a therapeutic milieu for the youngster, whereas now it has strong emotional associations with conflict and failure.

Had the parents been able to bring Jerry for treatment earlier, it is conceivable that an intervention designed along the lines of that presented in Case example A would have enabled the youngster to remain outside a hospital and make more appropriate use of the school system and his education. The parents could have been eased into the total program rather than coerced, and assigned a role compatible with their capabilities and with consideration of their resistances. There are no guarantees such an effort would have been successful with Jerry, but the results achieved with Terry and Sam certainly lend credibility to the notion.

SUMMARY

This paper has traced the historical lines of treatment of emotionally disturbed children, and shown that modes of practice must shift and change to compliment new insights, the emergence of diverse family constellations and individual personality constructs.

It highlights the importance of the school setting and teachers in the child's emotional, social, and intellectual life and proposes that a collaborative network between teachers, parents and therapist can provide a powerful base from which to launch a comprehensive treatment program for the child, which is particularly useful when parental limitations reduce the effectiveness of the contributions from the family sector.

The author reviews ways that such a network is established and utilized and presents three cases to illustrate the dynamic quality of this approach. The cases demonstrate how the functions of the components of the three-way alliance can be shifted to compensate for weaknesses in the system and thus maintain the integrity of the intervention.

An underlying theme of the chapter is the appeal for continued creativity and flexibility in working with children, and a caution against becoming so rigid in theory or specialized in training and practice that segments of the population are excluded from service.

REFERENCES

Berlin, I. N. Mental health consultation in schools as a means of communicating mental health principles. *Journal of the American Academy of Child Psychiatry,* 1962, *1,* 671–680.

Caplan, G. *An approach to community mental health.* New York, New York: Grune and Stratton, 1961.

Erikson, E. H. *Youth: Identity and crisis.* New York, New York: International Universities Press, 1968.

Finzer, W. and Waite, R. The relationship between accumulated knowledge and therapeutic techniques. *Journal of the American Academy of Child Psychiatry,* 1964, *3,* 709–720.

Freud, A. *Normality and pathology in childhood.* New York: International Universities Press, 1965.

Gordon, K. Psychotherapeutic technique: The application of psychoanalytic theory. *Journal of the American Academy of Child Psychiatry,* 1968, 152–160.

Hartman, H. *Essays on ego psychology,* New York, New York: International Universities Press, 1964.

Hersov, L. School refusal. In M. Rutter and L. Hersov (Eds.) *Child psychiatry: Modern approaches.* London: Blackwell Scientific Publication, 1977.

Josselyn, I. Child psychiatric clinics—Quo vadimus?. *Journal of the American Academy of Child Psychiatry,* 1964, *3,* 721–734.

Levy, L. Natural Service Delivery. In G. Specter and W. Clairborn (Eds.), *Crisis intervention.* New York, New York: Behavioral Publications, 1973.

Millar, T. Psychiatric consultation with classroom teachers. *Journal of the American Academy of Child Psychiatry,* 1966, *5,* 134–144.

12

The Effectiveness of Therapy with Disturbed Children

FREDERIC J. MEDWAY

Estimates indicate that as many as 12 million school-age children and adolescents in the United States suffer from some form of mental health disorder (Kramer, 1976). Although it has been argued that many of these children do not receive needed services (Cummings, 1979), a vast amount of work has been done that deals with the identification and treatment of emotionally disturbed children since the first accounts of psychotherapy with children in the early 19th century. Since that time, multitudes of children with a wide variety of emotional disorders have been seen in numerous settings by scores of mental health professionals. Yet, despite this long history of mental health interventions with children (Shore and Mannino, 1976) the need for these services has not abated, nor has there been any indication of a reduction in the incidence of emotional disturbance in the adult population (Levitt, 1971). Because of this, the value and impact of psychotherapeutic interventions with disturbed children has been seriously questioned.

This chapter evaluates the effectiveness of psychotherapeutic treatments with mildly and moderately emotionally disturbed children by reviewing the research and methodology in this area. The bulk of this chapter focuses on individual and group psychotherapy with children. For the purpose of this review psychotherapy includes a number of diverse, nonbehavioral approaches (e.g., psychoanalysis, client-centered therapy, and play therapy) which rely on

---

factors intrinsic to the therapist-patient relationship to relieve children's emotional disturbance and improve their socialization (Stuart, 1970). As in other discussions of this topic (e.g., Barrett, Hampe, and Miller, 1978), the research base of this paper excludes case studies and reports that do not contain some measure of psychotherapy outcome. In this review, only brief mention is made of outcome studies involving behavior therapy and family therapy. Both these topics are covered in other chapters of this book. Additionally, reviews of outcome research in behavior therapy (Kadzin, 1979; Ross, 1978) and family therapy (Gurman and Kniskern, 1978; Masten, 1979) have recently appeared in the literature.

Finally, although most of this paper reviews effectiveness data as indicated by studies of relatively brief clinical treatments, this chapter also summarizes a number of important considerations in the evaluation of large scale treatment programs for disturbed children. Given the already broad scope of the present discussion and space limitations, other topics have been entirely excluded from discussion. Among these topics are studies of treatment outcomes involving residential placement, correctional placement, mental health consultation, and primary prevention.

Any conclusions that can be drawn about the effectiveness of psychotherapy with children will be dependent upon the methodological rigor of the studies making up the reviewed data base. Although issues of reliability and generalization may be less important in examining mental health programs of clinics, schools, and other agencies than in examining evaluative research which seeks to make cause-effect interpretations (Koocher and Broskowski, 1977), there are a number of methodological issues that are unique to the area of intervention evaluation and a number of methodological weaknesses which have generally characterized previous studies. Thus, before examining this data base it is important to consider those methodological problems which have historically made it difficult to evaluate psychotherapy in general and those problems which have made it difficult to study specific applications of these procedures with children.

METHODOLOGICAL ISSUES IN PSYCHOTHERAPY EVALUATION

Misconceptions of the Psychotherapy Process

The roots of contemporary research on childhood psychotherapy can be directly traced back to the first program evaluation efforts of child guidance clinics which were started in the United States in the early 1900s. Since the purpose of such evaluations was to document the benefits of these clinics to children (Witmer, 1935), the research question was most often posed simply as,

"Is psychotherapy effective?" Although the simplicity of this question may have been adequate enough to serve as a general guideline for evaluating dismissed clinic cases, it served to reinforce a number of misconceptions about psychotherapy, many of which have persisted to the present day.

The first and perhaps most significant misconception is the belief that therapy represents a homogeneous treatment. This assumption underlies virtually every study which compares patients assigned to a therapy group and patients assigned to a control group. In refuting this misconception Strupp and Bergin (1969) argue:

> It is becoming increasingly clear that psychotherapy is not a unitary process but "a heterogeneous collection of ingredients or psychological conditions that produce varying degrees of both positive and deteriorative personality changes in patients" (Truax and Carkhuff, 1967, p. 21). Therefore, the term "psychotherapy," as traditionally used, encompasses a wide variety of techniques and procedures whose dimensions must be isolated and their relative contribution to the therapeutic process made explicit. (p. 24)

This misconception is inherent to virtually any treatment study that fails to define, comprehensively describe, or provide a rationale for the intervention under examination.

The belief that psychotherapy represents a homogeneous process dominated the thinking of researchers for many years. In the last quarter of a century, however, many researchers have circumscribed their focus and studied the effects of one specific type of therapy or have compared one method of therapy with another. Psychoanalysis, client-centered therapy, and behavior therapy have each been applied to a wide variety of mental health conditions and each one studied for its overall effectiveness or compared with one another. In other investigations, the effects of these therapies have been contrasted with indirect interventions such as consultation, or with family therapy, and crisis intervention.

Although specifying the model of therapy used is immensely preferable to examining some loosely defined treatment, this practice is based on a second questionable belief that there are clear-cut differences in the day-to-day administration of different types of therapy. Commenting on the differences in the application of distinct models of therapy, Strupp and Bergin (1969) observe:

> Even in those instances in which psychotherapy is focused upon a specific symptom, it is highly questionable that a *single* technique is being employed. The therapeutic influence (encompassing the person of the therapist in conjunction with specific techniques) is broad-gauged and always appears to proceed on a wide front. For example, the therapist's

influence in psychoanalytic therapy is not stringently or even approximately defined by the techniques of free association and interpretation; similarly, there is more to client-centered therapy than the therapist's empathy, congruence, and unconditional positive regard . . . and behavior therapy employs techniques besides those usually described as characterizing it. (p. 24)

In short, all therapists, no matter how distinct their theoretical statements, appear to share some common ground and "the practice of most therapists . . . always have been a mélange of eclecticism" (Strupp and Bergin, 1969, p. 25). Accordingly, studies which specify a general model of therapy but fail to provide details about the treatment and its application add little to the outcome literature.

Even when the treatment is specified in detail it is often difficult to replicate the results because of a third misconception, namely, that all therapists are similar. It is increasingly being recognized that "psychotherapists are quite heterogeneous along many dimensions (e.g., experience, attitudes, personality variables) and that these differences seem to influence patient outcome" (Kiesler, 1966, p. 112). As Fiske, Hunt, Luborsky, Orne, Parloff, Reiser, and Tuma (1970) observe:

> While the characteristics of the therapists have been considered separately from the description of the therapy, it is obvious that they interact, and their complete separation may not be possible. Thus, the therapist's belief in the efficacy of treatment is a variable of great significance. (p. 730)

Strupp and Bergin (1969) offer a comprehensive review of research on therapist characteristics, styles, and values.

The final misconception of much psychotherapy research is that of patient similarity. In challenging this "myth," Kiesler (1966) argues:

> Far from being relatively homogeneous, patients coming to psychotherapy are almost surely quite heterogeneous—are actually more different than they are alike . . . on just about any measure one could devise (demographic, ability, personality, etc.) these patients would show a remarkable range of differences. (p. 111)

The patient uniformity assumption is commonly made in research with disturbed children. Here it is not uncommon to find comparisons of emotionally disturbed children (or juvenile delinquents, conduct problem children, hyperactive children) and normal children when, in fact, many of the disturbed children are actually more similar to their normal counterparts than they are to other disturbed children. A significant flaw of much psychotherapy research, with adults and children, has been the failure to specify patient attributes and selection criteria (Fiske et al., 1979). When distinctions are made it is typically found that the treatment prognosis is worse for aggressive, acting-out children than shy, withdrawn children.

Spontaneous Remission

Researchers and practitioners have recognized for many years that there are many patients whose mental health problems lessen or disappear over time and with changing environmental circumstances in the absence of systematic therapeutic intervention. However, there has been considerable disagreement and controversy over the percentage of spontaneous remission (or more precisely, improvement as a function of unspecified helping sources) to be expected in the general population.

The controversy surrounding spontaneous remission rates was originally raised by Eysenck (1952). After examining two early survey studies of adult psychoneurotics who received minimal psychotherapy (Denker, 1947; Landis, 1937) Eysenck concluded that every two out of three supposedly nontreated patients showed significant improvement. The implication of this finding was that any therapist should be expected to be able to demonstrate improvement in at least 60% to 70% of their cases, and one would, of course, need to exceed this baseline figure in order to demonstrate the effectiveness of psychotherapy.

Since the publication of Eysenck's original article, his baseline recovery figures have been widely challenged on the grounds that the Denker and Landis studies did not carefully match experimental and control patients, did not employ control groups that did not receive any therapy, and did not use valid improvement and recovery criteria (Keisler, 1966; Rosenzweig, 1954). More recent estimates (Bergin and Lambert, 1978) indicate that the spontaneous remission rate for adult neurotic patients is closer to 43%.

Following Eysenck's lead, Levitt (1957; 1963; 1971) attempted to estimate the baseline rate of improvement for children in need of psychotherapy who did not receive it. Surveying two studies (Lehrman, Sirluck, Black, and Glick, 1949; Witmer and Keller, 1942), Levitt (1957) arrived at a 70% improvement rate for untreated children. In a later paper Levitt (1971) claimed that "results strongly suggest that the so-called spontaneous recovery rate lies somewhere between 60% and 70%, no matter how it is estimated" (p. 476). This conclusion was based on studies cited in Levitt's earlier papers and on the results of the Buckingham Child Survey in England (Shepherd, Oppenheim, and Mitchell, 1966) which compared 50 randomly chosen "neurotic" children with a matching control group of disturbed children who had not received treatment. In this study, clinical ratings of outcome indicated an improvement rate of 65% for the treated group versus 61% for the control group. Levitt was more careful than Eysenck to select better controlled studies on which to base his conclusions and, accordingly, his 60%-75% recovery rate for children has not been as widely challenged as Eysenck's figures for adults.

Recently, Tramontana (1980) has estimated the spontaneous recovery rate for adolescents to lie between 40% and 50%, a percentage closer to the baseline for adults (Bergin and Lambert, 1978) than for children (Levitt, 1971). According to Tramontana: "One can interpret this as suggesting that by adolescence, psychological problems tend to become more severe and chronic than in childhood and thus are less likely to improve without formal treatment" (p. 444). Although the figures reported by Levitt and Tramontana may be used as crude indices against which to judge changes due to child and adolescent psychotherapy, respectively, it is important to note that expected recovery rates vary dramatically from one study to the next, depending upon such factors as the ages and developmental level of children, the nature and severity of their symptoms, and the particular circumstances of their treatment and environments.

Outcome Measurement

The assessment of treatment outcome is a critical issue in psychotherapy evaluation. Since therapy involves an ongoing, dynamic process which varies greatly from one situation to another, numerous outcome measures have been used to evaluate its effects (Waskow and Parloff, 1975). Unfortunately, rarely has the choice of measurement procedure been dictated by an underlying conceptual theory. In addition, the relationships among these diverse measures has been small (Fiske et al., 1970).

Outcome measures used in psychotherapy studies vary on several dimensions. The first dimension involves whether the evaluation is based on internal experiential states such as are measured by questionnaires or personality tests, or whether the evaluation is based on an external measure of observable, discrete behavior. As noted by Strupp and Bergin (1969) the controversy over whether to use attitudinal or behavioral measures "emerges directly from the theoretical and technical controversies surrounding the confrontation between behavioral and more traditional therapies" (p. 57). Limiting assessment to either attitudinal or behavioral measures, however, makes it difficult to test propositions derived from competing or alternative notions of therapy.

A second dimension on which outcome measures vary is the source from whom the evaluation is obtained. In studies of adult psychotherapy the two most frequent evaluative sources are the therapist and the patient. When both therapist and patient ratings are obtained there may be marked variation in these measures depending upon the nature of the evaluation instrument such as the degree of inference required by the judgment and the time at which it is administered. In studies of child psychotherapy, the most frequent sources of information are therapist, family members, and other caretakers such as teachers. Those parties directly involved in the treatment are, however, more likely to report positive results than are independent observers (Garfield, Prager, and Bergin, 1971). For young children, peer ratings have been reported to be highly predictive of psychiatric difficulty (Cowen, Pederson, Babigian, Izzo, and Trost, 1973).

A third dimension is how effectiveness is evaluated. Psychotherapy researchers have generally used one or more of the following types of measures: (1) global ratings of the general state of patient functioning, (2) delimited ratings of specific states of functioning or behavior, and (3) tests varying in degree of standardization, reliability, and validity which attempt to measure patient functioning through objective or projective methods. The measures used in most psychotherapy research are global improvement ratings by the therapist. However, since the process of therapeutic change is considered to be multidimensional, the recommended procedure is to use diverse, multifactorial measures (Strupp and Bergin, 1969).

A fourth dimension involves the point in time at which assessment is taken. Some studies employ global improvement ratings made at the end of treatment. Other studies examine the difference between indices taken prior to treatment and indices taken at the close of treatment. And finally, still other studies use one of the above two methods and additionally incorporate in their design some type of follow-up or long-term evaluation. Global ratings of patient final status appear to be preferable to pre- and posttreatment difference scores in terms of reliability and freedom from measurement error (Green, Gleser, Stone, and Seifert, 1976).

In summary, the bulk of the research on psychotherapy effectiveness has employed many diverse global and nonoverlapping measures, many of which have been administered out of convenience or due to administrative considerations. Because of this, it is not surprising that the effectiveness rates reported in many studies have not exceeded those improvement rates that might be expected based solely on spontaneous remission. The present trend among researchers is to move away from global assessment toward the measurement of specific changes. Nonetheless, not all clients should be expected to show improvement on every measure, but only on those that are most related to the focus of the therapy. The issues involved in selecting outcome measures in psychotherapy are discussed in great detail in the sourcebook *Psychotherapy Change Measures* (Waskow and Parloff, 1975). This volume, sponsored by the National Institute of Mental Health, contains a number of excellent papers intended to aid the reader in selecting the most appropriate change measures. It concludes with a recommended battery for use with adults. Although the volume does not deal specifically with the assessment of children, many of the methodological points raised apply as well to this population, making the book must reading for anyone contemplating the evaluation of an ongoing treatment program.

Problems Specific to Child Psychotherapy Evaluation

The issues of misconceptions regarding the psychotherapy process, spontaneous remission, and outcome measurement apply to the evaluation of therapy programs with both adults and children. There are, however, certain problems that arise when one attempts to evaluate the impact of child psychotherapy that are more unique to this population.

With regard to the treatment of children with emotional disorders, one of the most important problems involves consensual identification and assessment. Despite considerable disagreement over what constitutes mental illness, it is generally conceded that adults with mild emotional disorders experience some combination of personal dissatisfaction, unhappiness, and anxiety that prevents them from functioning effectively in important areas of their lives. Many adults with mild emotional problems do not commit acts that seriously disturb other people or are contrary to social or societal standards. In short, the definition of emotional disturbance in adults is linked to failure to realize certain personal goals. By contrast, as Blau (1979) notes, "children are considered 'disturbed' when they behave in ways that are socially unacceptable to significant adults in their environment" (p. 969). Because the diagnosis and labeling of disturbed children is intimately related to the goals, values, and perspectives of the adult perceiver, normal children may at times exhibit behavior that is evaluated as disturbed and disturbed children may at times exhibit behavior that is evaluated as normal. The diagnosis of the behavior as disturbed will be related to the experiences of the child's socializing agents, the child's behavior in relation to age-appropriate acts, and the child's behavior in relation to social and cultural group standards. This situation has led some writers (e.g., Algozzine, 1977; Rhodes, 1967) to consider such children as "disturbing" rather than "disturbed." These definitional problems have important implications for the identification and treatment of emotionally disturbed children. The identification of emotional disturbance in children rests heavily on the use of rating scales (Quay and Peterson, 1975) and behavioral observations made by those individuals who find the behavior disturbing or who are asked to provide treatment. Many of these measurement procedures are of questionable reliability and validity. The treatment itself is often directed at the child who is presumed to "own" the problem (or at caregivers who are provided consultation to help them change the child) rather than at environmental or ecological determinants.

A second problem inherent in the evaluation of childhood therapy is that treatment programs for children often include significant persons in the child's life in the therapeutic process. In the past 25 years research and practice in family therapy (Sager and Kaplan, 1972), parent consultation and education (Fine, 1980; Graziano, 1977), and school consultation (Meyers, Parsons, and Martin, 1979) has grown dramatically. When the focus of treatment is not exclusively on the child it is difficult to evaluate the source or sources of therapeutic intervention. However, it does appear that many of the improvements noted in children's behavior can be traced directly to changes in the behavior of their parents and teachers. For example, research is beginning to accumulate indicating that parent consultation is at least as effective and oftentimes more effective than direct treatment of children themselves (Cobb and Medway, 1978). With reduced numbers of trained personnel to work directly with children and with the demonstrated effectiveness of indirect service approaches, less emphasis will be placed on direct treatment of disturbed children in the future. The need to separate effects due to treatment of the child as compared to treatment of the family (Levitt, 1971) does not seem to be of practical importance at this time and is less likely to be of importance in the future as the emphasis on preventive and indirect services increases.

EFFECTIVENESS OF THERAPEUTIC INTERVENTIONS WITH DISTURBED CHILDREN

This section describes the results of treatment outcome studies with disturbed children and adolescents. As indicated at the outset of this paper, most of this review focuses on the effectiveness of psychotherapy, although a short summary of the outcome data on behavior therapy and family therapy is also provided. An historical approach is used to review the psychotherapy effectiveness literature, starting with the early evaluation studies and proceeding up through present day research. This section owes much to earlier reviews of this topic (e.g., Barrett, Hampe, and Miller, 1978; Tramontana, 1980) which have summarized and integrated a considerable amount of data. Other than what has been discussed earlier, the methodological limitations pointed out by the individual reviewers are not mentioned until the end of this section. Although a number of methodological advances in psychotherapy research have been made over the years, several experimental flaws remain. These methodological problems are listed at the close so as to limit redundancy.

Research Findings

It will be recalled that the first systematic attempts to investigate the impact of mental health interventions with children date back to the 1930s when child guidance clinics sought to determine the general effectiveness of their practices. Levitt (1957) examined the results of 27 of these early effectiveness studies that were conducted between 1929 and 1955. The studies themselves were conducted at child guidance clinics and family service agencies. Children seen at these centers typically received some form of nonbehavioral therapy such as psychoanalytic, client-centered, or play therapy and the measure used to assess effectiveness was typically a global rating of improvement. Levitt computed improvement rates for 18 studies involving approximately 1200 children which assessed improvement at the close of therapy, and for 17 studies involving approximately 4200 children which assessed improvement at some follow-up period. Levitt's results indicated that approximately 67% of the cases showed some improvement at the close of the therapy and that approximately 78% of the cases showed some improvement at follow-up. Considerable improvement was seen in approximately 35% of the cases at close and 41% of the cases at follow-up.

Levitt claimed that his results indicated that the effectiveness of psychotherapy with children was weak since the improvement rates with therapy were comparable to those rates which might be expected merely on the basis of spontaneous remission. Because Levitt linked his results to the spontaneous remission issue, his conclusion as to the effectiveness of therapy with children was challenged (e.g., Heinicke and Goldman, 1960). In response to this controversy Levitt (1963) followed up his original article with another, more definitive review of an additional 22 studies involving approximately 1700 cases that were published up through 1960. Improvement rates found in these studies were strikingly similar to those found in the original body of studies. Table 1 presents a summary of Levitt's data from both the 1957 and 1963 reviews.

Levitt based his effectiveness rate estimates on generally well controlled studies (Barrett, Hampe, and Miller, 1978), though he did not eliminate studies on the basis of poor methodology. He also did not consider issues of who administered the treatment, how long it was administered, and under what conditions it was administered. Subsequent literature reviews, rather than lumping all outcome studies together as Levitt had done, examined what appeared to be the most experimentally sound outcome studies and drew conclusions based on this sample.

Wright, Moelis, and Pollack (1976) focused on studies which obtained treatment measures both at the close of therapy and at follow-up in order to more fully examine the phenomenon of greater improvement at follow-up than at close. The authors found that only one out of six studies reported improvement in a treatment group relative to a control group at the close of therapy, thus providing little evidence in favor of psychotherapy with children. However, at follow-up, four out of six studies indicated greater benefits for therapy than for control groups. Those studies which showed an increment in improve-

Table 1. Summary of Levitt's (1957, 1963) Findings of Child
Psychotherapy Outcome Studies[a]

Diagnostic group	Number of cases	Percent improved
Neurotic at close	4539	67.4
Psychotic at close	252	65.1
Acting-out at close	349	55.0
Total at close	5140	66.4
Neurotic at follow-up (median interval 4.8 years)	4219	78.2

[a]After Levitt (1971, p. 475).

ment rates from close to follow-up were ones that involved longer treatment programs. Based on these results, the authors argued that psychotherapy with children does appear to be effective, but that there may be a time lag between personality change and behavior change. Regardless of the adequacy of this explanation, their findings do strongly argue for the use of follow-up measures in child psychotherapy research.

Abramowitz (1976) reviewed 42 studies dealing with the effectiveness of group therapy with children published from 1964 to 1973. This research typically focused on the modification of disruptive classroom behavior, withdrawal, poor self-concept, and academic underachievement using a variety of group techniques including activity, play, verbal, analytic, nondirective, Adlerian, and eclectic approaches. Studies were analyzed according to the "box score" technique, that is, in terms of whether they found statistically significant results or not. Abramowitz found that "one third of the studies yielded generally positive results, one third generated mixed (i.e., some positive, some null, and/or some negative) results, and one third produced null findings" (p. 321). Behavior modification groups were found to have relatively good success rates. Abramowitz concluded that the present group therapy with children data base, though methodologically flawed, was not generally supportive of the effectiveness of this type of treatment.

By the mid 1970s the question "Does child psychotherapy work?" was gradually being abandoned and in its place investigators had begun to ask, "What type of therapy, under what type of condition, for what type of child with which emotional disorder has the greater benefit?" Starting with this question Barrett, Hampe, and Miller (1978) reviewed several studies that had not received attention in the previous literature. They did not directly challenge earlier conclusions about the limited effectiveness of psychotherapy with chil-

dren, but pointed out the need to examine important determinants of successful outcomes such as the age of the child and the child's developmental level.
They argued that the limited effectiveness of data may be due more to poorly
designed studies, insensitive measurement procedures, and the use of inappropriate treatment procedures than to weaknesses inherent in psychotherapy per
se.

The focus of the studies included in the aforementioned reviews was primarily on children up to about 13 years of age. Recently, Tramontana (1980)
reviewed the outcome research on therapy with adolescents that appeared between 1967 and 1977. Tramontana located 33 investigations of this topic
with most focusing on delinquents and adolescents with social adjustment
problems. The treatment in most of these studies was group therapy. Tramontana reported a positive outcome or improvement rate at close of 73% for
adolescents who had received approximately seven months of therapy as compared to an improvement rate of 29% for untreated adolescents. A follow-up
rate of 67% based on approximately a three year interval was found for treated
adolescents and a rate of 42% was found for untreated adolescents. The rates
at termination and follow-up were based on different samples, thus precluding
study of incremental effects. Although Tramontana interpreted these results
as indicating that adolescent psychotherapy is effective, he, like earlier reviewers, was less concerned with effectiveness rates per se than with the substantive
gaps in the knowledge base, particularly the dearth of studies seeking to identify factors predictive of successful treatment.

Behavioral Therapy

A considerable body of evidence exists strongly documenting the effectiveness of behavioral methods in treating emotional problems in children (Kazdin,
1979; Ross, 1978). Behavioral methods have been applied with success to the
treatment of childhood fears, social behaviors, hyperactivity, school phobia,
self-injurious behavior, aggression, and delinquency. Positive results have been
found with both direct treatment of children and with indirect treatment of
children using parents, teachers, and peers as behavioral change agents (Bergan,
1977; Graziano, 1977). Smith and Glass (1977), examining the results of nearly
400 studies of psychotherapy with both adults and children, did not find behavioral therapies to be more effective with neurotic clients than nonbehavioral
therapies. Similarly, behavioral parent training has not been found to be any
more effective than nonbehavioral methods (Cobb and Medway, 1978). Nonetheless, it is quite likely that behavioral methods are preferable to nonbehavioral
approaches for certain types of problems, especially for children, who appear to
be particularly responsive to modeling treatments (Rachman, 1972).

Family Therapy

"A therapist engages in family therapy when he sees natural units as parents and children, spouses, or members of the extended family, together as a group over most of the duration of treatment with the goal of improving their functioning as a unit" (Wells, Dilkes, and Trivelli, 1972, p. 191). The practice of family therapy has grown immensely in the past 25 years. Over 200 effectiveness studies have been conducted (Gurman and Kniskern, 1978), occasioning several research reviews which address the effects of such treatments on children (Gurman and Kniskern, 1978; Masten, 1979; Wells and Dezen, 1978).

Research on family therapy generally suffers from the same methodological flaws as that on individual and group therapy (e.g., lack of control groups). Additionally, like research in these other areas, estimates of gross improvement rates convey little information without an examination of the conditions under which family therapy is effective with disturbed children. Nevertheless, general improvement rates do allow for a crude comparison with other forms of treatment.

Most reviewers generally agree that family therapy is no worse than and is often better than individual child therapy or some other type of treatment such as crisis intervention. Gurman and Kniskern (1978) located 19 studies of nonbehavioral family therapy where children or adolescents were the identified patient and found an improvement rate of 71%. This rate is similar to that found for individual therapy of these groups and is not significantly different from the improvement rate of adults in family therapy. This improvement rate is based primarily on measures administered to therapists and patients and therefore is open to the criticisms cited earlier. Behavioral family therapy has also been found to be effective. However, in this type of therapy as compared to the nonbehavioral methods, the child is often not directly involved in the treatment and the dependent measures are parental reports. There is thus a thin, almost indistinguishable line between the term behavioral family therapy and terms involving behavioral counseling, consultation, or training of parents. Guerney's (1964) "filial therapy" has been reported to be particularly successful with children.

Methodological Considerations

Although the research methodologies used in child psychotherapy outcome studies have been subjected to considerable criticism (Abramowitz, 1976; Barrett, Hampe and Miller, 1978; Wright, Moelis, and Pollack, 1976), at the outset of this section it must be acknowledged that psychotherapy research is difficult to conduct in such a way that experimental control is ensured and applicability to real-life issues is preserved. The psychotherapy researcher must be prepared to live with and learn from the variability inherent in different patients, therapists, treatments, and settings. Because of the difficulty in doing systematic research in this area it is no wonder that most articles on child psychotherapy are simply descriptions of clinical procedures or case studies with no real outcome measurement or analysis. Such articles, however, shed little light on particular procedures that may be used successfully with particular types of disturbed children.

Within the last 10 years there have been some significant improvements in the research methods used in psychotherapy studies. Unlike those studies that appeared between 1930 and 1970, most recent outcome studies include some type of control or comparison group with more and more studies recognizing the importance of using placebo-attention control groups (Kendall and Wilcox, 1980; La Greca and Santogrossi, 1980); include more than one or two measures of psychotherapy outcome and sample from wider domains of behavior than global improvement ratings, such as sociometric standing and prosocial behavior (Camp, Blom, Hebert, and van Doorninck, 1977; Gottman, Gonso, and Schuler, 1976); focus on the specific processes associated with therapy success; take place in nonclinic and residential settings such as the schools; and examine the therapeutic impact of personnel indiginous to those settings and paraprofessionals (Fo and O'Donnell, 1974; Tefft and Kloba, 1981).

Nevertheless, a discouraging picture of much present as well as past outcome research remains. The meaningfulness of any conclusions about the effectiveness of therapy with disturbed children would be considerably improved if in the future researchers would:

1. Attempt to relate their therapeutic procedures to one or more conceptual models of behavior or therapy.

2. Provide a detailed description of the type of therapy under examination and present objective evidence that the therapy was being administered as intended.

3. Provide a detailed description of participant and environment variables. Specific information should be presented on the following: (a) the background history and present developmental level of the child, (b) the specific nature of the emotional problem and the means used to identify it, (c) the training, personality characteristics, and expectancies of the therapist (many outcome studies use minimally trained graduate students as therapists), (d) the therapeutic setting including relevant organizational or administrative factors, (e) the extent of group member composition influences in group treatments, and (f) the nature of ongoing supplemental and collateral treatments administered directly to the child or to his or her caretakers.

4. Report the reliability and validity of dependent measures.

5. Collect data at several points in time. This allows one to study changes that may occur during treatment in addition to changes that may be present at close and follow-up.

6. Collect data on individual treatment components. Most outcome studies examine net effectiveness. Although an overall treatment package may be evaluated as unsuccessful, one or more subcomponents may be valuable.

7. Consider the practical significance of reported changes for the child. Researchers should keep in mind that statistically significant results may have little real value in terms of practical and meaningful changes in child functioning.

The Bottom Line

At this point it should be clear that the question, "How effective is psychotherapy with disturbed children and adolescents?" cannot be answered in any way that will meaningfully advance practice in this area. As Bergin (1971) has emphasized: "It is impossible to conclude very much from gross studies of therapeutic effects. It is only when we break therapy down into its components that we begin to obtain clearer results" (p. 238).

Recognizing this fact one still can conclude that the weight of the evidence is supportive of therapy with children. This is important to note since consumers and others who evaluate the effects of therapy often pose their queries in a global way. Not only have methodological advances been made in recent years, but techniques, being increasingly applied to narrow domains of disturbance, are yielding greater results. The effectiveness of these techniques cannot be explained by spontaneous remission. Finally, in a general sense, certain therapeutic approaches do appear to be more effective. These include parent consultation, family therapy, behavioral group approaches involving modeling (Camp et al., 1977; Gresham and Nagle, 1980), and those involving prolonged treatment (Wright, Moelis, and Pollack, 1976).

PROGRAM EVALUATION

Up to this point the present chapter has been restricted to a discussion of the outcomes and methodologies of treatment research. Treatment research involves controlled studies that are designed to obtain reliable information about the effects of one or more specified treatment procedures that may be generalized across different programs and settings. However, often individuals working with emotionally disturbed children need to demonstrate the value of a multifaceted treatment program with a wide range of diverse, interacting services such as may be associated with a community mental health center, a clinic, or one of any number of residential settings. The evaluation and management of large-scale treatment programs is not limited exclusively to measuring the impact of treatments on the lives of children but extends to helping "a program recognize the relationship between what it wants to do and what it actually is doing" (Durkin and Durkin, 1978, p. 321).

"Program evaluation is a type of applied research in which program processes and outcome characteristic are explicitly related to a set of values, such as program goals, objectives, and costs" (Hagedorn, Beck, Neubert, and Werlin, 1976, p. 1). It "is an aspect of program management, and its purpose is to inform program decisions and improve the effectiveness of the specific program being evaluated" (Hagedorn et al., 1976, p. 202). Compared to treatment research, program evaluation is less concerned with issues of reliability, validity, and adequate sample size, and more concerned with how to monitor a program so that it is running as planned and how to obtain periodic evaluative feedback so that midcourse corrections in the program may be made. In evaluating a comprehensive treatment program there are a greater number of variables to study than in researching a single treatment and there is often little real information available on how these diverse variables interrelate.

An evaluation of a treatment program for emotionally disturbed children may be undertaken for one of several reasons. These include: making modifications in the program; demonstrating the effectiveness of the program to local funding sources, state legislators, insurance reimbursers, and the general public; justifying the existence of the program in the face of criticism and opposition, demands for accountability, and potential malpractice suits; and, in the case of community mental health centers, monitoring the program to comply with federal legislation. Public Law 94-63 mandates that federally funded mental health centers allocate not less than two percent of their previous year's operating expenses for continuing program evaluation.

The effectiveness of a mental health program for children is typically measured in terms of (1) its impact on children and their families, (2) the cost of the services, (3) the patterns, usage, and acceptability of the services, and (4) the availability and accessibility of the services. Within these broad domains, a variety of factors are evaluated, including the resources that go into the system, the formal and informal goals of the program, the clarity of personnel role and function, the interrelationship of subcomponents of the system and the relationship of institutional characteristics to organizational goals, the task and maintenance functions of the social system, and the relationship of the program to other systems such as other agencies and the community at large. Multiple outcome criteria are typically employed in program evaluation since different external interest groups may have different views on what constitutes an effective program. Fiester (1978) suggests that successful evaluation systems (1) are responsive to children's individual needs, (2) are comprehensive in the sense of measuring multiple aspects of program functioning, (3) are responsive to therapeutic goals and processes, (4) allow for input from the recipients of the services, (5) disseminate their results in a way that is easily understandable by the lay public, (6) allow for frequent data feedback to the clinical and administrative staff, (7) are minimally intrusive into day-to-day operations, (8) ensure respondent confidentiality, and (9) are cost effective.

Many of the questions asked when measuring the impact of programmatic mental health services on children are similar to those asked in treatment studies. These questions include, Does the treatment help?; In what way?; How much?; How much more than would be expected given spontaneous remission?; and How much more than other treatments? As in a treatment study, the assessment of this data in program evaluation is generally made using therapists' ratings of improvement, some rating of the child's symptoms, some rating of the child's personal, social, and community adjustment, and some evaluation by the child or their parents of satisfaction with the treatment program and clinical personnel.

One technique which is increasingly being incorporated in the evaluation of services to meet children's mental health needs is Goal Attainment Scaling (Kiresuk and Sherman, 1968). Goal Attainment Scaling is a procedure for assessing the accomplishment of specific treatment goals on an individualized basis for each child. This procedure involves the following sequential steps: (1) an identification and negotiation of treatment goals by the therapist and client (or parent), (2) a weighting of the goals in terms of importance relative to one another, (3) a specification of several possible outcomes for each goal varying in terms of how much that particular goal was accomplished, (4) derivation of a total score based on individual goal attainment at some follow-up interval, and (5) comparison of this attainment score to client status at intake. Fiester (1978) developed a modified version of Goal Attainment Scaling called The Automated Comprehensive Children's Evaluation System (ACCES) which is specifically designed to measure utilization, availability, and quality of children's mental health services.

Cost-outcome assessment is another important part of program evaluation that is not as salient in treatment research. The questions asked here are: for a given cost, what program produces the best outcome?; and, which program uses the fewest system resources to produce the best outcome? For each treatment or program all costs and benefits, including social and community ones, are calculated and compared. The procedure involves first delineating the treatment goals for the clients; second, indicating programs to be compared; third, determining program costs for each client; fourth, assessing the effectiveness of the treatment; fifth, comparing cost and outcome data for each program; and sixth, comparing cost and outcome data across programs. The choice of a treatment program is first dictated by its overall effectiveness and then its cost when more than one program is equally effective.

Program evaluation also makes use of descriptive information on the pattern and usage of services. One aspect of this is an evaluation of the therapeutic process as it unfolds in the course of treatment. Huberty, Quirk, and Swan (1973) note "one of the primary mistakes of traditional treatment has been the emphasis on gross change. Restoration of the disturbed child comes, in most cases, from small bits and pieces in the motoric, cognitive, and emotional areas" (p. 77). In their description of the therapeutic program at the Rutland Center for emotionally disturbed preschool and primary school-age children in Athens, Georgia, Huberty, Quirk, and Swan describe the use of an in-process observational system which measures the extent to which children are engaging in various behaviors at different times during treatment. Pattern and usage of services may also be evaluated in terms of an agency's ability to train therapists and paraprofessionals, and to involve the family in children's treatment.

Availability and accessibility involve the extent to which needed services exist and familiarity of the community with the services, and potential cost, location, and/or transportation barriers to effective community utilization of these services. Availability and accessibility can be measured with consumer satisfaction questionnaires (Fiester, 1978). Finally, effectiveness, availability, accessibility, and acceptability of a program may be examined in terms of changes in the prevalence rates of childhood psychopathology in the community, reduction in crime statistics for adolescents, changes in community attitudes about emotionally disturbed children, and lastly, changes in legislation affecting children with mental health problems.

SUMMARY

This chapter has reviewed a number of issues relevant to the evaluation of therapy with disturbed children. The research on the effectiveness of therapy has been summarized and several methodological issues have been highlighted. In addition, an overview has been provided of important issues in the evaluation of treatment programs with these children.

Despite some variability in terms of the methodological rigor of treatment studies conducted over the past 50 years, it can generally be concluded that therapeutic interventions with emotionally disturbed children have demonstrated usefulness. Although success rates of these outcome studies may not be as high as some therapists might like, there is little reason to believe that childhood psychopathology improves as much and as quickly in the absence of systematic intervention as it does with therapy. This is particularly true in the case of the adolescent. Nonetheless, it has been noted that, at best, gross improvement rates provide only a crude estimate of therapy effectiveness; at worst, they are misleading or uninterpretable. Researchers have yet to isolate one homogeneous method that "works the best" with all or most emotionally disturbed children and there is little reason to believe that such a method will ever be found. It has been amply demonstrated that the effectiveness of therapy is dependent upon a complex network of interacting variables involving the treatment, the therapist, the treatment setting, the child, the symptoms, and the child's environment. Furthermore, effectiveness itself can be defined in several ways and includes more than just a reduction in symptomatology. When evaluating a treatment program, issues of cost, efficiency, availability, and accessibility come into play. Because of this, both the focus of much present treatment research and program evaluation is on the specific processes that determine successful outcomes. Success itself is being defined as making small, delimited, but meaningful improvements in the mental health of children. Although the present knowledge base of these determinants of therapeutic success is not as large as might be hoped for, until researchers have further unraveled the variables that make therapy work for children, individual mental health workers and therapists must have a broad-based knowledge of treatment approaches, be flexible enough to use different methods with different children, and be familiar with the evaluation issues raised in this chapter in order to convincingly demonstrate the effectiveness of their efforts.

REFERENCES

Abramowitz, C. V. The effectiveness of group psychotherapy with children. *Archives of General Psychiatry,* 1976, *33,* 320–326.

Algozzine, B. The emotionally disturbed child: Disturbed or disturbing? *Journal of Abnormal Child Psychology,* 1977, *5,* 205–211.

Barrett, C. L., Hampe, I. E., and Miller, L. C. Research on child psychology. In S. L. Garfield and A. E. Bergin (Eds.), *Handbook of psychotherapy and behavior change* (2nd ed.). New York, New York: John Wiley and Sons, 1978.

Bergan, J. R. *Behavioral consultation.* Columbus, Ohio: Merrill, 1977.

Bergin, A. E. The evaluation of therapeutic outcomes. In A. E. Bergin and S. L. Garfield (Eds.) *Handbook of psychotherapy and behavior change.* New York, New York: John Wiley and Sons, 1971.

Bergin, A. E. and Lambert, M. J. The evaluation of therapeutic outcomes. In S. L. Garfield and A. E. Bergin (Eds.) *Handbook of psychotherapy and behavior change* (2nd ed.). New York, New York: John Wiley and Sons, 1978.

Blau, T. H. Diagnosis of disturbed children. *American Psychologist,* 1979, *34,* 969–972.

Camp, B. W., Blom, G. E., Hebert, F., and van Doorninck, W. J. "Think Aloud:" A program for developing self-control in young aggressive boys. *Journal of Abnormal Child Psychology,* 1977, *5,* 157–169.

Cobb, D. E. and Medway, F. J. Determinants of effectiveness in parent consultation. *Journal of Community Psychology,* 1978, *6,* 229–240.

Cowen, E. L., Pederson, A., Babigian, H., Izzo, L. D., and Trost, M. A. Long-term follow-up of early detected vulnerable children. *Journal of Consulting and Clinical Psychology,* 1973, *41,* 438–446.

Cummings, N. A. Funding for children's services. *American Psychologist,* 1979, *34,* 1037–1039.

Denker, P. G. Results of treatment of psychoneuroses by the general practitioner: A follow-up study of 500 cases. *Archives of Neurology and Psychiatry,* 1947, *57,* 504–505.

Durkin, R. P. and Durkin, A. B. Evaluating residential treatment programs for disturbed children. In M. Guttentag and E. L. Struening (Eds.) *Handbook of evaluation research* (Vol. 2). Beverly Hills, California: Sage, 1975.

Eysenck, H. J. The effects of psychotherapy: An evaluation. *Journal of Consulting Psychology*, 1952, *16*, 319-324.

Fiester, A. R. The Access system: A procedure for evaluating children's services at community mental health centers. *Community Mental Health Journal*, 1978, *14*, 224-232.

Fine, M. J. *Handbook on parent education*. New York, New York: Academic Press, 1980.

Fiske, D. W., Hunt, H. F., Luborsky, L., Orne, M. T., Parloff, M. B., Reiser, M. F., and Tuma, A. H. Planning of research on the effectiveness of psychotherapy. *Archives of General Psychiatry*, 1970, *22*, 22-32.

Fo, W. S. and O'Donnell, C. R. The Buddy System: Relationship and contingency conditions in a community intervention program for youth, with nonprofessionals as behavior change agents. *Journal of Consulting and Clinical Psychology*, 1974, *42*, 163-169.

Garfield, S. L., Prager, R. A., and Bergin, A. E. Evaluation of outcome in psychotherapy. *Journal of Consulting and Clinical Psychology*, 1971, *37*, 307-313.

Gottman, J., Gonso, J., and Schuler, P. Teaching social skills to isolated children. *Journal of Abnormal Psychology*, 1976, *4*, 179-197.

Graziano, A. M. Parents as behavior therapists. In M. Hersen, R. M. Eisler, and P. M. Miller (Eds.) *Progress in behavior modification* (Vol. 4). New York, New York: Academic Press, 1977.

Green, B. L., Gleser, G. C., Stone, W. N., and Seifert, R. F. Relationships among diverse measures of psychotherapy outcome. *Journal of Consulting and Clinical Psychology*, 1976, *42*, 689-699.

Gresham, F. M. and Nagle, R. J. Social skills training with children: Responsiveness to modeling and coaching as a function of peer orientation. *Journal of Consulting and Clinical Psychology*, 1980, *48*, 718-729.

Guerney, B. L. Filial therapy: Description and rationale. *Journal of Consulting Psychology*, 1964, *28*, 304-310.

Gurman, A. S. and Kniskern, D. P. Research on marital and family therapy: Progress, perspective, and prospect. In S. L. Garfield and A. E. Bergin (Eds.) *Handbook of psychotherapy and behavior change* (2nd ed.). New York, New York: John Wiley and Sons, 1978.

Hagedorn, H. J., Beck, K. J., Neubert, S. F., and Werlin, S. H. *A working manual of simple evaluation techniques for community mental health centers*. Washington, District of Columbia: U.S. Government Printing Office, 1976.

Heinicke, C. M. and Goldman, A. Research on psychotherapy with children: A review and suggestions for further study. *American Journal of Orthopsychiatry*, 1960, *30*, 483-494.

Huberty, C. J., Quirk, J. P., and Swan, W. W. An evaluation system for a psychoeducational treatment program for emotionally disturbed children. *Education Technology*, 1973, *13*, 73-80.

Kazdin, A. E. Advances in child behavior therapy. *American Psychologist*, 1979, *34*, 981-987.

Kendall, P. C. and Wilcox, L. E. Cognitive-behavioral treatment for impulsivity: Concrete versus conceptual training in non-self-controlled problem children. *Journal of Consulting and Clinical Psychology*, 1980, *48*, 80-91.

Kiesler, D. J. Some myths of psychotherapy research and the search for a paradigm. *Psychological Bulletin*, 1966, *65*, 110-136.

Kiresuk, T. J. and Sherman, R. E. Goal attainment scaling: A general method of evaluating comprehensive community mental health programs. *Community Mental Health Journal*, 1968, *4*, 443–453.

Koocher, G. P. and Broskowski, A. Issues in the evaluation of mental health services for children. *Professional Psychology*, 1977, *8*, 583–592.

Kramer, M. *Report of the President's Biomedical Research Panel*. Washington, District of Columbia: U.S. Government Printing Office, 1976.

La Greca, A. M. and Santogrossi, D. A. Social skills training with elementary school students: A behavioral group approach. *Journal of Consulting and Clinical Psychology*, 1980, *48*, 220–227.

Landis, C. A. Statistical evaluation of psychotherapeutic methods. In L. E. Hinsie (Ed.) *Concepts and problems of psychotherapy*. New York, New York: Columbia University Press, 1937.

Lehrman, L. J., Sirluck, H., Black, B. J., and Glick, S. J. Success and failure of treatment of children in the child guidance clinics of the Jewish Board of Guardians. *Jewish Board of Guardians Research Monograph*, 1949, *1*, 1–87.

Levitt, E. E. The results of psychotherapy with children: An evaluation. *Journal of Consulting Psychology*, 1957, *21*, 186–189.

Levitt, E. E. Psychotherapy with children: A further evaluation. *Behavior Research and Therapy*, 1963, *60*, 326–329.

Levitt, E. E. Research on psychotherapy with children. In A. E. Bergin and S. L. Garfield (Eds.) *Handbook of psychotherapy and behavior change*. (2nd edition) New York, New York: John Wiley and Sons, 1971.

Masten, A. S. Family therapy as a treatment for children: A critical review of outcome research. *Family Process*, 1979, *18*, 323–335.

Meyers, J., Parsons, R. D., and Martin, R. *Mental health consultation in the schools*. San Francisco, California: Jossey-Bass, Inc., 1979.

Quay, H. and Peterson, D. *Manual for the behavior problem checklist*. Mimeographed, 1975.

Rachman, S. Clinical applications of observational learning, imitation, and modeling. *Behavior Therapy*, 1972, *3*, 379–397.

Rhodes, W. The disturbing child: A problem of ecological management. *Exceptional Children*, 1967, *33*, 449–455.

Rosenzweig, S. A transvaluation of psychotherapy: A reply to Hans Eysenck. *Journal of Abnormal and Social Psychology*, 1954, *49*, 298–304.

Ross, A. O. Behavior therapy with children. In S. L. Garfield and A. E. Bergin (Eds.) *Handbook of psychotherapy and behavior change* (2nd edition). New York, New York: John Wiley and Sons, 1978.

Sager, C. and Kaplan, H. *Progress in group and family therapy*. New York, New York: Brunner/Mazel, 1972.

Shepherd, M., Oppenheim, A. N., and Mitchell, S. Childhood behavior disorders and the child guidance clinic: An epidemiological study. *Journal of Child Psychology and Psychiatry*, 1966, *7*, 39–52.

Shore, M. F. and Mannino, F. V. Mental health services for children and youth: 1776–1976. *Journal of Clinical Child Psychology*, 1976, *5*, 21–25.

Smith, M. L. and Glass, G. V. Meta-analysis of psychotherapy outcome studies. *American Psychologist*, 1977, *32*, 752–760.

Strupp, H. H. and Bergin, A. E. Some empirical and conceptual bases for coordinated research in psychotherapy: A critical review of issues, trends, and evidence. *International Journal of Psychiatry*, 1969, *7*, 18–90.

Stuart, R. A. *Trick or treatment: How and when psychotherapy fails.* Champaign, Illinois: Research Press, 1970.

Tefft, B. M. and Kloba, J. A. Underachieving high school students as mental health aides with maladapting primary-grade children. *American Journal of Community Psychology,* 1981, *9*, 303–319.

Tramontana, M. G. Critical review of research on psychotherapy outcome with adolescents: 1967–1977. *Psychological Bulletin,* 1980, *88*, 429–450.

Truax, C. B. and Carkhuff, R. R. *Toward effective counseling and psychotherapy: Training and practice.* Chicago, Illinois: Aldine Press, 1967.

Waskow, I. E. and Parloff, M. B. *Psychotherapy change measures.* Washington, District of Columbia: U.S. Government Printing Office, 1975.

Wells, R. A., and Dezen, A. E. The results of family therapy revisited: The nonbehavioral methods. *Family Process,* 1978, *17*, 251–275.

Wells, R. A., Dilkes, T. C., and Trivelli, N. The results of family therapy: A critical review of the literature. *Family Process,* 1972, *11*, 189–207.

Witmer, H. L. A comparison of treatment results in various types of child guidance clinics. *American Journal of Orthopsychiatry,* 1935, *5*, 351–360.

Witmer, H. L. and Keller, J. Outgrowing childhood problems: A study of the value of child guidance treatment. *Smith College Studies in Social Work,* 1942, *13*, 74–90.

Wright, D. M., Moelis, I., and Pollack, L. J. The outcome of individual child psychotherapy: Increments at follow-up. *Journal of Child Psychology and Psychiatry,* 1976, *17*, 275–285.

Index

Adolescents, disturbed
  spontaneous remission rates for,
    250
  statistics on, 179
  treatment of, 6
Affective education, 126, 127
Affective growth, 82
Analogic rules, 136
Anger, 192, 196
Anxiety, 110, 111
Automated Comprehensive Children's
  Evaluation System, 261

Behavior
  acceptance of differing, 20
  antiseptic bouncing for control of,
    78
  appeal to values in management of,
    78
  classroom program restructuring for
    controlling, 78
  in conflict cycle model, 65
  demystification of, 5–7
  disturbed vs disturbing, 44
  drugs in control of, 34
  ecological concepts applied to,
    157–158
  excess or deficit in, 90
    duration recording of, 94–95
    event recording of, 94
    identification and operational
      definition of, 91–93
    interval recording of, 95
    observation of, 94–95

[Behavior]
  [excess or deficit in]
    settings and circumstances asso-
      ciated with, 93
    supporting contingencies for, 94
    time sampling of, 95
  holistic approach to assessment of,
    216–218
  hurdle help for controlling, 77–78
  of hyperactive children, 33, 34
  interest boosting for controlling, 77
  learned, 8, 87
  nonconstructive, managing, 76–79
  object removal for control of, 78
  operant, 90
    antecedent and consequent
      events in, 90
    extinction concept and, 97–98
    identification of, 91, 92
    reinforcement programs and,
      96–97
  person–environment interaction in, 6
  physical restraint for control of, 78
  planned ignoring of, 77
  proximity control of, 77
  purposes served by, 11
  redirecting, 73
  reinforcers of, 96–97
  self-control, 79–80
  settings for, 158–159
  signal interference of, 77
  social reinforcers of, 96
  structured routines for controlling,
    78

267